Recovering Co

Recovering Couples Anonymous:

A Twelve-Step Program For Couples

4th Edition of the Basic Text

RCA®

Call toll free in the U.S. and Canada 1-877-663-2317
Email: info@rca-wso.info
Website: http://www.recovering-couples.org

First Edition published in 1991
Second Edition published in 1992
Third Edition published in 1996
Third Edition (revised) published in 2003
Fourth Edition (draft) published in 2005
Fourth Edition (draft two) published in 2006
Fourth Edition Published in 2011
Printings: 2nd–2013; 3rd–2016; 4th–2018; 5th–2020

The Twelve Steps and Twelve Traditions are reprinted and adapted by permission of Alcoholics Anonymous World Service, Inc.

The Preamble is reprinted and adapted by permission of A.A. Grapevine, Inc.

The Tools of Recovery are reprinted and adapted with permission of Workaholics Anonymous.

The Unity Prayer is printed with permission (1993) of the author, Rosanne S. In Overeaters Anonymous it is called "The OA Promise."

The transcription of the Founder Address, the adaption of the Serenity Prayer, and Reflections One through Thirty printed by permission of Dr. Patrick J. Carnes.

Cover Design: Susan A. Lobachyov
Composition: Anne M. Landgraf, Brooklyn BookWorks LLC

RCA Fellowship Approved Literature.

ISBN 978-0-9637495-1-2

Contents

Chapter III

Introduction to the Fourth Edition

Since the printing of the Third Edition of *Recovering Couples Anonymous* our fellowship has continued to grow and endure, establishing a website making it much easier for those couples who still suffer to find RCA, and a meeting in their area. As with most other Twelve-Step fellowships, RCA has not been without its "growing pains." And, as pain was the great motivator that brought many of us into recovery in the first place, it can also be the motivator to bring RCA as a fellowship into becoming a healthy and flourishing service organization able to effectively carry the message of hope and recovery to couples who still suffer.

RCA obtained permission to use the Twelve Steps, the Twelve Traditions, and the Preamble from Alcoholics Anonymous in 2005 as they appear in this edition. To develop a book reflecting RCA experience, and to sample the RCA Group Conscience of all the RCA Membership, a new fourth edition of the Blue Book has been written. It was written in draft form and presented to the RCA Membership just before the 2005 Convention for general distribution. Questionnaires were included with the draft copies and a website organized with questions. Both the questionnaires and the website were used to obtain feedback from the RCA membership as to how the fourth edition reflected the experience, strength, and hope of the membership. The data were collected and used to modify the first drafts. This process was repeated. This draft has been extensively modified, then presented to the fellowship, and approved by them. This is the first time we have had a fellowship–approved Blue Book.

Foreword

"The only requirement for membership is the desire to remain in a committed relationship."

We are members of Recovering Couples Anonymous (RCA). Some of us began our Twelve Step recovery in RCA, but many of us who had begun to recover in individual programs found we could no longer relate to our partners in the same old dysfunctional ways. Many of us separated, coming close to permanent separation or divorce. Unwilling to abandon our partners, we sought ways to heal our coupleships. Through RCA we learned new ways of relating and solving problems. We discovered greater levels of intimacy.

We feel the need to share this program with others. This book contains suggestions we have followed in recovery. We publish these to give hope to others. We emphasize this is not a cookbook or a self-help book to be used alone. We discourage trying to work this program alone. Most of us have been helped by working with others. We worked the Steps with a sponsor couple, or at least in a knowledgeable supportive system. We attended RCA meetings, and we passed on what we had learned to others by sharing, service work, or being sponsor couples ourselves. We think of this book as a guide book, a general description of how we improved our coupleships. We hope you find recovery for your coupleship also.

Chapter I

An Invitation to Healing

Who We Are

We are couples committed to restoring healthy communication, caring, and greater intimacy to our coupleships. We suffer from many problems, some identified and some not, some treated and some not. We also come from different levels of brokenness. Many of us have been separated or near divorce. Some of us are new in our coupleships and seek to build intimacy together. We have all sought healing in Recovering Couples Anonymous (RCA).

Although we have many relationships, we have only one coupleship. We restrict ourselves to one partner for the full expression of our physical, emotional, sexual, and spiritual love. We try to honor the special nature of our love by doing spontaneous things with our partners. It can be easy to become so preoccupied with our work, children, elderly parents, or other distractions that we neglect our partners. We may feel there will always be time for our partners later so we do not pay them the special attention they deserve today. A nurturing, healthy coupleship requires regular attention to function at a level that gives the highest satisfaction. Keeping our focus on our love can bring pleasures we never believed possible.

Our History

Recovering Couples Anonymous was founded in the fall of 1988 in Golden Valley, Minnesota. Several couples completed a "We Came To Believe" program, which focused on working the Twelve Steps in intimate relationships. RCA groups were formed independently in California at about the same time. Couples from the groups discovered over time that the same Twelve Steps that had helped them recover individually from different addictions also helped to build the health of their coupleships.

Our Steps and Traditions are based on and adapted from those of Alcoholics Anonymous. The Minneapolis fellowship revised the Twelve Steps, Twelve Traditions, How It Works, and The Promises to reflect couple language and issues. They also developed a meeting guide and a list of characteristics of dysfunctional relationships.

RCA groups can be found in many cities in the United States, Canada, and Europe, and are spreading to other areas. RCA group meetings are listed in the RCA International Meeting Directory on the RCA website: http://www.recovering-couples.org.

The World Service Organization (WSO) serves as a connecting point for all groups and as a clearinghouse for new material. The RCA International Convention is held annually. The WSO office was originally located in Minnesota, moved to St. Louis, Missouri, and then to Oakland, California in 2000. In 2009, the WSO office became a "virtual" office instead of a physical one.

Who Comes to RCA

The following profiles are common to many of us. If any of these characteristics are causing problems in your coupleship, you have come to the right place, and help is available. For some of us, being enmeshed and totally dependent on our partners was perceived as being in love. Others came to RCA dealing with conflict by getting totally out of control. Many of us felt it was safer to be with other people than to be alone and intimate with our partners. Not all couples will have all of these issues, but most couples will have some of them. Perhaps one of these issues provided the pain that brought you to RCA. If so, you have come to the right place and the Steps and Tools of RCA can work for you.

The following are quotes from RCA Couples. If you identify with one or more, RCA may offer hope and help for you.

> *"We believed that we had to agree on everything. We believed that we had to enjoy the same things and have the same interests. Being together and unhappy was safer than being alone."*

> *"We felt it was safer to get upset about little issues than to express our true feelings about larger ones. It was easier to blame our partners than it was to accept our own responsibility."*

"We feared that if we let our partners know who we really were—what we had done or what we were feeling and thinking—we'd be abandoned. We either avoided our problems or felt we were individually responsible for solving the problems we had as a couple. It was easier to hide (medicate) our feelings through compulsive behavior than it was to express them."

"We found it difficult to ask for what we needed, both individually and as a couple. We dealt with conflict by not arguing at all. We equated being sexual with being intimate."

"We had forgotten how to play and have fun together. We were ashamed of ourselves as a couple. We worried that we were not socially acceptable, that we were inadequate parents."

"The analogy of coupleship as a dance helps us keep our interaction in perspective. In a dance, my partner and I have our respective responses, whether it's a tango, or a dance of avoidance, a dance of anger, or a dance of denial. To change the dance, either of us can change just one step—as individuals, or as a couple."

Our Philosophy

RCA is a tool for recovery and not an end in itself. It exists to promote caring, communication, and intimacy. A successful formula of RCA is: my individual recovery plus your individual recovery plus our couple recovery equals a healthy recovering coupleship. These three are all important factors in the serenity, stability, and intimacy we each seek.

To be successful in any Twelve-Step program, at a minimum there's something you need to do. In AA you stay sober, in OA you stay abstinent, in NA you stay clean, and in RCA you *stay committed*. This commitment to not leave the coupleship, even if you find it necessary to live apart, provides a foundation on which you can grow as a couple.

We believe that a coupleship needs constant nurturing and care from both partners. It is important that each partner accept mutual responsibility for the problems and progress of the coupleship—and furthermore, that each recognizes individual recovery as an important factor in couple recovery.

Our philosophy also includes the need for a couple to treat their coupleship as an *entity, distinct* and *separate* from their individual recoveries. This "entity," or "coupleship," resembles a little child needing to be nurtured by its parents (the two members of the coupleship) and needs the same nurturing and recovery as individuals. As couples we need meetings, sponsors, service, and a Twelve-Step program.

The process of healing the coupleship stimulates a feeling of hope. We are developing new, healthy behaviors, and being more respectful of each other. We are beginning to forgive ourselves and look forward to our future. We believe healing begins when we first commit to recover *together*. For many of us this date has become a second anniversary.

Honesty and personal responsibility are keys to this program. Before recovery many of us did not feel OK about ourselves, and we blamed somebody or something else—usually our partners. We focused on how we wanted to change our partners rather than recognizing how we needed to change ourselves. The blame was always on our partners. As we worked the Twelve Steps of RCA, we began to recognize we were the source of our own problems. We could only change ourselves, and we needed to change if we were going to feel better. We needed to reverse the process of blaming our partners by taking responsibility for our own behavior. Slips or relapses occur when we refuse to accept responsibility for our actions, expressed as blaming behavior and not working the program together. Usually we know when we make slips because we become distant from our partners. Many of us escape, or go numb, in a variety of ways that we have known since childhood. This distance may lead to relapses in our individual recoveries as we revert to old ways of coping. However, even though slips in our individual programs usually affect our relationships, they may not lead to slips in couple recovery, if we are honest.

In the RCA program, we are learning to face our problems as a couple. We are learning to express our true feelings—even about large issues. We are learning to fight fairly. Some of us are writing fair fighting contracts to help us express conflict respectfully (see Appendix for a sample fair fighting contract, pp. 351–353).

We are recognizing and breaking the patterns of dysfunction we learned from our families of origin. As we grow through using the Steps, Tools, and Traditions in our coupleships, we learn to play and have fun together, and to be proud of ourselves as couples.

RCA Philosophy in a Group Reading Format

In RCA we believe that a coupleship is like an infant needing constant nurturing and care from both partners. It is important that each partner accept mutual responsibility for the problems or progress of the coupleship, and furthermore, that both recognize their own individual development and recovery as essential factors for couple recovery.

In RCA we think of our lives in coupleships as being represented by a three-legged stool: commitment, communication, and caring. All are important "legs" to the serenity, stability, and intimacy we each seek. The legs can also represent our individual recovery, our partner's recovery, and our coupleship recovery.

We all have family-of-origin issues and a history of past relationships. We may not have gotten what we needed—emotionally, physically, mentally, or spiritually—when we were growing up. There may have been physical, sexual, spiritual, or emotional abuse. There may have been abandonment or neglect. We bring "baggage" to the coupleship. Thus, we deal with memories of past hurts, misbehavior, and perhaps vows violated. Blaming our partners is likely the most devastating aspect of dysfunctional relationships. Blaming becomes so second-nature that we are often unaware when we do it.

We are each responsible for the absence of intimacy between us. As soon as we accept responsibility, we are ready for RCA recovery. Each person must act as if that individual carries 100% of the responsibility for intimacy in the coupleship, since the only thing we can change is ourselves, certainly not our partner.

Without help our anger, hurt, and mistrust are too great for us. At RCA meetings we learn how the program works, how to practice the Twelve Steps together as a couple, and how to replace old unhealthy behavior patterns with healthy ways of relating. The Steps teach us how to look at our "baggage" and how to reverse the process of blame. These are the Steps we took, which are suggested as a program of recovery (read the Twelve Steps of RCA; see p. 52).

Characteristics of Functional and Dysfunctional Couples

1. **Dysfunctional:** Being together and unhappy is safer than being alone.
   Functional: Being alone is comfortable, but working together can bring us greater joy and happiness. We are together because we want to be.

2. **Dysfunctional:** It is safer to be with other people than it is to be alone and intimate with our partners.
   Functional: Being alone and intimate with our partners is becoming safe because we are learning to be open and honest.

3. **Dysfunctional:** If we really let our partners know what we have done or what we are feeling and thinking (who we are), we will be abandoned.
   Functional: When we let our partners know what we have done or what we have been thinking (who we are), surprisingly, it is generally met with acceptance and actually increases our intimacy.

4. **Dysfunctional:** It is easier to hide or medicate our feelings through compulsive behaviors than it is to express them.
   Functional: We are learning to express our feelings, no longer needing to hide or medicate them.

5. **Dysfunctional:** Being enmeshed and totally dependent on each other is perceived as being in love.
   Functional: Being interdependent adds strength to our coupleship.

6. **Dysfunctional:** We find it difficult to ask for what we need, both individually and as couples.
   Functional: We are learning that it is acceptable to ask for what we need, both individually and as couples.

7. **Dysfunctional:** Being sexual is equal to being intimate.
   Functional: Being lovingly sexual can enhance our coupleships, but there are many additional ways of being intimate.

8. **Dysfunctional:** We either avoid our problems or feel we are individually responsible for solving the problems we have as couples.
   Functional: We are learning to face our own problems but not to feel individually responsible for solving all the problems we have as couples. It is normal for couples to have problems that are not immediately resolvable.

9. **Dysfunctional:** We believe that we must agree on everything.
   Functional: We are learning it isn't necessary to agree on everything to be happy.

10. **Dysfunctional:** We believe that we must enjoy the same things and have the same interests.
    Functional: We are learning that we can have many different interests and still enjoy being together.

11. **Dysfunctional:** We believe that to be good couples we must be socially acceptable.
    Functional: We believe that to be good couples we must be true to ourselves, to our coupleships, and to our principles.

12. **Dysfunctional:** We have forgotten how to play together.
    Functional: We are discovering lightheartedness and the joy of playfulness.

13. **Dysfunctional:** It is safer to get upset about little issues than to express our true feelings about larger ones.
    Functional: We are learning to appropriately express our true feelings about issues both large and small.

14. **Dysfunctional:** It is easier to blame our partners than it is to accept our individual responsibilities.
    Functional: We are learning to accept our individual responsibilities rather than focusing on our partners.

15. **Dysfunctional:** We deal with conflict by getting totally out of control or by not arguing at all.
    Functional: We are learning to deal with conflict appropriately and to fight fairly.

16. **Dysfunctional:** We experience ourselves as inadequate parents.
    Functional: We are coming to accept our limitations as parents.

17. **Dysfunctional:** We are ashamed of ourselves as couples.
    Functional: We are proud of the progress we are making as couples.

18. **Dysfunctional:** We repeat patterns of dysfunction from our families of origin.
    Functional: We are recognizing the patterns of dysfunction from our families of origin—and breaking them.

RCA Membership

The only requirement for RCA membership is a desire to remain in a committed relationship.

Ultimately, we feel it is important for both members of a couple to be involved in individual recovery, or other spiritual work, for real progress to be made in the coupleship. It is not, however, a requirement to get started in couple recovery. RCA is a safe place to begin that healing process, and it offers support for continued individual work. We refuse no couple who wishes to recover.

Each partner needs to take responsibility for the dysfunction of the coupleship. We do not seek to blame our partners. Our partners may have chosen to medicate the pain of their loneliness with various addictions. We do not seek to take responsibility for these behaviors. As two people, however, we both bring family-of-origin messages, abuse experiences, expectations, abilities, and individual coping mechanisms (including addictions) into the relationship. We must take responsibility for these behaviors and learn new ways to deal with them.

Many of us had discovered that we expected our partners to solve our own family-of-origin or other individual issues. We were often angry with our partners because they didn't resolve feelings that actually belonged to us individually. Unless our individual recoveries are strong, and we can take ownership of our "baggage," couple recovery will be difficult. In many ways, *couple* Twelve-Step work depends on and accompanies *individual* Twelve-Step work.

This requires a strong commitment to the Twelve-Step process. We strongly suggest that both members of the coupleship be in individual Twelve-Step programs. Both members are encouraged to be open to the Twelve-Step process and be willing to learn more about it. We recognize there are times when the pain of a relationship is so great that it needs the immediate support of our Fellowship, even if one partner is new to recovery, or both are.

Coupleship Challenges

In RCA, we are fortunate to realize we are no longer alone with our problems. We have found that couples fight and get into serious trouble around a number of common issues. Not all couples will have all of them, but most of us will have some. The following is just a partial list of common issues and is not in any particular order:

- Money
- Sex
- Children
- Power issues: roles, rules, and boundaries
- Fear
- Resentment
- Attempting to control one's partner's behavior
- Partner's family
- Communication
- No mutual interests

Many RCA couples overcome these challenges by benefiting from other couples' experiences. Understanding that we are not unique and having support from the group gives us courage to look at these obstacles to happiness. This support helps us develop new ways of living and loving. And as we progress through the Steps, we begin to see them not just as challenges, but also as opportunities for growth and healing.

Chapter II

A Guide to RCA's Twelve Steps

Working the Steps Together

RCA is first and foremost a Twelve-Step program. Working the Twelve Steps of RCA together, *as a couple,* offers a unique recovery experience. This process opens doors to both *individual* and *couple* recovery. It is important for couples to create a safe environment for their Step work. The suggestions offered here have worked for others; however, they are not the only way to work the Steps. The needs of each couple should be taken into consideration. Many couples choose sponsor couples to help them work the Steps. This book is only a general guide, showing how we changed our coupleships for the better. Each couple will have specific situations best dealt with by working with a sponsor couple.

We encourage couples to use the process suggested in the First Step to get a sense of the powerlessness each partner has over the relationship. It can be powerful to look at how our family-of-origin relationships—and possibly other relationships—have influenced the way we relate to our partner.

We suggest that each couple decide in advance how much time they will spend doing Step work at each sitting. Frequently one partner is willing, even eager, to do Step work, while the other partner may be reluctant. We have found that when we honor the less enthusiastic partner by agreeing to a relatively brief time period, especially in the beginning, the reluctant partner often becomes more enthusiastic as that partner experiences the safety of the process. For some, the thought of doing this work for more than fifteen to twenty minutes at a time may be challenging. For other couples, an hour at a time is no problem.

We encourage couples to set aside a regular time to do Step work. If for some reason the agreed-upon time is missed, we suggest that you establish a new time right away. This is helpful to ensure the Step work continues to be a priority in the coupleship.

Many experienced couples feel it is important to work the Steps *in order.* Some couples might be tempted to fix specific problems in the coupleship before Step work has been completed. Generally, we feel this shortcut will not work without the foundational work done in the Steps.

Many of us came into RCA because we were in pain and conflict. We found it helpful to *begin* working the Twelve Steps together right away. As we focused on the Steps, we worked together for a common goal of healthy intimacy. For some of us, one obstacle to working the Steps was that as we started talking honestly about our relationships, we opened up emotionally charged issues. As a result of this, it was difficult for one or both partners to stay with the process. Since our situation frequently gets worse before it gets better, we suggest that you agree not to leave the coupleship before spending a certain amount of time working the program—preferably six months. Many of us found it helpful to make a simple commitment contract in which we agreed to work specific Steps for a limited period of time:

Sample Contract

(This is a sample of a Step Contract. More sample contracts can be found in the Appendix.)

I, ______ , commit to work Steps One, Two, and Three with you, ______ , for ___ hours each Saturday morning for the next three months.

I, ______ , commit to work Steps One, Two, and Three with you, ______ , for ___ hours each Saturday morning for the next three months.

We agree that we will start by saying the Serenity Prayer in the "we" format, followed by the Safety Guidelines. We agree not to interrupt our partner. We agree to keep the focus on ourselves, not on our partner. We commit to stay present and not make any "dramatic exits." If we find either of us needs to take a break, before we leave, we commit to reschedule a time to continue. We commit to close each session with the Serenity Prayer.

We agree if we are unable to make progress in two consecutive sessions we will ask another RCA couple for support.

We agree to negotiate an extension to this contract if we have not finished our three Steps during the last week of the three-month period.

Signed, ________________ Date _____________

Signed, ________________ Date _____________

Witnesses ____

Inviting Higher Power Into Step Work

Many couples have found it helpful to invite their Higher Power into their Step Work starting with Step Two. Couples may invite their Higher Power in whatever manner feels right to them. Most of us have found that only by inviting our Higher Power into our coupleships have we received the serenity we sought. Some of us say a Third Step Prayer to reflect couples' language. Below is one possible version:

Higher Power, we offer our coupleship to you
to transform us and to do with our relationship
as you believe is best.
Take away the selfishness we show toward each other
and others in our lives, so that we may better do your will.
Take away our dysfunctional patterns
of caring, communication, and intimacy,
that overcoming them may be a testimony of
your power, your love, and your way of life—
to each other, and to those we might help.

Step Study Questions

The following are the Steps which have lead many RCA couples to better coupleships. Most of us know what an unhealthy relationship involves—*attempted control of the other.* Step One is where we admit we are powerless and need help. Step Two is where we come to believe that a Higher Power can help us do what we cannot do ourselves. Step Three is where we invite our Higher Power into our coupleship to find spiritual ways to deal with our problems. In Step Four we uncover the problems in our coupleship. In Step Five we admit to our Higher Power, to each other, and to another couple that these problems do exist, and we accept our individual parts in them. In Steps Six and Seven we ask for help to change our behaviors. Steps Eight and Nine are for repairing our past mistakes. Step Ten empowers us to reverse the process of blame and shame, and inspires us to view our partners with gratitude and appreciation. Step Eleven allows us to have a deeper sense of being guided and sustained, by these Steps and by a Higher Power, as we work together. Step Twelve has us carry the message to other suffering couples—a major spiritual experience for many of us.

Step One

We admitted we were powerless over our relationship—that our lives together had become unmanageable.

Most of us have family-of-origin issues and all of us have a history. We may not have gotten what we needed emotionally, physically, mentally, or spiritually. When we were growing up there may have been abuse (physical, sexual, spiritual, or emotional), abandonment, or deprivation. We all bring "baggage" to the coupleship. The Steps teach us how to look at our baggage and how to reverse the process of blaming.

Each of us is responsible for the presence or absence of intimacy between us. As soon as each of us accepts responsibility, we are ready for Step One of RCA. Step One involves taking full responsibility for the health or disease of the relationship. Each person carries 100%.

Occasionally some couples might not be far enough along in their individual recovery (or not in recovery at all) to be able to answer the following questions, or they might get into fights or other dysfunctional behavior simply by raising certain issues. In these cases, we encourage Step work be done only in the presence of a sponsoring couple.

Couples come into RCA at different stages. Step One involves understanding dysfunctional patterns. It also involves understanding family-of-origin issues, personality traits, and other individual issues that affect our current coupleship.

Writing is important for clarity and thoroughness. We suggest that you:

1. Read aloud the "Safety Guidelines" (see p. 55).
2. Take one pencil and one piece of paper and begin the process together. RCA is about the "we-ness" and "us-ness" of our relationship. In RCA, we open ourselves up to a new way of thinking and living in coupleship.
3. Make couple decisions: Who will hold the pencil and do the writing? Are you able to share, negotiate, or compromise? Is there a power struggle? Are you ready to take the First Step?
4. Divide the paper in half with a vertical line down the middle.
5. Make lists of the coupleship issues over which you feel powerless.
6. As an alternative, divide the duties of writing and dictating, or each write your own part.

We suggest you answer the following questions:

1. What dysfunctional roles have you brought from your family of origin?
2. What have your family-of-origin models taught you about relationships?
3. If you have had experiences of abuse, how have those affected your ability to relate, to be intimate, and to be sexual?

4. How do your individual addictions or dysfunctions affect your coupleship?
5. What are recurring issues you never seem to resolve (e.g., how you spend money, how you spend your time together, parent, divide the household duties, celebrate the holidays, etc.)?
6. How do these issues bring you to anger and what are your patterns of expressing anger?
7. In what ways do you feel hopeless about your coupleship?
8. In order to save your coupleship, what measures have you tried that haven't seemed to work?
9. How do you fight unfairly?

Understanding the powerlessness and unmanageability of your relationship is key. Remember, you are a beautiful and unique couple and you deserve recovery. Having surrendered thus far, you are ready to take Step Two.

Step Two

We came to believe that a power greater than ourselves could restore us to commitment and intimacy.

In Step One we admitted we were powerless over our relationship. Step Two involves coming to some mutual understanding of what we trust as a couple, and what we believe. This is the beginning of a spiritual quest. We seek to blend our traditions and to find meaning as a couple. We do this by first identifying our individual beliefs about a Higher Power. Once both partners have their own vision of a Higher Power, we can seek those aspects that are common to both of us; these become our couple's Higher Power. Individuals within the coupleship may each have a separate vision of a Higher Power, but many couples believe there should be a goal of a mutual Higher Power shared by both partners.

One approach we find helpful is to cut sayings and pictures out of magazines that make us think of our Higher Power. We make collages to have a visual picture of our Higher Power. In making collages we share a deep, intimate look at our beliefs and feelings. As we share parts of ourselves, we may find a special connection. We find it helpful to frame and keep these collages accessible for our coupleship and to share them with other couples. We are willing to accept our Higher Power and nurture our relationship with a sense of hope and freedom.

We also find writing Step Two a useful tool. We suggest you share one pencil and piece of paper as you do the Step. The following is a list of questions you may wish to consider to assist in your journey of recovery. We suggest that you pause and read aloud the Safety Guidelines (see p. 55) before moving forward:

1. What family-of-origin messages about religion or spirituality have you brought into the coupleship?

2. What kinds of instruction, modeling, teaching, etc. about religion or spirituality have you experienced?
3. What forms of spiritual guidance have you received from your parents?
4. Are there abuses or dysfunctional beliefs regarding couples you have learned from your religion?
5. Are there healthy and supportive beliefs you have learned from your church, synagogue, or other spiritual path?
6. Are there spiritual abuses you have experienced?
7. Are there examples of one of your parents being the Higher Power in your family of origin?
8. Are there examples of clergy or religious teachers being unkind, shaming, blaming, or belittling?
9. Are you angry about religion, God, or your heritage?
10. What do you accept or reject of the spiritual beliefs of your partner?
11. Describe your vision of your Higher Power.
12. What would it be like to have a relationship with this Higher Power?

Many of us made our partner our Higher Power. We focused on our partner and gave our partner the power to regulate our lives. Because of this, we found it necessary to find a spiritual connection with a Higher Power, a center for our lives, rather than focusing on what others were doing. When we are spiritually centered, our partner's actions do not bother us nearly as much as when we are not. Additionally, it may be helpful to remember to HALT. When we are <u>H</u>ungry, <u>A</u>ngry, <u>L</u>onely, or <u>T</u>ired we can lose touch with our spiritual center. We need to return to our spiritual center rather than fight with our partner.

Step Two allows us to believe that a Higher Power can restore us to commitment and intimacy. Step Three gives us an opportunity to develop a relationship with our Higher Power.

Step Three

We made a decision to turn our wills and our life together over to the care of God as we understood God.

Together two people in a committed relationship form a coupleship, a oneness, *a distinct and separate entity*. This coupleship has a life of its own and needs to be nurtured. Couple recovery depends on this nurturance. Each partner needs individual recovery such as meetings, sponsorship, support groups, spirituality, recreation, vocation, and individual interests. The coupleship needs these same elements for couple recovery.

Trust is a major issue for most couples, since almost all couples have had trust violated in the past. Just as Step Two focused on what we decided to trust together, Step Three focuses on how we decide to turn our coupleship over to our Higher Power.

Letting go of outcomes is especially helpful. Many of us feel compelled to control events, believing that our happiness depends on resolutions favorable to us, only to find disappointment when the happiness we expect is only temporary or nonexistent. In spiritually centered coupleships, we simply do our best, while leaving the outcome to our Higher Power.

Some couples find "Higher Power Boxes" helpful to visualize relinquishing control. Couples write their relationship problems down and place them in the box, symbolically turning them over to their Higher Power. Similarly, some couples make a ceremony of burning their problems or having the tide wash them away.

The practice of meditation and prayer, especially the Serenity Prayer, is the spiritual bulwark of most couples. Focusing on insight, courage, willingness, and acceptance seems to be the key to letting go.

Becoming more integrated in an RCA group is a vital part of any Third Step. Sharing our fears and stories at the group and sponsor level is an emotional letting go. It also allows us to relate to others, breaking our sense of isolation and uniqueness. Participation in a meeting can lead to a change in perspective and a return to sanity. "Letting go" also means "not going alone."

Many couples go on a "spiritual quest" as part of their Third Step. Spiritual quests vary widely, but could include the following:

- Starting each day with thanksgiving
- Reading spiritually significant literature together
- Meditating
- Going to a house of worship or other spiritually significant place
- Going to recovery groups
- Praying
- Going on a spiritual retreat together

These quests could take days, months, or even years. We hope that your own spiritual outlook as a couple will be deepened. We encourage you to write down a quest agreement. This could be in longhand or printed suitable for framing and witnessed by friends or your sponsors. This is a truly warm, supportive, and validating experience for all involved. Additionally, we suggest that you chair an RCA Step meeting, and share your experience, strength, and hope with other couples.

Ultimately, Step Three involves turning our relationship over. Many of us find it important to do something significant, even formal, to celebrate our spiritual renewal, such as a rededication of couple vows in the presence of friends. This may occur anywhere: in a place of worship, at an informal gathering such as a picnic, or at home. We invite you to be creative and have a personally memorable event celebrating your increasing commitment to each other and to the relationship.

We recognize that we are on a spiritual path together. Placing our relationship in our Higher Power's hands would mean the end of power struggles and seeking to control. We make a decision. We surrender. This is the spiritual principle upon which Step Three rests.

Step Four

We made a searching and fearless moral inventory of our relationship together as a couple.

We suggest you look at the impact of your individual behavior on the coupleship. First you may share your individual inventories. Next you can complete your coupleship inventory. The goal of these inventories is to gain awareness of the extent of our dysfunction. We all need to be fearless in our inventories. When a couple is able to face their reality honestly, they can grow in their love. Here are some questions that may help you in your individual inventory:

1. **Unfinished Business:** In what ways have I failed to raise issues with my partner, letting those unresolved issues build resentments?
2. **Hypervigilance:** In what ways have I looked for things to go wrong?

3. **Self-Responsibility:** In what ways have I failed to take responsibility for my actions?
4. **Comfort and Feelings:** In what ways have I not shared uncomfortable feelings with my partner?
5. **Accuracy and Honesty:** In what ways have I placated my partner or avoided sharing my own perceptions?
6. **Connection:** In what ways have I not been available to my partner? In what ways have I sought to connect?
7. **Stress:** In what ways have my overextension and stress affected my partner?
8. **Separateness:** In what ways have I developed a separate life from my partner?
9. **Personal Needs:** In what ways has my partner needed to guess or been expected to know my needs? Have I clearly asked for these needs to be met?
10. **Shaming and Blaming:** In what ways have I sought to shame or blame my partner?
11. **Pain Thresholds:** In what ways have I tolerated emotional pain that was unnecessary and caused distance from my partner?
12. **Choice Clarity:** In what ways have I been unclear about my choices, leaving things undecided or up to my partner?

To complete your couple inventory, review together the following questions and record your answers on paper. Writing helps to organize your thoughts and beliefs. Please begin by reading aloud the Safety Guidelines (see p. 55).

Please answer the following questions as a couple:

1. In what ways have we let fears or resentments interfere with our coupleship? How has that affected our intimacy?
2. In what ways have we created crises when there weren't any?
3. In what ways have we fought that never accomplished anything?
4. In what ways have we neglected our coupleship?
5. In what ways have we avoided being intimate?
6. In what ways have we pretended our problems did not exist?
7. In what ways have we isolated from couples and friends who could have supported our coupleship?
8. In what ways have we allowed ourselves to become depleted, leaving nothing to give to each other?
9. In what ways have we tolerated abuse?
10. In what ways have we had losses (never having achieved financial goals, having children with problems, having a dysfunctional sexual relationship, etc.)?
11. In what ways have we grieved these losses?
12. In what ways have we treasured our partner and the coupleship? What are our strengths as a couple?

Having gained a better understanding in Step Four of how frequently our problems arose from within us rather than as a result of external hostile forces, many of us found it very freeing to reveal our problems to another couple—often our sponsor couple. Although sharing our problems was often intimidating, the relief we felt was enormous when we found that we were accepted. While we may have believed that we were unique in our problems before taking Step Five, we often learned that the couple with whom we shared our inventory had experienced many of the same issues.

Step Five

We admitted to God, to each other, and to another couple the exact nature of our wrongs.

Most of us choose to share our Fifth Step with a sponsoring couple or another couple who has been in the RCA program long enough to have worked the Twelve Steps. It is also important to share this inventory with a couple who seems to be living the program. This process of doing the Fifth Step is a vehicle to self-acceptance. This may be difficult because of shame. However, this is your opportunity to have shame transformed into humility.

We suggest you begin with a moment of silence and then the Serenity Prayer, followed by reading the Safety Guidelines (see p. 55). We encourage you to record your experiences in a journal and to get feedback from the sponsoring couple. We find sharing honestly and openly with other couples to be healing, because we realize our coupleship is accepted in spite of our dysfunctional behavior. Step Five frees us to begin anew.

(For information on sponsors and what to do if sponsors who have worked the Steps are not available, see the section on sponsorship in Chapter IV, pp. 97–112.)

Step Six

We were entirely ready to have God remove all these defects of character, communication, and caring.

Step Six has a clear message—get ready for some changes! The first three Steps showed us we couldn't change on our own, but that we could find the power needed to change. Then Step Four helped us recognize our defects. Step Five allowed us to get rid of much of our shame. With Step Six we become willing to have our Higher Power remove these defects. We don't have to let go of *behaviors*. We just need *willingness* to allow our defects to be removed. The more we work the RCA program, the more willing we become.

Every recovering couple has dysfunctional patterns of behavior. These patterns typically occur at times of stress, overextension, or depletion. Often these happen during an opportunity for intimacy. One or both partners elect to avoid closeness by going to their old patterns. Recovering couples need to recognize these patterns.

Here are some warning signs that old patterns are resurfacing:

- Arguing repetitively
- Falling into frequent periods of denial
- Communicating nonproductively
- Suffering extreme overextension or depletion
- Making statements we do not really mean
- Taking actions we regret
- Fighting about issues that are not important
- Stating "You *always* . . . " or "You *never* . . . "

We suggest listing your dysfunctional patterns. Make these lists together and pick a time to talk when you are both feeling balanced. You are now ready. Enjoy the process. See the humor.

Open up to healing in your coupleship. Always start by reading the Safety Guidelines (see p. 55) aloud. Take your piece of paper and gather more information for your coupleship by answering the following questions:

1. What are your dysfunctional patterns of relating?
2. What are your dysfunctional patterns of communicating?
3. What are your dysfunctional patterns of caretaking?
4. What are your dysfunctional patterns of nurturing each other?
5. What are your dysfunctional patterns of being sexual?
6. What are your dysfunctional patterns of fighting?

If, as a couple, we don't work on our relationship, similar issues will likely surface with subsequent partners. This means that we should practice couple recovery with our partner *now*. Our couple issues in this relationship are probably the same as they were in previous relationships.

Step Seven

We humbly asked God to remove our shortcomings.

In Step Seven, we need to form a working partnership with our Higher Power. We seek humility. *Humility* is defined in many ways, including the ability to face reality; knowing there is a Higher Power, and we, or our partner, are not it; not thinking less of ourselves, but thinking about ourselves less; being spiritually no better than, but no less than, anyone or any other couple. The real change happens as we let go of our false pride and work to change in partnership with our Higher Power.

We frequently ask our Higher Power to remove our shortcomings. We know we can't change our old ways of doing things on our own, but in partnership with our Higher Power, we can. The more we work the RCA program, the more our shortcomings are relieved. Many of us found contracts to be a vital tool in overcoming these shortcomings by adding accountability (see contract information in Appendix, pp. 342–353). We learn to avoid being too Hungry, Angry, Lonely, and Tired (HALT), as these states seem to make our shortcomings worse. At the very least, we avoid making crucial decisions while experiencing these states.

A suggested Seventh Step Prayer (or meditation topic):

I want to be more sensitive to my partner,
as sensitivity to my partner opens awareness of my innermost self.
Higher Power, help me become more open and aware.

I need to see my own fear behind my shortcomings:
my tendency to be sarcastic and stubborn,
my tendency to blame and make my partner wrong,
my need to make my partner feel disrespected and "less than."
Higher Power, help me find the courage to acknowledge my own shortcomings,
instead of focusing on those of my partner.

I promise to try to use the coupleship tools I have learned
to stop interrupting my partner,
to speak from "I" statements,
and to acknowledge the strengths my partner brings to our coupleship.
Higher Power, teach me humility and remove my character defects so that I may love more sincerely and completely.

Amen.

Step Eight

We made a list of all persons we had harmed and became willing to make amends to them all.

Step Eight is about those people—including ourselves—who have been harmed by our couple dysfunction, such as family members, children, friends, and co-workers. In this Step, we continue to take our coupleship inventory. This Step helps us to interact with other people in new ways. It calls for *changes* in our behavior.

In Step Eight we need to determine the harm that we have caused. What is the exact nature of this harm? It helps to categorize our wrongdoing into the following four groups:

Emotional Wrongs

Raging
Holding grudges
Withholding information
Giving our partner "the silent treatment"
Making shaming or blaming statements

Material Wrongs

Borrowing, spending, or withholding money selfishly
Cheating, or not abiding by terms of couple contracts
Disregarding others' boundaries regarding personal things
Destroying or violating joint property

Moral Wrongs

Setting bad examples
Engaging in infidelity, broken promises, lying
Engaging in emotional, physical, sexual, or verbal abuse

Spiritual Wrongs

Neglecting obligations to ourselves, family, support group, or community
Avoiding self-development
Lacking gratitude
Neglecting our spiritual quest
Lacking humility
Being self-righteous
Preoccupying ourselves to the point of emotional unavailability

Now we suggest that you look at the facts and ask yourselves:

1. What are your thoughts and feelings about the harm you have done?
2. What are your fears about making amends?
3. What causes your resistance to making amends?
4. What consequences of your harmful behavior are you willing to accept?
5. What are the ways you plan to make amends?

Now that you have a better idea how your coupleship dysfunction has affected yourselves and others, make a list of people you have harmed, including yourselves. Review your amends list with your sponsor couple. Now ask for guidance on how to make amends that will not hurt others. When direct amends are not appropriate or possible, we suggest you devise alternative amends, such as praying for the well-being of those people, being kind and responsible to your partner and others, doing community service, or donating to a charity.

We become willing to make amends to our partner, ourselves, and others by admitting the harm we have done. As we become willing to look at our own behavior, we tend to become more tolerant and forgiving, less rigid and judgmental. Our viewpoints, attitudes, and beliefs will begin to change as a result of our participation in this process. Now we should be ready to move on to Step Nine.

Step Nine

We made direct amends to such people wherever possible, except when to do so would injure them or others.

This is another action step and requires a willingness to confront our issues. In order to avoid unintended harm, you may wish to review your proposed amends with your sponsor couple. For example, parents or children might be harmed by learning of compulsive behaviors. This Step takes courage, good judgment, and a careful sense of timing.

Many of us begin our Ninth Step with our children. Depending on their maturity, we discuss our unhealthy behaviors only when it is clear they will not be harmed. We make further amends to our children by respecting them as individuals, by maintaining our own recovery, and by striving to be healthy and happy adults ourselves.

We caution you not to confuse *apologies* with *amends*. Sometimes apologies are called for, but apologies are not amends. Amends are made by repairing damage when possible, and then acting differently. For example, we can apologize ten times for being late to a meeting, but this does not "*amend*" the issue. Being on time and changing our behavior becomes our amends.

As we repair the damage done to others, we are healing our own coupleship. We find satisfaction in knowing we are doing all we can to pay off emotional, material, moral, and spiritual debts.

In preparation for the actual making of the amends we suggest that you:

1. Read the Safety Guidelines (see p. 55)
2. Devote time to prayer or meditation
3. Think about what you want to say
4. Be clear—possibly writing out your amends
5. Create a comfortable, safe setting

In making the actual amends we suggest that you:

1. Keep it simple
2. Express a desire and/or ask permission: "I (we) need to admit the harm I (we) have done and take responsibility for my (our) actions. I (we) would like to make amends to you. Are you willing to receive an amends?"

The form of our amends may be something like this:
I (We) want to make an amends about ____________ .
I (We) ask for your forgiveness.
I (We) plan to change my (our) behavior by ____________ .

In making amends, we also need to make amends to ourselves and our partner. How do we make amends to ourselves? We develop new attitudes that reflect a willingness to love and forgive ourselves. The format for making an individual or coupleship amends may be similar to other amends, but you may want to use this suggested format:

I want to make an amends to our coupleship about ______ .

I would like you to forgive me for all the words that were said out of fear (thoughtlessness, inconsideration, anger, immaturity, self-righteousness, selfishness, etc.) and out of my own confusion.

I ask for your forgiveness.

I plan to change my behavior by ______________________ .

As a result of doing our amends we are developing ourselves as persons within a healthy relationship. We ask our Higher Power for the courage and wisdom to face each new challenge in our coupleship. We take responsibility for our mistakes and learn from our experiences.

The final three Steps are about practicing what we learned in the first nine Steps.

Step Ten

We continued to take personal inventory and when we were wrong promptly admitted it to our partner and to others we had harmed.

Step Ten is about continuing to take inventory of our coupleship by reviewing our behavior. A suggested way of taking this inventory is to ask: "What has my partner done to help the coupleship?" and "What have I done to harm the coupleship?" Also, "What have we, as a couple, done to harm or help others?" This can be done daily or weekly, privately or publicly. Much of our harmful behavior involves blaming our partner. A daily or weekly inventory tends to reverse the process of blaming. It also expresses what we like and appreciate in our partner. In first doing the Tenth Step, it may be helpful to write this inventory. By its nature Step Ten is an ongoing process, repeated as often as necessary. The hope is that this new behavior will become familiar and automatic.

Ongoing practice of Step Ten maintains our honesty and humility. If we become comfortable and start believing we don't need to continue practicing Step Ten or regularly attending meetings, we tend to become irritable and short-tempered, think negatively, and may relapse. Examples of relapse behavior might include avoidance, excessive working, compulsive spending, isolation, busyness, control, manipulation, withholding feelings, and difficulty with intimacy. Nothing stays the same in our life or coupleship. We are either growing or regressing.

RCA suggests three types of ongoing inventories:

1. *Spot-check inventory:* Whenever agitated or fearful, you might pause and spot-check your underlying motives.
2. *Daily or weekly inventory:* What have I done that is harmful to our coupleship? What has my partner done to support our coupleship?
3. *Long-term periodic inventory:* Perhaps an annual spiritual retreat focused on how your coupleship has grown (or not), and your role and your partner's role in this growth.

Step Ten is ongoing and never fully completed. However, having demonstrated a willingness to fully understand our own role in the dance of the coupleship, we should be ready to move on to the spirituality of Step Eleven.

Step Eleven

We sought through our common prayer and meditation to improve our conscious contact with God as we understood God, praying only for knowledge of God's will for us and the power to carry that out.

In Step Eleven we have an opportunity to develop a deeper relationship with our Higher Power. This Step is about our spiritual awakening. We improve conscious contact with our Higher Power through prayer and meditation. Appropriate prayer is sincere, humble, and not for our own selfish gain. We pray for knowledge of our Higher Power's will for us and for willingness to act on it. Meditation is an ancient art of quieting the mind. Some of us find it difficult to sit quietly and relax or quiet our racing mind, but this becomes easier with continued practice.

Couples achieving some progress with this Step may develop a greater sense of gratitude. Many of us feel a sense of being connected, guided, and sustained as we work together as a couple.

It is beneficial to spend daily intimate time together. We find that intimacy with our partner depends not only on connecting emotionally, but also spiritually. As we develop more trust in our Higher Power we can become more vulnerable and find a deeper acceptance of each other. At this point you may want to revisit your spiritual quest in Step Three to review what you want to add or change.

If you have difficulty praying, or lack experience with prayer and meditation, we suggest that you use the Serenity Prayer:

God grant us the serenity
to accept the things we cannot change,
courage to change the things we can,
and wisdom to know the difference.

God grant us the serenity

Serenity means no longer recoiling from the past, no longer living in fear because of our present behavior, nor worrying about the future. To maintain serenity, we regularly seek healthier behaviors. We try to avoid depletion, which tends to make us vulnerable to despair and old, self-destructive patterns.

To accept the things we cannot change

Acceptance means acknowledging that there are situations over which we have no control. By changing our behavior, we avoid the suffering that comes from clinging to that which no longer exists.

Courage to change the things we can

Courage to change involves giving up our attempts to control outcomes, but it does not require that we give up our boundaries or best efforts. It does mean an honest appraisal of the limits of what we can change.

And wisdom to know the difference.

Wisdom in RCA often comes from painful experiences in which we tried to control situations that frightened us, only to discover that we could not. Wisdom is our ability to evaluate our past experiences, learn from them, and let them go. Wisdom is critical in determining which things we can change and which we can't. Once we arrive at a degree of acceptance and begin to let go, we find a new energy and enthusiasm for life.

Step Twelve

Having had a spiritual awakening as the result of these Steps, we tried to carry this message to other couples, and to practice these principles in all aspects of our lives, our relationship, and our families.

Step Twelve is about taking the message of couple recovery to other couples. Those who have worked the Twelve Steps have much to offer other couples. When we are able to shine the light of our own recovery experiences in such a manner that others find their own way, we are practicing the Twelfth Step.

We find that spiritual awakenings are seldom sudden occurrences, but more generally gradual shifts in perspective. These spiritual awakenings often take place through couples working the Steps of RCA together. We typically gain an awareness of the importance of our coupleship as *"a oneness and an entity,"* and thus reach new levels of commitment. When we learn that *neither one of us is the center of the universe,* we may be able to see how we fit together and how our coupleship fits into the rest of the world. These awakenings transform us both individually and as a couple.

We acquire new depth and understanding of the wisdom of the Twelve Steps. As we watch other couples around us being transformed, we witness the spiritual nature of the program in action. We come to believe in miracles.

Just as in our individual programs, in the RCA fellowship we carry the message in many ways including:

1. Sharing as a couple in RCA meetings
2. Seeking and accepting service positions
3. Being sponsors and temporary sponsors

4. Carrying the message of hope to others:

    - at retreats
    - in our individual program meetings, for example, by posting flyers and ads, as well as talking about RCA to people who have "couple issues"
    - by informing the helping community (spiritual, medical, legal, and counseling)
    - by making a schedule of RCA meetings available

5. Supporting the national convention through participation, voting as a group delegate couple, and making financial contributions

6. Serving on the World Service Organization (WSO) Board of Trustees, or on a WSO Service Committee, or volunteering

7. Writing our couple story and sharing it with others (especially by having it published in the RCA *Blue Book*)

Having worked these Twelve Steps, it is important to remember that Step work is meant for a lifetime. As we practice these Steps we have a better understanding of our history, our lives, our coupleship, and our Higher Power. As we share our experience, strength, and hope, we see the positive effects on our relationships, and if we have children we can break the chains that have bound families for generations. We learn from those couples who have gone before. The message we carry is a liberating one. Working with newcomers is not only a rewarding experience; it shows where we have been and where we need to go.

Chapter III

RCA Groups and Meetings

The Importance of Meetings

We attend RCA meetings to learn how the program works, and to share our experience, strength, and hope with other couples. We learn that our struggles are not unique, and we gain the hope and assurance that our own coupleships can recover and grow.

Couples who come to RCA may not be certain that the RCA program is right for them. Attending meetings may help them see how the program may be useful to them. Some groups recommend that a couple attend at least six meetings before deciding whether or not to continue. Some of us have found that we needed to attend RCA meetings and hear about the recoveries of other couples before we could trust that we could get along well enough to participate in our own couple recovery work.

It is in meetings that we glimpse the power of the spiritual connection that distinguishes successful *coupleships* from just *relationships.* And it is in meetings that we observe other couples and hear how they are using the suggestions of RCA to restore, build, or improve their coupleships. Seeing effective couples shows us who we may choose as sponsor couples, which is an important element in couple recovery. Most RCA couples agree that regular meetings are essential to the spiritual growth of our coupleships.

Giving the Program a Fair Chance

We encourage new couples to remain committed to each other for a specific period of time as they attend RCA meetings together. Some couples are eager to get a sponsor couple and to begin working the Steps together right away. For other couples, the first few months in RCA can be overwhelming. Just learning to listen and not fight is a reasonable initial goal. If you need to sit and absorb the meeting process for a few months, we encourage you to do so. Through attending meetings, we learn to trust the process of working the RCA program together.

Intimacy Backlash

Meetings often bring couples closer and encourage communication. But many couples have their biggest fights after a first, or an especially intimate, RCA meeting. We call this phenomenon **intimacy backlash.** This is not exclusive to newcomers. We have found it helpful to remind everyone about intimacy backlash. It is important to remember that when this happens, we are temporarily reverting to old behaviors. We need to remind ourselves and each other that this is a *temporary* backlash. We are actually right on track, and making progress. Keep coming back.

Sharing At Meetings

Many of us believe that our coupleships recover in direct proportion to our willingness to share. It is through listening and participating *honestly* that we find the recovery we seek. Being honest and vulnerable in front of our partners is frightening but well worth it. We then experience the power of the program, and find hope and spirituality. But some couples may not want to discuss some things in a meeting. We can talk with our sponsor couple about issues we would rather not share with the entire RCA meeting.

Meeting Diversity

RCA is open to all committed adult couples seeking to create or restore a caring, committed, and intimate monogamous relationship regardless of age, sexual orientation, gender identification, religious background, culture, race, class, national origin, physical or mental challenge, or political affiliation. The RCA fellowship actively supports valuing differences both within a coupleship and among couples of diverse backgrounds. In our coupleships and in our groups, we are committed to valuing our differences and surmounting the barriers to serenity. Diversity is important to our coupleships and to the RCA fellowship because each of us, being different, makes a richer contribution to the whole. Each individual meeting is autonomous except in matters affecting other groups and RCA as a whole. We encourage you to check the directory on our website, www.recoveringcouples.org, and call or email the Group Contact Couple (GCC) listed before attending a new meeting.

Creating a Safe Environment in Our Meetings

When couples come to RCA they bring with them the same kinds of baggage that alcoholics, co-dependents, or addicts bring to their individual recovery programs. The main difference between the person who comes to an individual recovery program and the couple that comes to RCA is that the RCA couple attends *as a couple*. This might not seem like such a big problem, but we have found this can be a major difficulty!

Placing principles before personalities becomes one of the biggest challenges. Not only is there interaction between one member of a couple and the other member, but there is interaction *between* the coupleships, and interplay between all the people individually in all the couples. Principles become very important.

Getting one person to come to Twelve-Step recovery is very difficult. Getting two people in a coupleship to come to RCA can be even harder. Getting two partners to work together towards the same goal must be handled by a Higher Power! Trying to not judge one another in our own coupleship is hard. Getting several couples not to judge or to take others' inventories is even harder. Most groups find that using the RCA Safety Guidelines (see p. 55) in their meetings is essential to creating a safe environment.

We have found that just as a coupleship flourishes in an atmosphere of safety, a meeting grows when safety is established. Communication is important, yet many couples come to RCA *fighting* instead of *communicating*. Some couples don't fight. They just isolate and shut down. To promote intimacy, we strive for safe communication so couples can deal with conflict in a healthier way. We have found that as human beings, it is OK to have feelings, and to express them clearly and respectfully. It is OK to make mistakes, and to make appropriate amends. It is OK to disagree, and become accepting of our disagreement. It is OK to have needs and learn to respectfully ask for them to be heard.

Honoring the Safety Guidelines

In order to follow the Safety Guidelines (see p. 55) during the meeting, most groups read them aloud, usually just before the sharing begins. In some groups, the Chair makes sure the Safety Guidelines are followed; in other groups, the Timekeeper has that task.

Keeping the RCA Focus

Our RCA World Service Organization offers RCA-approved literature. Much of this is included in the RCA Meeting Starter Packet. We stay focused on the message of Recovering Couples Anonymous by using these materials in our meetings. The Meeting Format and many of the customary readings that are suggested for group use are offered on the official website and in the Meeting Readings following this section. By using this material, we create the opportunity for couples to find an RCA "home" anywhere in the world.

Planning Our Meeting Format

Each group is autonomous and is free to establish a meeting format that best fits the needs of its members. We suggest that meetings be mindful of the Traditions when establishing a meeting format. The RCA Traditions (see pp. 56–57) provide guidelines for how we conduct ourselves in RCA.

We suggest that each meeting have a written format adopted through the group's informed conscience. There are many options for RCA meetings. Speaker couples may share their story or share their experiences with a Step or a Tool of RCA, either in person, by phone connection, or by playing a tape or CD. Some groups have a Literature Study focus. There are "Share and Feedback" meetings, Step Meetings, Reflection Meetings, Tradition Meetings, and Topic Meetings. Some groups have a different focus each week of the month. A suggested Basic Meeting Format follows, and there are many examples of meeting formats on the website www.recovering-couples.org.

Suggested Meeting Format

(Please adapt for your own group purposes.)

Pass out for members to read:

- The Preamble (see p. 50)
- How It Works Part 1 (see p. 51)
- The Twelve Steps (see p. 52)
- How It Works Part 2 (see p. 54)
- The Twelve Traditions (see pp. 56–57)
- The Safety Guidelines (see p. 55)
- The Promises (see pp. 59–60)

Readings may also include:

- The Reflections (see pp. 233–296)
- Characteristics of Functional/Dysfunctional Couples (see pp. 7–9)
- The Tools (see p. 58)

"Welcome to the ***(group name or meeting day/time)*** meeting of Recovering Couples Anonymous. My name is (***give your name***) and I'm a member of Recovering Couples Anonymous. We hope you will find in this fellowship the help and friendship we have been privileged to enjoy. Let's open the meeting with a moment of silence, followed by the Serenity Prayer. In this group, the Serenity Prayer uses the words 'we' and 'us.'" (see p. 60.) ***(Group recites the Serenity Prayer.)***

"A member will read the RCA Preamble." (see p. 50.) ***(Member does so.)***

"A member will read How It Works Part 1." (see p. 51.) ***(Member does so.)***

"A member will read the Twelve Steps of RCA." (see p. 52.) ***(Member does so.)***

"A member will read How It Works Part 2." (see p. 54.) ***(Member does so.)***

"A member will read the Tradition of the month **(or all Twelve Traditions)**." (see pp. 56–57.) ***(Member does so.)***

<u>*Optional Readings.*</u> ***(Groups usually seek to balance the time allocated for the various readings with the time allocated for couple-sharing.)***

"Now is the time we introduce ourselves. I'm ***(give your name)*** and I'm in recovery with ***(give your partner's name)." (Partner responds similarly. Group greets the couple.)*** "Hello_______." "Hello_______." ***(Other attendees continue the process, giving their names using a similar formula. All are greeted by the group in turn.)***

"We will circulate our meeting's phone and email list. People who put their names on this list are willing to receive program calls and emails. Phone calls and emails are helpful program tools. Leave your number and email address if you like." ***(Chair [or Secretary, Meeting Facilitator, etc.] circulates the phone and email list.)***

Rules of the house ***(e.g., no smoking, where to park, no cross-talk, literature, bathrooms, coffee, no scents, etc.)***

"The format of this meeting is _________. ***(Speaker Couple, or Step Study, or Reflection, or Tradition, etc. Often the format will rotate within the month. For example: Week 1: Speaker Couple. Week 2: Step of the month. Week 3: Reflection. Week 4: Tradition of the month. Week 5 (if there is one): Special topic [e.g., how to make an informed group conscience, sponsoring, what RCA has done for our coupleship, value of RCA retreats, potlucks, conventions, etc.])***

"This is the time for sharing our experience, strength, and hope. If one member of a couple shares, the other member may share next or pass. Please keep your shares brief. We ask that we avoid cross-talk. Avoiding cross-talk means that when we speak, we address the meeting as a whole."

(If this is a Speaker Couple meeting, the Chair says): "The speakers will have about 10 minutes each to share on a topic they have chosen. ***(Chair introduces speakers.)*** "Now let's welcome our speakers for tonight." ***(If this is a Step Study or Reflection or Tradition meeting, the Chair asks,)*** "Will whoever has the ***(Step or Reflection or Tradition)*** please read it?" ***(or)*** "Will you read the first paragraph and pass it to your neighbor?"

(When the reading or speakers are finished, the Chair asks): "Will a member please read the Safety Guidelines?" (see p. 55)

(When the Safety Guidelines have been read, the Chair says): "The meeting is now open for sharing." ***(In some meetings the shares are timed. If this is the case, the Chair will then say):*** "Sharing is limited to _____ minutes. At the end of _____ minutes, please wrap up your sharing as rapidly as possible, so that all may have a chance to share."

(Members share.)

(At about 15 minutes before closing, the Chair may say) "Would any of our newcomers like to share?" ***(and/or)*** "Does anyone have a real need to share?"

(The Chair ends the sharing at 5 minutes before the close of the meeting by saying): "Now we practice the Seventh Tradition, which states that every RCA group ought to be fully self-supporting, declining outside contributions. Our contributions go for rent and literature, and for support of our National Service Organization."

(If this has been a Speaker Couple meeting, the Chair says): "Let's thank our Speakers."

"Our next business meeting will be ______________________."

"Are there any other RCA or related announcements?"
(Members give their announcements.)

"A member will now read the Promises." ***(see pp. 59–60, Member does so. Chair distributes copies of The Unity Prayer.)***

"Let's end our meeting with The Unity Prayer." ***(see p. 60; or the Serenity Prayer, see p. 60, or another prayer).***

(The meeting is now over.)

Suggested Meeting Readings

Preamble

(Adapted with the permission of AA Grapevine, Inc.)

Ours is a fellowship of recovering couples. We suffer from many addictions and dysfunctions, and we share our experience, strength, and hope with each other that we may solve our common problems and help other recovering couples restore their relationships. The only requirement for membership is the desire to remain committed to each other and to develop new intimacy.

There are no dues or fees for membership; we are self-supporting through our own contributions. We are not allied with any organization. We do not wish to engage in any controversy, neither endorse nor oppose any causes.

Although there is no organizational affiliation between Alcoholics Anonymous and our fellowship, we are based on the principles of AA. Our primary purpose is to stay committed in loving and intimate relationships and to help other couples achieve freedom from dysfunctional relationships.

How RCA Works—Part I

Adapted from the book, *Alcoholics Anonymous*

Rarely have we seen a couple fail who has thoroughly followed our path. Those who do not recover are people who cannot or will not completely give themselves to this simple program. They are naturally incapable of grasping and developing a manner of living which demands mutual and rigorous honesty. There are those, too, who cannot or will not make a commitment to their partner. There are those who suffer from grave emotional and mental disorders, but many of them do recover if they have the capacity to be honest.

Our stories disclose in a general way what we used to be like, what happened, and what we are like now. If you have decided you want what we have and are willing to go to any length to get it, then you are ready to take certain steps.

At some of these we balked. We thought we could find an easier, softer way. But we could not. With all the earnestness at our command, we beg of you to be fearless and thorough from the start. Some of us have tried to hold on to our old ideas, and the result was nil until we let go absolutely.

Remember that we deal with addictions—cunning, baffling, powerful. We also deal with all those memories of past hurts, misbehavior, and vows violated. Without help our anger, hurt, and mistrust are too great for us. But there is one who has all power; that one is God. May you find God now.

Half measures availed us nothing. We stood at the turning point. We asked God's protection and care with complete abandon. Here are the steps we took, which are suggested as a program of recovery.

The Twelve Steps of RCA

1. We admitted we were powerless over our relationship—that our lives together had become unmanageable.
2. We came to believe that a power greater than ourselves could restore us to commitment and intimacy.
3. We made a decision to turn our wills and our life together over to the care of God as we understood God.
4. We made a searching and fearless moral inventory of our relationship together as a couple.
5. We admitted to God, to each other, and to another couple the exact nature of our wrongs.
6. We were entirely ready to have God remove all these defects of character, communication, and caring.
7. We humbly asked God to remove our shortcomings.
8. We made a list of all persons we had harmed and became willing to make amends to them all.
9. We made direct amends to such people wherever possible, except when to do so would injure them or others.
10. We continued to take personal inventory and when we were wrong promptly admitted it to our partner and to others we had harmed.
11. We sought through our common prayer and meditation to improve our conscious contact with God as we understood God, praying only for knowledge of God's will for us and the power to carry that out.
12. Having had a spiritual awakening as the result of these Steps, we tried to carry this message to other couples, and to practice these principles in all aspects of our lives, our relationship, and our families.

Adapted from The Twelve Steps of Alcoholics Anonymous which read: 1. We admitted we were powerless over alcohol—that our lives had become unmanageable. 2. Came to believe that a Power greater than ourselves could restore us to sanity. 3. Made a decision to turn our will and our lives over to the care of God as we understood Him. 4. Made a searching and fearless moral inventory of ourselves. 5. Admitted to God, to ourselves and to another human being the exact nature of our wrongs. 6. Were entirely ready to have God remove all these defects of character. 7. Humbly asked Him to remove our shortcomings. 8. Made a list of all persons we had harmed and became willing to make amends to them all. 9. Made direct amends to such people wherever possible, except when to do so would injure them or others. 10. Continued to take personal inventory and when we were wrong promptly admitted it. 11. Sought through prayer and meditation to improve our conscious contact with God, as we understood Him, praying only for knowledge of His will for us and the power to carry that out. 12. Having had a spiritual awakening as the result of these Steps, we tried to carry this message to alcoholics, and to practice these principles in all our affairs. (The Twelve Steps and Twelve Traditions of Alcoholics Anonymous have been reprinted and adapted with permission of Alcoholics Anonymous World Services, Inc. (AAWS). Permission to reprint and adapt the Twelve Steps and Twelve Traditions does not mean that AA is affiliated with this program. AA is a program of recovery from alcoholism only—use of AA's Steps and Traditions or an adapted version of its Steps and Traditions in connection with programs and activities which are patterned after AA, but which address other problems, or use in any other non-AA context, does not imply otherwise.

How RCA Works—Part II

Adapted from the book, *Alcoholics Anonymous*

Many of us exclaimed, "What an order! We can't go through with it. Our love is lost, our vows forever violated, our communication destroyed, our families broken beyond repair."

Do not be discouraged. No couple among us has been able to maintain anything like perfect adherence to these principles.

We are not saints, our love is not perfect, our energy not unbounded, nor our relationships ideal. There is no such thing as the ultimately caring and nurturing partner or perfect intimacy. The point is that we are willing to grow together along spiritual lines. The principles we have set down are guides to progress. We claim spiritual progress rather than spiritual perfection. In our spirituality we claim the goal of greater caring, communication, and intimacy.

Our understanding of our addictions, dysfunctions, and our personal histories before and after recovery make clear three pertinent ideas:

1. That our relationship had become unmanageable. That despite our best efforts we were headed for separation and/or divorce.

2. That probably no human power could have restored us to commitment and intimacy.

3. That God could and would if God were sought.

RCA Safety Guidelines

Anonymity and mutual respect of boundaries are essential to providing a healing experience to each of us. Most of us have had great difficulty establishing our boundaries, assertiveness, and personal space. We are sensitive to cross-talk. Our purpose is not to give advice or try to fix one another, but rather to create a safe environment where we can experience and share our pain. We have found that:

1. It is OK to feel.
2. It is OK to make mistakes.
3. It is OK to have respectful conflict.
4. It is OK to have needs and ask for them to be met.
5. It is important to respect others (partners and others in the group). It is important to avoid self-righteous statements, baiting or button-pushing statements, case-building statements, and the taking or sharing of another person's inventory.
6. It is important to respect ourselves and to avoid self put-downs and self-pity. It is helpful to take ownership of our own story and to take credit for our progress and work in recovery.
7. Anonymity is our spiritual foundation. Whom you see here, what you hear here, when you leave here, let it stay here.

We have care and concern for ourselves and our coupleships. We meet to both receive and provide the nurturing our relationships need to grow and endure. For that reason, it is important for us to act and speak respectfully to our partners and others. As we do this, we value the group and the relationships in it.

The Twelve Traditions of RCA

1. Our common welfare should come first; couple recovery depends upon RCA unity.
2. For our group purpose there is but one ultimate authority, a loving God as known in our group conscience. Our leaders are but trusted servants; they do not govern.
3. The only requirement for RCA membership is a desire to remain in a committed relationship.
4. Each group should be autonomous except in matters affecting other groups or RCA as a whole.
5. Each group has but one primary purpose, to carry its message to recovering couples who still suffer.
6. RCA ought never endorse, finance, or lend the RCA name to any related facility or outside enterprise, lest problems of money, property, and prestige divert us from our primary purpose.
7. Every RCA group should be fully self-supporting, declining outside contributions.
8. Recovering Couples Anonymous should remain forever nonprofessional, but our service centers may employee special workers.
9. RCA, as such, ought never be organized; but we may create service boards or committees directly responsible to those they serve.
10. Recovering Couples Anonymous has no opinion on outside issues; hence the RCA name ought never be drawn into public controversy.

11. Our public relations policy is based on attraction rather than promotion; we need always maintain personal anonymity at the level of press, radio, TV, and films.

12. Anonymity is the spiritual foundation of all our traditions, ever reminding us to place principles before personalities.

Adapted with permission from the Twelve Traditions of Alcoholics Anonymous, which read: 1. Our common welfare should come first; personal recovery depends upon AA unity. 2. For our group purpose, there is but one ultimate authority—a loving God as he may express Himself in our group conscience. Our leaders are but trusted servants; they do not govern. 3. The only requirement for AA membership is a desire to stop drinking. 4. Each group should be autonomous except in matters affecting other groups of AA as a whole. 5. Each group has but one purpose—to carry its message to the alcoholic who still suffers. 6. An AA group ought never endorse, finance or lend the AA name to any related facility or outside enterprise, lest problems of money, property and prestige divert us from our primary purpose. 7. Every AA group ought to be fully self-supporting, declining outside contributions. 8. Alcoholics Anonymous should remain forever nonprofessional, but our service centers may employ special workers. 9. AA, as such, ought never be organized; but we may create service boards or committees directly responsible to those they serve. 10. Alcoholics Anonymous has no opinion on outside issues; hence the AA name ought never be drawn into public controversy. 11. Our public relations policy is based on attraction rather than promotion; we need always maintain personal anonymity at the level of press, radio and films. 12. Anonymity is the spiritual foundation of all our traditions, ever reminding us to place principles before personalities.

RCA Tools of Recovery

We find these recovery tools useful for restoring and sustaining the commitment, intimacy, and joy in our coupleships. (See Chapter IV, pp. 106–112 for more detailed explanation of the Tools.)

1. Attending and sharing at meetings
2. Calling a Meeting of Two
3. Calling a Moratorium or "Time-Out"
4. Conflict resolution contracts and written agreements (see Appendix, pp. 349–353)
5. Developing a support system within and outside of RCA
6. "I" statements
7. Listening and communicating
8. Reading and working the Steps
9. Reading recovery literature
10. Service
11. Sponsorship
12. Using The Safety Guidelines (see p. 55)

Closing Readings

The Promises of RCA

Adapted from the book, *Alcoholics Anonymous*
Chapter 6—"Into Action" (Page 86)

If we are honest about our commitment and painstaking about working the Twelve Steps together we will quickly be amazed at how soon our love returns. We are going to know a new freedom and a new happiness. We will learn how to play and have fun together. As we experience mutual forgiveness we will not regret the past nor wish to shut the door on it. Trust in each other will return. We will comprehend the word serenity, and we will know peace.

No matter how close to brokenness we have come, we will see how our experiences can benefit others. That feeling of uselessness, shame, and self-pity will disappear. We will lose interest in selfish things and gain interest in our partners, families, and others. Self-seeking will slip away. Our whole attitude and outlook on life will change. Fear of people and of economic insecurity will leave us. We will intuitively know how to handle situations which used to baffle us. We will be better parents, workers, helpers, and friends. We will suddenly realize that God is doing for us what we could not do for ourselves.

Are these extravagant promises? We think not. They are being fulfilled among us-sometimes quickly, sometimes slowly. They will always materialize if we work for them.

For those of you who are new to our fellowship there are no problems that you have experienced that are not common to many of us.

Just as our love for our partners has been imperfect, we may not always be adequately able to express to you the deep love and acceptance we feel for you. Keep coming back, the process of loving and communication grows in us and with each other one day at a time.

Remember always, what is said here stays here.

Unity Prayer

(The Unity Prayer is printed with permission (1993) of Rosanne S., the author. In Overeaters Anonymous it is known as the OA Promise.)

I put my hand in yours,
and together we can do what we could never do alone.
No longer is there a sense of hopelessness.
No longer must we each depend
upon our own unsteady willpower.
We are all together now, reaching out our hands
for a power and strength greater than ours.
And as we join hands, we find love and understanding
beyond our wildest dreams.

Serenity Prayer for Couples

God, grant us the serenity
to accept the things we cannot change,
courage to change the things we can,
and wisdom to know the difference.

Some Suggested Meeting Topics

1. A coupleship is a oneness.

Together two people who are in a committed relationship form a *coupleship*, a *oneness*, a distinct and separate *entity*. This coupleship has a life of its own and needs to be nurtured appropriately. Couple recovery depends on this nurturance. Both partners in a dysfunctional relationship need individual recoveries: meetings, sponsors, therapy, a support group, spirituality, recreation, vocation, and individual interests. A coupleship needs these same elements for couple recovery. There are, then, three elements of couple recovery. Our individual recoveries are the two basic components. Our couple recovery is the third component. One of the symbols of RCA is the three-legged stool.

Each leg represents one of these components. If one leg is missing, the stool will fall. If one component is missing, the coupleship may fail.

This is why, for example, many of us know how hard it is for one partner to be identified as the addict and in recovery while the other partner has no individual recovery. One partner grows and the other doesn't. Individual recovery for only one partner will, therefore, produce more distance in the coupleship.

2. In addictive relationships, the partner of a primary addict is referred to as the co-addict.

Addiction theory suggests that one or both partners is often a co-dependent and/or an enabler. Some co-addicts have assumed that if the addict gets sober, they will no longer be co-addicts. This is not true. Co-addiction is a disease in and of itself. Co-addicts often grow up in families where they learn to cope with addictions of all kinds. They may find that throughout their lives they have related to a series of addicts. Their current partner may be just another in a long list. They find themselves attracted to the familiar, and thus may unconsciously choose their current partner. They will not get well just because their partner is in recovery. They must learn how to break the pattern of co-addiction themselves. Co-addicts need to be in recovery *for themselves.*

Sobriety for co-addicts includes:

- learning about healthy self-nurturing;
- clear communication of feelings, needs, and concerns;
- respectful detachment.

Using the RCA tools of recovery, co-addicts learn to develop personal boundaries and to express their individuality. Co-addicts may have their own primary addiction(s). It is not uncommon for two addicts to be in a relationship and co-addicted to each other. For both the addict and the co-addict, lessons learned in their family of origin may be the culprit.

Sometimes current crises trigger unhealthy coping behaviors. For example, co-addicts might turn to food when feeling abandoned by the addict. The use of food as a mood elevator or a symbol for love might have been learned in childhood from a parent who filled the emptiness inside by eating. Other co-addicts might turn to work or excessive "busyness." Both partners need to work on their individual recoveries if their coupleship is to recover, and if they wish to stop their family legacies from affecting their children and future generations.

3. Both partners must accept responsibility for the health or dysfunction of their coupleship.

Both partners bring their own addictions, personalities, family-of-origin messages, and individual dysfunctions into the coupleship. The coupleship doesn't create dysfunctions, though it may trigger or reinforce them. It is the elements *brought by both partners* that contribute to the nature of the coupleship.

This does not mean that one is responsible for any of the addictive or dysfunctional behaviors of one's partner. Those behaviors are their responsibility and reflect choices that they make in order to cope with feelings (including the feelings generated by the current state of the coupleship). *Both partners* are responsible for the presence or absence of intimacy.

4. Both partners may be co-dependent.

Mutual co-dependency may be an aspect of co-addiction. Partner co-dependency may be based on fear of abandonment, deep shame, or a need for approval. Enmeshed partner attachments may result, causing both partners to seek to control each other, usually to prevent their partner from leaving.

There can be two styles of control: *manipulative* and *domineering*. The *manipulative* co-dependents seek to secure their partners by always doing what their partners need or want. This compels these co-dependents to lose their independent identity and sometimes to almost literally die for their partners. This style, which is usually unconscious, might also include portraying themselves as victims, which projects images of being such poor, wretched, mistreated people that no one could ever leave them.

The *domineering* style is more directly controlling. In this style, the co-dependents use anger (or even rage), harsh orders, demands, argumentation, threats, and suggestions (in a variety of subtle and not-so-subtle ways) that they are superior and should control the behavior of their partners.

Whichever style is present, *both partners fear the other's leaving* and use their own personal co-dependent style to prevent abandonment. In recovery, partners can learn how to be in the coupleship *by choice.* Before such recovery, co-dependent partners lack choice. They are in the coupleship out of necessity—the compulsion of their shared addiction to each other.

5. Both partners probably suffer from intimacy disorder.

Intimacy disorder is based on the individual feeling of shame that says, "*If you really knew me, you would hate me.*" This disorder produces a fear of intimacy and an inability to be honest and vulnerable with one's partner.

One of the maxims of intimacy disorder is that one will be *least honest with the person one is most afraid of losing.* Those of us who live with intimacy disorder often experience great resentment because our partners appear able to be totally honest with relative strangers but not with us. We need to realize that being the last to know is not because our partner is willingly trying to deceive us or doesn't care for us, but because of a deep fear of being abandoned.

Ultimately, intimacy is a matter of practicing honest risk-taking. We must learn to take great risks telling the truth about ourselves—the truth about current behaviors, feelings, attitudes, preferences, and needs, as well as old behaviors when this revelation will not hurt the other. As we take these risks, we find that our partners usually don't leave, that instead they are grateful for the honesty. Practicing honesty can build trust and intimacy; lack of honesty cannot.

6. Both partners usually have significant family-of-origin issues.

The limited amount of research that has been conducted with addicted couples suggests that both partners may be victims of some kind of neglect or abuse. Addicted couples may have learned unhealthy styles of relationships in their families of origin, where they did not receive healthy modeling of nurturing and intimacy.

Each partner may be the victim of violation of personal boundaries—emotional, physical, sexual, or spiritual. Such violations often create suppressed rage, coupled with profound fear and anxiety. Addictions may develop as ways of coping with these feelings.

Both partners also may be victims of abandonment, in which their basic needs for nurturing and security were not met by one or both of their parents (or primary caretakers). This form of abuse can leave emotional voids full of great loneliness.

Individuals may suppress memories of this abuse. The feelings, however, can be provoked without the past memories becoming conscious. Our partner may say or do something that unconsciously reminds us of our abuse. This may trigger our old, buried feelings. Our reactions of terror, despair, or rage may seem out of proportion to the current event.

Many couples, for example, fight over trivial matters. Their rage or sadness may seem totally inappropriate or unconnected to anything in the present. Unresolved arguments and "mysterious" emotional reactions can often be traced to family-of-origin issues.

Abandonment in one's family of origin may create the co-dependency described in Meeting Topic 4. Co-dependency is based on fear of abandonment. Often we fantasize our partners will make us feel OK. We may think that our partner will be the nurturing parent(s) we didn't have in childhood. Consequently, the partner expected to fulfill this role may rebel, saying, *"I'm not your mother (or father)."*

No partner can ever take the place of a parent. When partners realize this, pressure to be people they can never be is relieved. True partner intimacy may then become possible.

7. In order to stay together, either or both partners may need to divorce their parents.

This assumes that at least one parent has been abusive. We may need to create boundaries around the abusive parent(s), even if only in our memory of them. This can mean a variety of things, from not seeing or talking to that parent, to limits on the frequency or nature of visits. This will be particularly true if there is fear that the parent will continue the pattern of abuse with their grandchildren.

If there has been abandonment, we will need to grieve the loss. This might involve significant amounts of counseling and/or group support. We have found that *grief work needs to be verbalized.* When this happens pressure is taken off our partner to be the perfect nurturer. *If we can divorce ourselves from our abusive parents, we won't need to divorce each other.*

8. Couples are full of illusions about ideal relationships.

Addicted couples may have lists of requirements for what they believe makes a "Good Couple." For example, the partners may think if they have violated their marital vows, have money problems, or are not perfect parents, they can never be acceptable as a couple.

Sometimes standards are reinforced by idealistic beliefs or religious values. For example, couples might think, *"The sun should never set on our anger."* Such couples might argue well into the night trying to *"get it right."*

We encourage recovering couples to make a list of these ideals, and try to determine which expectations may be totally unrealistic. For example, some couples may never obtain the happiness they thought they would have or should have. Their children will never be perfect. To prevent living a life based on disappointments, couples need to let go of those false ideals and perhaps grieve their losses.

Perhaps the addicted partners expect to have a certain amount of money. If so, they may need help to learn how to set reasonable spending plans, to balance the checkbook, or to make wise investments. For support in reaching these goals, the partners may choose specific sponsors, such as a couple with financial expertise, or they may attend a group focusing on financial health.

Reaching out for help is an essential and valuable tool for resolving these illusions. Recovering couples need to learn that they are not alone. They also need to accept that they have limitations.

9. Just as individuals have slips, so will couples.

Just as individuals in recovery know that addiction lasts a lifetime and they must continue their programs for life, so partners learn they must maintain recovery in their coupleship for life. If couples stop working their program, experience has taught us that old patterns of dysfunction will likely return. Just as individual addicts have slips, so will couples. Slips occur in coupleships when:

- communication breaks down,
- old fights and patterns of interaction return, and
- partners start distancing from each other.

Couples in recovery learn to sense these patterns, and can feel when intimacy is breaking down. They can recognize that familiar feelings of isolation and loneliness are returning to haunt them. Old angers and resentments are resurrected, and fears of abandonment are elevated. Hopelessness can overcome suffering couples when they have relapsed into the old dance of dysfunction.

When feelings of loneliness return, old individual patterns of addiction may recur. In response, partners may criticize some of each other's old addictive patterns, which in turn may cause their partners to further distance themselves. This creates a relapse into dysfunction that causes the partners to distance further and further from each other—a "couple addictive cycle."

At times like these we need to admit again to ourselves our powerlessness and lack of control and to use the Tools of RCA to get out of the abyss by reaching out to our sponsor couples and attending meetings for couple support.

10. There may be little social support for the recovering coupleship.

When couples enter recovery, the social system around them may not comprehend or accept the changes both partners are making, and may not support the partners in their efforts. We have found RCA to be a useful support for us in our efforts to change.

Certain family members or old friends who are not in recovery may have an investment in maintaining the old ways of interaction and may discourage any changes. This unhelpful dynamic may include a couple's children, who may not embrace their parents' new way of life. Children may have grown accustomed to their old dysfunctional relationship with their parents. As changes in recovery alter family dynamics and power relationships, these changes can be unsettling for the children. They may also have learned to play one parent against the other, often by triangulating to "win" a parent's approval. Too often this approval can come at the expense of maintaining healthy relationships in the family.

A healthy balance of some time together as well as time apart is the formula for creating a vibrant recovering family. The family situation will improve if members focus on their own recoveries as well as couple recovery. As the parents' world expands, children may demonstrate behaviors that indicate their fear of abandonment. Both partners can show love by assuring their children they are loved and making sure each are given special time and attention.

Non-recovering old friends may not understand the changes in a recovering couple. Relations with these old friends may become strained. Furthermore, continuing to connect with them may lead to old addictive patterns. While no one wants to abandon old friends, it is important to be careful. Eventually both partners will find that new recovering friends likely will be the ones to whom they gravitate.

Social and economic conditions may not be supportive of couple recovery. For example, both partners typically need to earn an income, leaving time for the coupleship at a premium. If partners try to share responsibility around the home plus care for the children as well as for elderly parents, employers may not understand or accept the need for creative scheduling. Additionally, couples may feel threatened by old debts or other economic concerns. A recovering couple may find that its savings have been depleted by out-of-control behaviors. With creative budgeting, and support from their sponsors, partners may find that they can manage to live within their means.

Ultimately, a recovering couple must be ready to go to any lengths to recover. If the partners work on their own personal as well as couple recovery, they should be able to make the lifestyle changes needed to support their recovery. They may need to grieve the loss of family support, friendships, and even former jobs, houses, or communities. It may become necessary for couples to remove themselves from "slippery" people, places, and things that jeopardize their recovery.

11. Resolving underlying relationship issues supports both personal and coupleship recovery.

Divorce or separation, usually are not solutions to dealing with coupleship problems. If the partners in a coupleship don't work on their issues in the current coupleship, these same issues will likely resurface in future relationships. We have found that accepting this premise has increased our incentive to work on our couple recovery with our current partner.

Often, as new RCA members with years of individual recovery, we find to our amazement and disappointment that our "new" couple issues are the same as the ones we experienced in previous coupleships. We may have worked to become the "healthiest" person possible, but our relationship issues will continue to be the same, unless we face certain underlying issues in couple recovery. Resolving these issues can help us heal with our partners; we can transform our coupleships, while at the same time becoming healthier, happier individuals.

However, this does not mean everyone should stay in a coupleship at all costs. If one or both of the partners are *abusive* it might be a matter of emotional or physical safety to get out of harm's way and work on one's own individual recovery in safety. In RCA, we aspire to grow by learning healthy ways to relate to our partner, our Higher Power, and ourselves. Ultimately, both partners must accept the paths revealed by their own Higher Power.

12. Couples will experience shame, just as individuals do.

We must be aware that our individual shame is doubled in coupleship when we become convinced that we are a terrible couple. Sometimes we may feel we are "terrible" friends, parents, sexual partners, communicators, managers of money—seemingly not doing as well as other couples in RCA, etc. This is called *couple shame.* We may think that we are in the worst coupleship imaginable. In this state of mind, it may seem to us that the only solution is to end the coupleship.

The answer for couple shame is the same as for individual shame. As we tell our story to other couples, we learn that we are not alone in our problems. In this way, we can also experience affirmation for our progress in recovery. Additionally, by getting a sponsor couple, working the Steps, and working our own individual recovery programs we will begin to heal. Gradually, over time, we can experience intimacy that few other couples know.

If we understand the dysfunctions of addictive couples, we can also reduce our shame. Since we typically come from dysfunctional families, is it any wonder that we have difficulty with intimate relationships? As a recovering couple, we need to learn to nurture our relationship. A loving, nurturing relationship is possible, but only as we as a couple practice the Twelve Steps and grow together in its recovery.

Developing RCA Groups

An Informed Group Conscience: Where Does RCA Get Its Guidance?

The Second Tradition states, "For our group purpose there is but one ultimate authority—a loving God as known in our group conscience. Our leaders are but trusted servants; they do not govern." When a group needs to address an issue, the members get all the information they can and come together to discuss it. We seek to be guided by a Higher Power in reaching a decision that will be good for the group as a whole. This decision is normally called the *group conscience,* and it is usually wiser than any individual member's conclusion.

One issue common to many RCA groups is that of the founding couple becoming the *de facto* final authority for the group. In these instances—and often with the best of intentions—personalities have been placed before principles. With honest sharing and through the process of group conscience, often difficult issues like this can be addressed gently, positively, and in the spirit of loving discussion.

In RCA, as in all Twelve-Step fellowships, our leaders are simply trusted servants exercising only limited authority. When a group is starting up, usually more experienced couples guide the meeting, attending to most of the tasks. Once the group is firmly established, however, these couples prudently tend to retire to the sidelines where they may be consulted but not interfere with the principle of rotation of service. Sharing responsibilities and working together are the underpinnings that promote the effective development of the group conscience.

Since the concept was first developed in Alcoholics Anonymous, years of Twelve-Step experience have demonstrated that the group conscience process *does work.* More than simply majority rule, the *group conscience* is the powerful notion that if people have a common spiritual commitment and respectfully listen to one another until a shared view emerges, they can rise above petty individual concerns and unite in a common purpose. In RCA our overarching purpose is to stay committed in intimate and loving relationships and to help other recovering couples restore their coupleships.

How Does the Group Conscience Differ From a Majority Vote?

What exactly is the group conscience? And how does it differ from a group opinion or a majority vote? And what is the best way to "get there"?

A true group conscience strives for consensus, not simply majority rule. This involves respectful and open-hearted listening to all viewpoints, as well as to the quiet voice of our Higher Power. Working deliberately, following the RCA Steps and Traditions, and placing principles before personalities, gradually a collective view tends to evolve. The group needs to hear all of its members, often more than once, so that the group's collective insight prevails rather than the opinions of a dominant few. At its best the group conscience is the coming together of the entire group in a common purpose, a true spiritual expression of the whole group. It is based on mutual trust and respect, not simply the winning of one faction over another.

As one RCA member shared about the evolution of her understanding:

> *"At first, group conscience simply was a 'vote.' You get your side and I'll get my side, and then we'll vote. Now my concept of group conscience has grown as I begin to understand each of the words in the Second Tradition. The informed group conscience means to me that we try to profit from those who have gone before us; whether these are majority or minority experiences. And then we seek a collective understanding of the*

guidance of our Higher Power. And with this we try to fulfill the primary purpose of our group—increasing the commitment and intimacy of our own relationships, and helping other recovering couples."

How Important Is the Word "Informed"?

A central element of the concept of *group conscience* should be the word "informed"—something often left out of the discussion. Without the word "informed," a fellowship's group conscience could mean almost anything, easily becoming the rule of a dominant clique. When a group's sense of what is appropriate is "informed," and their deliberations respectful, the results are usually enlightened and well thought out. Without sufficient insight, respect, and deliberation, the group conscience can stray from RCA principles.

How Does a Group Get Informed?

First, if we are to achieve an informed group conscience, we will learn about our RCA Traditions. We will read our literature and be willing to share that knowledge with newcomer couples. We will understand and participate in our service structure. To ensure that we truly have group conscience meetings, we will seek guidance through prayer or meditation. The only authority in a group conscience is our Higher Power.

The Formula for Getting the Group Conscience

An effective formula for an informed group conscience calls for:

- a straightforward explanation of the issue at hand in all its aspects;
- the Chair polling the group members for their views (this should be less a debate than a calm and respectful airing of views);
- the rotation around the group continuing a second time, a third time, or until all have had their turn, giving even the shyest person an equal voice (the idea is not to "win" but to come together as a group on a topic).
- The Chair will usually speak only after everyone else has talked.

We have found that when we continue discussion in this way, we can usually achieve a united group conscience. When the group agrees that discussion has been completed, the Chair will summarize the discussion. If we cannot reach consensus, it is a good idea to postpone a decision to a later date. Only if a decision must be made *immediately* should a vote be taken, voting as individuals rather than as couples. A group conscience does not mean that everyone is happy with a decision, but that we are satisfied that it is the best one we can make under the circumstances.

Issues and Problems for the Group Conscience Process

The impact of group conscience decisions can be seen in numerous ways: from the election of officers to the selection of our World Service Organization Board; from how a group chooses to handle people with special issues to the development and publication of RCA literature. Here are just a few of the issues some RCA groups have dealt with through the process of informed group conscience:

- How do we as a group respond when formerly active RCA couples separate?
- What qualifications do we want for our group's Contact Couple to the World Service Organization?
- How do we handle a local TV station's request for an RCA couple to appear on one of their shows?
- How do we address a member's motion to change our meeting day, time, or location?
- How do we establish a prudent reserve for our group?
- How do we address a member's motion to increase the Seventh Tradition's suggested contribution?
- How does a group develop its guidelines on cross-talk?

Tips to Help Your Group Thrive

For a meeting to remain successful, it is best the meeting be held at the scheduled time, unless weather conditions, or an emergency, etc. prevents it. In that case, the leaders need to call people as soon as they know. Some groups keep and maintain a phone list of the group and encourage couple-to-couple outreach calls. Some groups provide an opportunity for couples willing to sponsor other couples to be recognized. Some successful RCA groups emphasize that socializing outside of RCA meetings is important for long-term success of the group. Coffee after the meeting, pot-luck dinners, meditation sessions, local weekend retreats, holiday socials, and bowling parties can all provide additional opportunities for sharing and bonding with other couples committed to recovery. In fact, it appears that groups that do not socialize outside the recovery meetings have a less than average chance of survival.

How to Grow a Meeting—A Suggested Checklist

- Make everyone feel welcome.
- Be open to diverse couples.
- Have a local web page for group meeting information, convention information, links to the RCA/World Service Organization website, a bulletin board page to post questions, etc.
- Have a "greeter couple" who greets all who attend (especially newcomer couples), and talks to new couples after the meeting.
- Have a "follow-up couple" who calls new couples after the initial meeting, and calls couples who haven't attended for a while. (The follow-up call is for making people feel welcome, as well as letting them know they are not alone, and that the group is there when they are ready.) Have a phone list and email list (to offer information, inspiration, communication, etc.)
- Have regular (e.g., monthly) speaker meetings (couples sharing their story with the group).
- Have weekend retreats for couples to do the Steps. This can vitalize the group.
- Have a Step study meeting (e.g., a two-hour session) once a month. (The RCA Blue Book can be used as a resource.)
- Have RCA potluck dinners for fun and socialization with other couples.
- Go out to dinner after the meetings.
- Have a "meeting after the meeting" to connect with other couples.
- Elect officers for local meetings, which gives everyone a role and responsibility.
- Consider addressing baby-sitting needs if possible.

- Keep a log of who chaired, the topic, next Chair couple, etc. to be aware of service contributions and to avoid redundancy of topics.
- Have a newcomer's gift bag.
- Create consistency for newcomers with a "greeter couple" one week who chairs the meeting the following week.
- If the regular "greeter couple" is not present, ask another couple during the meeting to serve as greeter couple.
- Send information to churches, therapists, and other Twelve-Step groups about RCA.
- Place flyers about RCA on bulletin boards in Twelve-Step meeting places.
- Be vigilant that the group not become little more than a clique or social club.
- Provide sponsorship for working the program, and sharing experience, strength, and hope.

More ideas for Meeting Guidelines are posted on www.recovering-couples.org

Group Business Meetings

Group business meetings are generally scheduled regularly—monthly, every other month, or quarterly according to the group conscience. The meetings are usually led by the Chair for that day. It is during these meetings that the members review how well the group is doing in following the Twelve Traditions and may set new objectives and goals. Reports are usually given by the Chair, the Treasurer, the Literature couple, and the Public Information couple.

Suggested Procedure for Business Meetings

As in any other meeting, some structure is needed. Most groups find using Robert's Rules of Order helpful in bringing some structure to their meeting. In addition, the following are usually emphasized:

1. Only one person may have the floor (speak) at a time.
2. Members address their remarks to the Chair and not to other members.
3. To keep our meeting focus on service to our fellowship, we follow the Safety Guidelines. We avoid using statements that are baiting, button-pushing, case-building, self-righteous, judgmental, or taking or sharing another person's inventory. It is important for us to act and speak respectfully to each other. If someone needs to be confronted, do it directly, privately, and in person if possible, or in a direct phone call.
4. We use the Informed Group Conscience Process:
    - The person raising an issue gives its background.
    - Speaking in order, everyone has time to comment on the issue. A few circuits around the group may be necessary to come to a consensus.
    - After a consensus has been reached, a motion may be made.
    - Only one main motion can be considered at a time.
    - Once a motion is made, we take time to make sure the motion is clear.
    - Keep discussion focused on issues and principles, and not on personalities.

- After the discussion, *if a consensus can not be achieved*:

  1. Non-urgent matters may be postponed for further discussion.
  2. For urgent matters, the motion is put to a vote.

- Although we strive for consensus or concordance, *the majority rules.*

Group Inventory

A group inventory is used for assessing group health, and can be an excellent tool for refocusing our energy and vision to serve our local RCA community. How often this occurs is for individual groups to decide, but annually would be the choice of some. Here are some suggested questions to assist in your group inventory:

1. In what ways do we concentrate on the program's ideas, purposes, and results in interesting and helpful ways?
2. In what ways do we encourage participation by all couples?
3. In what ways do we prevent one person/couple from dominating the meeting (i.e., how do we keep the common welfare first)?
4. In what ways do we make use of RCA literature for meeting topics?
5. In what ways can we avoid forming cliques?
6. In what ways are we giving new couples information, sponsorship, and support?
7. In what ways are we performing outreach (Public Information)?

8. In what ways are we following the Traditions?
9. What are we doing well?
10. What would we like to improve?
11. What is our vision for the future?
12. Who will implement any plans we have made for our growth?

Group-Sponsored Monthly Step Workshops

- The monthly Step workshop, by moving couples through the Steps, creates a larger pool of couples available to sponsor within the local area, which helps the community to grow. It is facilitated by an experienced couple who has worked the Steps of RCA.
- Usually the facilitating couple has a sponsor couple.
- The workshop can provide a place for couples to work through the Steps when there are too few sponsors.
- The workshop encourages couples to continue their Step work between the monthly meetings.
- Couples are encouraged to commit to a regular time to do their Step work; often this is done on a weekly basis.
- Each monthly workshop is centered on a particular Step, and couples are encouraged to come no matter what Step they are working on.
- A potluck before or after the workshop promotes fun and fellowship.

RCA Monthly Step Study Suggested Meeting Format

Opening

- Serenity Prayer (see p. 60)

Customary Readings

- The Preamble (see p. 50)
- How It Works Part 1 (see pp. 51)
- The Twelve Steps (see p. 52)
- How It Works Part 2 (see p. 54)
- The Twelve Traditions (see pp. 56–57)
- The Safety Guidelines (see p. 55)

Check-In

Couples are offered a chance to give a brief check-in sharing or Tenth Step Sharing (which is a daily or weekly inventory: What have I done that is harmful to our coupleship? What has my partner done to support our coupleship?) This gives couples a chance to become present with the group. It provides a time of transition of emotions and spirit to the workshop.

Step Presentations

The facilitating couple shares their experience, strength, and hope about the current step briefly describing their experience with this step.

RCA Twelve Traditions Long Form

Tradition One

Our common welfare should come first; couple recovery depends upon RCA unity.

As a fellowship we have seen that by working the Twelve Steps of the RCA program, our coupleships have grown in commitment and intimacy. The Twelve Traditions provide guidance and direction for the RCA fellowship. In order for the fellowship to flourish, the Twelve Traditions need to be understood and applied.

The Traditions are the glue and backbone of RCA itself. These Twelve Traditions come to us from the program of Alcoholics Anonymous and were adapted to the needs of our fellowship. We follow the Traditions to ensure the RCA fellowship will always be available for those couples who are recovering from addictions or dysfunctional behaviors that have affected their coupleships.

Many of us have found that doing service has helped to speed our healing process. We have a new sense of belonging when we learn to not isolate and to work with other couples.

Before recovery, many of us thought our own personal approach was the only correct one. However, we learned in our RCA groups to listen to our partner as well as other couples. We learned from other couples that partners have differing opinions and viewpoints. We became able to listen without judgment. We learned to share time with each other and not monopolize the group with "Oh, ain't it awful" stories. In our meetings, we learned to stay focused on the meeting topics. We learned to follow the Safety Guidelines and group conscience process. Learning to respect the needs of the group taught us to respect the needs of our coupleship.

In addition to our own recovery, we have a responsibility to express ourselves to promote group unity. We have experience, strength, and hope to share. Our stories need to be heard, and they show others that we are not unique. As couples, we sometimes share just by listening and being present to hear other couples' stories. However, if we consistently remain silent, it inhibits group unity.

Making newcomers feel welcome promotes RCA growth and unity. Some of the ways we have found helpful in making newcomers welcome are: providing temporary sponsors; giving out newcomer chips; sharing how RCA has been helpful to us, handing out newcomer packets with phone numbers of active members; and of course, chatting informally with newcomers before and after the meeting.

Tradition Two

For our group purpose there is but one ultimate authority—a loving God as known in our group conscience. Our leaders are but trusted servants; they do not govern.

Locally, we have service or leadership positions such as Secretaries or Chairs, Treasurers, Group Contact Couples, and Delegate Couples. Nationally and internationally we may see people serving on the Board of Trustees of the World Service Organization, or on its committees.

These are individuals and couples who are willing to devote time, work, and energy to the RCA Fellowship. These RCA members serve and direct our fellowship by following our group conscience. The positions do not give authority beyond the consent of the fellowship. *Ultimate RCA authority is from the bottom up, not the top down.*

Rotation of officers gives equal opportunity for service, and restricts dominance by any individual or couple. This rotation emphasizes group conscience rather than control by any individual. Following this Tradition emphasizes equality among all members, teaching us that equality is the cornerstone of our coupleships.

Even when there is difficulty in finding someone to take a leadership position, it is important *not* to allow an individual or couple to continue doing the work indefinitely simply because they are willing to do so. People who remain in leadership positions too long can begin to feel they're indispensable, or conversely, feel put upon or used. Therefore, we search for and encourage couples and members to volunteer for positions. Service helps a couple experience growth in their coupleship.

The Second Tradition reminds us not to assume authority over a sponsee couple. Our purpose is not to give advice or impose a decision. Sponsor couples agree to share their own experience, strength, and hope. They are "fair witnesses," helping sponsee couples see their own processes as well as providing a safe space to work on their issues and options.

Longtime RCA couples may be helpful in starting new groups. Their role should be to guide the development and structure of the meetings, but then encourage other couples to assume the leadership roles as they gain program knowledge and experience.

The group conscience is what governs the group, and we arrive at this conscience by open discussion. We set limits on holding office. We share the workload. This Tradition protects and safeguards all of us and our group. When this Tradition is followed, a state of humility exists because the source of authority is our Higher Power.

Tradition Three

The only requirement for RCA membership is a desire to remain in a committed relationship.

Tradition Three tells us who is eligible to be a member of RCA. We are couples committed to restoring healthy communication, caring, and greater intimacy to our coupleships. We suffer from addictions, co-addictions, or other dysfunctions, some of these identified and some not, some treated and some not. We also come from many levels of brokenness. Many of us have been separated or near divorce.

Some of us are new in our coupleship and seek to build intimacy as we grow together as a couple. We refuse no couple who wishes to recover.

Ultimately, we feel it is important for both partners to be involved in *individual* recovery for real progress to be made in our coupleships. However, individual recovery is not a requirement to get started in couple recovery. RCA is a safe place to begin the healing process, and it offers support for continued individual work.

Any two or more couples gathered together for restoring commitment, communication, and caring to their relationships may call themselves an RCA group, provided that, as a group, they have no other affiliation.

Tradition Four

Each group should be autonomous except in matters affecting other groups or RCA as a whole.

Each RCA group is autonomous and responsible to its own group conscience. However, we strive to conduct our work in the program according to the spiritual principles outlined in the Traditions. Following our Traditions safeguards our program, guiding us while not controlling us, allowing us to act independently but reminding us to be ever mindful of our group as part of the larger fellowship.

RCA is less a top-down organization than a bottom-up fellowship made up of couples in recovery. But when our plans concern the welfare of neighboring groups, those groups ought to be consulted. No group, regional committee, couple, or individual should ever take any action that might affect RCA as a whole without conferring with the World Service Board. On such issues our common welfare must be paramount.

Each group is responsible for conducting itself in a way that is good for the fellowship as a whole. The Safety Guidelines and suggested meeting format in the RCA Blue Book explain how to conduct meetings. Each group is free to choose its own meeting format and topics for discussion, and to decide where and when it will meet and how the funds it collects will be apportioned.

We all strive to carry a *unified* message to the couples who are still suffering. To do this, it is RCA's intention to be open to all sincere couples, to use approved literature, and to provide a safe place for the sharing of our pain and hope. To check how well we are doing this, it is suggested that each meeting regularly take its own inventory (see pp. 81–82). Further, it is suggested that local groups conduct periodic business meetings, where discussion at length may be indicated. Minority opinions are to be aired and taken into consideration. Each RCA group is responsible for taking the time to know the Traditions and understand why they are important to the Fellowship.

Tradition Five

Each group has but one primary purpose—to carry its message to recovering couples who still suffer.

Tradition Five suggests that we will best be able to help other couples who are still suffering when we first help ourselves practice the Twelve Steps. The Twelve Steps give us the guidance we need to: 1) share our own experience, strength, and hope with other couples; 2) give comfort to other couples; and 3) listen to other couples. Each Recovering Couples Anonymous group ought to be a spiritual entity having but one primary purpose—to carry its message of intimacy and commitment to couples who still suffer.

Many couples come to RCA not knowing if they belong. Some may not even be aware that anything is wrong with their coupleship. In RCA we have a list of "Characteristics of Functional and Dysfunctional Couples," (see pp. 7–9) to help couples identify problem areas in their coupleships. Couples do not have to relate to all of these to admit their coupleships are suffering or to seek help or guidance. The identification of such characteristics serves to let us know that we are not alone in our struggle to find intimacy.

RCA believes that a coupleship is like an infant, needing constant nurturing and care from both partners. It is important that each partner accepts responsibility for the problems or progress of the coupleship, and that each recognizes individual recovery as an important factor for couple recovery. In RCA we think of coupleship as being represented by a three-legged stool; our individual recovery, our partner's recovery, and our coupleship recovery are all important "legs" that support the serenity, stability, and intimacy we seek.

When we welcome newcomer couples to our fellowship, we share our experience, strength, and hope. We offer spiritual support and the opportunity to connect with other couples, typically through sponsorship, meetings, and RCA social events. We provide RCA-approved literature, the Blue Book, the newcomer brochure, and where possible, a listing of meetings in the area and local phone numbers. Tradition Five emphasizes that in order to "get the program," we must "give it away"!

Tradition Six

RCA ought never endorse, finance, or lend the RCA name to any related facility or outside enterprise, lest problems of money, property, and prestige divert us from our primary purpose.

The purpose of RCA is to carry its message to recovering couples who still suffer. Tradition Six is an elaboration on the many possible ways a group might *not* stick to its primary purpose, as well as a reflection on how to avoid actions which could lead to disunity. It establishes boundaries for our fellowship, much as we set boundaries in our personal relationships.

Problems of money, property, and prestige may easily divert us from our primary aim. Therefore, significant property should be separately incorporated and managed.

An RCA group, as such, should never go into business, but we need to cooperate with many other entities that have similar or supportive aims. Without this cooperation we could not let couples that suffer know of our existence and our program.

But while an RCA group may cooperate with anyone, such cooperation ought never go so far as affiliation or endorsement, actual or implied. Adjuncts to RCA, such as clubs, therapists, and couples counseling entities, ought to be separately incorporated. They should not use the RCA name. Their management should be the sole responsibility of those people who financially support them.

An RCA group can bind itself to no one. It has been our experience that outside organizations are attracted to RCA. They send members to us. RCA has a common bond with other Twelve-Step programs such as AA—that of recovery—but even though we have similar aims, we should not affiliate with them.

When we adhere to the principles of Tradition Six we are able to carry the message and interact with others, knowing that we will not compromise our purpose. Some of the principles that help us observe Tradition Six include humility, integrity, faith, harmony, and anonymity.

Tradition Seven

Every RCA group should be fully self-supporting, declining outside contributions.

The principle is simple—being self-supporting is a tremendous source of strength and self-respect. This Tradition places the responsibility for supporting our groups on our own shoulders. We do not accept outside contributions. We do not sell our independence. We do not owe anyone favors. We do not give anyone special treatment. We are responsible for our own financial survival as a fellowship, just as we are responsible for our progress in recovery as couples.

This tradition should govern the actions of the World Service Organization just as it does the individual groups in Recovering Couples Anonymous. We do not use the RCA name in connection with any allied enterprise. We believe that accepting gifts or contributions carrying any obligation is unwise. Joint ventures with outside organizations or individuals always contain downside obligations. They should be rigorously avoided.

In keeping with Tradition Seven, the membership supports the World Service Organization (WSO) by group contributions, individual donations, and the sale of approved literature and other materials from the WSO. Although there are no dues or fees for membership, voluntary contributions are typically collected when each meeting practices the Seventh Tradition.

It is a tradition of RCA to not accumulate funds in excess of that needed for basic RCA functions. If excess money were accumulated, problems could arise that would divert us from our primary purpose. Funds beyond normal operating expenses and a prudent reserve should be forwarded to the WSO.

Tradition Eight

Recovering Couples Anonymous should remain forever non-professional, but our service centers may employ special workers.

Tradition Eight provides guidance for our trusted servants as well as to RCA members who may be in the helping professions, such as counselors, therapists, clergy, physicians, social workers, and other professionals. Sharing at meetings should be about personal couple recovery. No one should participate in a professional capacity or as a therapist. We help each other as equals. Our work with others is done to further our own spiritual growth—not for money or from any position of superiority. RCA committee and subcommittee work is unpaid Twelve-Step service work.

Service workers may be contracted to do work in our service centers. These paid service positions are not limited to those in the RCA fellowship, as they normally do not involve Twelve-Step work. Twelve-Step work should never be compensated.

Tradition Nine

RCA, as such, ought never be organized, but we may create service boards or committees directly responsible to those they serve.

Like AA, RCA is a fellowship where the power resides in the fellowship and not the officials. The officials are just "trusted servants." Service positions may be called Secretary, Chair, Vice Chair, Trustee, Facilitator, Treasurer, Literature Person, Sponsor, or Group Contact Couple. These positions should rotate on a regular basis so that all couples involved have a chance to share responsibility. No couple directs nor controls the other couples in the group.

The spirit of RCA is service. All couples are encouraged to volunteer their services. All local groups are encouraged to have Group Contact Couples who facilitate communication between the groups and the Board of Trustees. Our World Service Organization (WSO) Board of Trustees is directly responsible to the fellowship of RCA. The WSO service providers are directly responsible to the WSO Board of Trustees, providing literature and information to the fellowship as well as the general public. *Hand In Hand* is the official publication of RCA and is generally issued quarterly.

Tradition Ten

Recovering Couples Anonymous has no opinion on outside issues; hence the RCA name ought never be drawn into public controversy.

An RCA group should not express any opinion on outside issues, nor should couples, if they are speaking for RCA. The Recovering Couples Anonymous groups neither endorse nor oppose other organizations or their causes, particularly those concerned with controversies, politics, addiction reform, sectarian religion, or particular therapy programs. RCA couples come from all walks of life and hold diverse opinions; little binds us together except our primary purpose—to carry RCA's message to recovering couples who still suffer. If we focus on other issues, either inside or outside the group meeting, we run the risk of alienating other RCA couples or other allies in recovery, and possibly shattering the fellowship.

Tradition Eleven

Our public relations policy is based on attraction rather than promotion; we need always maintain personal anonymity at the level of press, radio, TV, and films.

Tradition Eleven is our guide whenever there is an opportunity to be public. We are reminded to preserve our anonymity, emphasizing that it is RCA that is important—not the individual.

Public relations is ongoing in the program. For example, when we desire to "carry the message," we may provide information or locations of meetings, using only the first names of the Group Contact Couples. We may also leave RCA information on bulletin boards or at treatment centers to let other couples know there is hope for intimacy in their coupleships through a

Twelve-Step program. We also maintain RCA websites where interested people may find information about couple recovery.

Our RCA public relations policy not only means providing information to the public but reaching out from couple to couple. When couples in RCA practice their recovery and live in the solution, they become more healthy and attractive. This in itself can elicit an attraction to the program from people who have seen a couple struggle, and now see them with a sense of serenity and spirituality.

Tradition Twelve

Anonymity is the spiritual foundation of all our Traditions, ever reminding us to place principles before personalities.

In RCA, as in all other Twelve-Step programs, the concept of personal anonymity serves as a multi-layered protection. At its most basic level, being anonymous protects us from public disclosure of our addictions and other dysfunctions. Doubtless, it was in this sense that the concept was first used in Twelve-Step programs. However, as the concept has become a fixture of Twelve-Step culture, it has come to be understood as having more far-reaching benefits. Simply put, we tend to relapse or otherwise act out in ways that could bring the organization of RCA into disrepute. By remaining anonymous, we protect RCA from our public personal failures.

Still more important are the implications of anonymity for ourselves. No matter who we may be in the outside world, in the rooms of RCA we are just another couple trying to heal our coupleship. Anonymity tends to focus us away from the "I" and towards the "we"; away from personalities and towards principles; and away from egotism and towards a true humility.

Anonymity is a simple concept. It doesn't "preach," but leads us gently by example. We all need healing. And as we reveal ourselves to one another in these rooms, we come to understand that it is less the "I" than the coupleship that is important. And the more we understand our commonality instead of our distinctiveness, the more we heal.

Thus, we of Recovering Couples Anonymous believe that the principle of anonymity has particular spiritual significance. It reminds us that we place principles before personalities and that as we practice a genuine humility, we heal. Moved by the spirit of anonymity, we give up desire for personal distinction as members of RCA and before the general public. We believe that each of us is responsible to take part in the protection and preservation of RCA as a whole in order to grow and work in unity.

Chapter IV

Coupleship Healing

Sponsorship

Those of us working individual recovery programs are familiar with sponsorship. In RCA we find it helpful to choose a couple that we can relate to and trust, and who appears to have what we need. Talking with a sponsor couple with whom we feel safe is essential. If we are comfortable talking with them, we may be more willing to discuss issues that seem shameful to us. And discussing our shame is key to our healing.

RCA is a "we" program. We cannot do this work alone. Many of us come to RCA after trying everything we can think of to make our relationships work. Working with a sponsor couple is the beginning of exploring new behaviors for most of us. It demonstrates that we as a couple are willing to try something different and are beginning to understand our powerlessness and inability to heal alone.

What Is a Sponsor Couple?

Sponsor couples provide a safe environment and witness our process. They hear our stories, are honest with us, and support our coupleship. They hold us accountable for our RCA program, and help us work the Steps. They don't take sides or favor one partner over the other.

In RCA it is the *coupleship* that is being sponsored, not the individuals in the coupleship. It is essential that all four members be present, either in person or on the phone, when sponsors and sponsees meet. Sponsor couples help us to overcome shared denial, and they are there for us during tough times. The recovery tool of RCA couple sponsorship usually works best when both partners of the recovering couple are active in their individual recovery.

The Gifts of Sponsorship

Sponsor couples have fresh points of view based on their experience using the RCA program. As partners in turmoil, we usually have differing perspectives on the nature of our coupleship problems. Through sharing with a sponsor couple, we have the opportunity to evolve toward a mutual understanding of our major issues, and then we can search for solutions as a team.

The love and acceptance of a sponsor couple is healing for the sponsored partners, both individually and as a couple. We find that with the experience, strength, and hope our sponsors share with us, we can work through many things that we thought impossible. Our sponsor couple's support is affirming to our coupleship!

One of the important aspects of couple recovery is learning to become open and honest. Accepting help from other couples is vital to our recovery together as well. Having a sponsor couple is a tool that helps us to become more open and honest, and at the same time helps us to learn to accept help from another couple.

Barriers to the Gifts of Sponsorship

Some of us have found it difficult to ask for help, but when we ask another couple to be our sponsor, and take what may feel like a risky step by telling them our stories, we almost always discover that we are neither as alone nor as unique as we had feared. We find that our sponsors have had many of the same problems that we have experienced—and are recovering from them. We find acceptance and understanding, and this gives us something that may have been missing from our relationship—hope! The following are some of the barriers we have found to accepting the gift of sponsorship.

Couple Shame

Couple shame can play a major role in preventing us from seeking the sponsorship we need. We begin to address this by attending RCA meetings and sharing. Finding a sponsor couple can be the next step. In RCA we disclose personal issues to our sponsors. This kind of intimacy and vulnerability may feel threatening, even overwhelming, to some couples. We may have shame about the difficulties we face in our coupleship. We may feel that our dysfunctions are much greater than anyone else's, or that we do not deserve another couple's help.

Hopelessness

Some of us have feared that we were hopeless cases, and that it was therefore no use to find and work with a couple sponsor. However, couple sponsors can help us to remember that although everyone faces different challenges, there are no perfect coupleships. All couples in the RCA program have difficulties and dysfunctions they need to work through. Sponsors are not there to judge us, but rather to share their experience, strength, and hope with us, reminding us that we are capable of working through our dysfunctions with the help of the RCA program.

Procrastination

Many couples find that one or both partners just don't feel ready to choose a sponsor couple. Our fears cause procrastination. We might find ourselves frustrated if we are ready when our partner is not. In RCA we work towards letting go of our need to control our partner. It may help to talk with our partner about our feelings. We may talk with other couples about how they became ready to choose a sponsor couple. If we are the partner who is not yet ready, it may help to talk to our partner about our fears. It is important to understand that we don't have to *feel* ready to do the right thing; if we do the right thing long enough, it may feel right after awhile.

Vulnerability

We may wonder what good it will do us to bring up issues from the past. We may be reluctant to "air our dirty laundry" in front of another couple. Or we may have been taught from an early age that problems within a family are private and not to be disclosed to anyone else. In RCA, we try to remember that, "we are only as sick as our secrets." We need to agree with our partner that it is safe to disclose the exact nature of our issues to a sponsor couple.

One of the amazing gifts of the RCA program is that we finally are able to find a safe place to become open and talk about our pain. When we share about ourselves honestly, we are better able to let go of our anger and hurt. We find we are not alone. Our common issues help us to bond with our sponsor couple, as well as with the other couples we have come to know in RCA.

Choosing a Sponsor Couple

It can be helpful for both partners to say out loud and write on paper the qualities we would like in a sponsor couple. Frequently both partners are seeking similar qualities. Some questions to consider in choosing a sponsor couple might be:

- Does the couple work the Steps?
- Do we relate to their story?
- Does the couple appear to be using the Tools of RCA?
- Does it sound like and look like the couple is recovering?
- Do we think we could work with this sponsor couple?
- Would our coupleship be better if we had more of the recovery they have?

If we are reluctant to reach out for assistance, we talk to other couples who have sponsor couples. We consider selecting sponsors on a temporary basis. Once we choose a sponsor couple, we are always free to change to a different sponsor couple if either partner does not feel safe or comfortable with them.

When interviewing potential sponsor couples we may want to ask them what they expect of couples they sponsor. Some sponsors insist that those they are sponsoring call at certain times, or follow certain instructions, while other sponsors leave it to the sponsee couple to set the pace. It is helpful to know what we need from a sponsor couple, and what they expect of us.

Asking for a sponsor couple usually means admitting the powerlessness and unmanageability of our relationship together. We now have acquired the willingness to begin working the Twelve Steps of RCA together.

Working with Our Sponsor Couple

Couple sponsorship is a major part of working the RCA program. In RCA the Fifth Step says: "We admitted to God, to ourselves, and to another couple the exact nature of our wrongs." The main function of a sponsor couple is to support couples in working the Twelve Steps. In RCA, a couple works the Steps not as individuals, but together in coupleship. But as we work the Steps and explore the dynamics of our coupleship, conflict may erupt. If this happens, some of us find it safer to do our Step work in the presence of our sponsor couple or others. Sponsor couples frequently have had many of the same issues, and are recovering from them. They help maintain a safe environment for the sponsored couple by pointing out where to apply the RCA Safety Guidelines and witnessing the couple's process.

The process of exploring issues by working the Steps and answering the questions outlined in this book with a sponsor couple will usually reveal the true nature of our problems. Some of our underlying problems may involve issues of *trust, safety, abandonment,* or *disrespect of personal boundaries.* Often a sponsor couple can see the needs of the couple, and can help them feel safer. Sometimes contracts or agreements allow couples to work safely while they develop more lasting solutions. We find that contracts, or agreements, are most effective when written, signed, and dated by each partner and witnessed by the sponsor couple.

Most of us make it a practice to meet with our sponsor couple and read what we have written for each Step. This helps our sponsors to better understand our coupleship, and to affirm our work and progress in recovery. Our sponsor couple can be a mirror, guiding us to see our relationship more clearly. We do all of the Steps as a couple, sharing with our sponsor couple as we progress.

Working with Others

We cannot continue to progress in our own recovery unless we share it with others. Working with others is a spiritual process based on sharing our personal experiences of working the program. It is often said that we "keep it by giving it away," meaning that it is through sharing what we have learned as couples in working our RCA program together that we can continue to grow and heal in our coupleships.

An important part of being ready to sponsor is becoming willing. We can ask how our partner feels about the prospect of becoming a sponsor couple if the opportunity presents itself. We can ask ourselves if we feel that we've turned our wills and our life together over to the care of our Higher Power. When we can answer yes, it may be time to let go of fears we have around being a sponsor couple. We can let go and trust that our Higher Power has sent us just the right opportunities for our coupleship to grow. We can allow ourselves to open up to the experience of using a new Tool for the recovery of our relationship.

Suggested Guidelines for Working with Another Couple

Because Twelve-Step work is different from other approaches, we have found the guidance in these principles to be beneficial in working with couples we sponsor:

1. We listen, listen, and listen. Especially when we feel like interrupting, we listen.

2. We validate feelings and respond to content; we strive to understand not only what is being said, but also what is being felt. We try to remember that all feelings are valid, and to be supportive when we give feedback.

3. We use prayer and meditation, as suggested in Step Eleven, as a means of becoming centered.

4. We are a safety net for our sponsee couple. We feel adherence to the Safety Guidelines is a sacred trust.

5. If we find ourselves arguing, becoming involved with our sponsees' anger and anxiety, or trying to control and fix them, we try to stop these behaviors, acknowledge our slip, and apologize!

6. We are honest, kind, and dependable to the best of our abilities. We encourage our sponsees to attend meetings and suggest they use the Tools of RCA, as these have helped us and other couples. We share our experience, strength, and hope rather than give advice.

7. We recognize that there may be situations that are beyond the scope of any sponsoring couple. There are times when it is most appropriate and supportive to suggest that the couple seek outside help. One such situation is when one or both partners' safety is threatened, such as a threat of abuse or of suicide. The best help we can offer at such times is knowing when to step back and allow professionals to step in.

8. There are no right or wrong answers. We can share what worked for us, but the sponsee couple may find that other tools work better for them. We are cautious about providing the "right answer" to them, rather than providing the support and encouragement which helps them find their own answers.

9. We continue to work our own program. The best preparation for helping others is the work that we do on our own recovery: attending meetings, working the Steps, working with our own sponsor couple, and "walking the talk."

We are recovering couples who are willing to share our experience, strength, and hope, and to grow along spiritual lines.

We are not perfect, and we are not counselors. It is not our job to "fix" anyone. All couples have the responsibility to work their RCA program to the best of their ability, and the success or failure of sponsee coupleships are the couples' own responsibility. It is not the job of sponsor couples to ensure that sponsee couples stay in a committed and loving relationship, but rather to give acceptance, guidance, and suggestions.

As the RCA fellowship grows, the need for sponsor couples grows too. We hope some of these suggestions will help you feel more comfortable offering yourselves as sponsor couples.

> *"Acting as sponsors for other couples helps bring our coupleship closer."*

> *"In RCA we are learning to be 'a team.' We learn to go from 'my game plan' and 'your game plan' to 'our game plan.' As we turn our lives together over to a Power greater than ourselves, we turn away from 'my way' and 'your way' toward 'God's way.' In RCA we call this the 'Third Way.'"*

RCA Tools of Recovery (Long Form)

We have found these recovery tools useful for restoring and sustaining commitment, intimacy, and joy in our coupleships.

Attending and Sharing at Meetings

We attend RCA meetings to learn how the program works, and to share our experience, strength, and hope with other couples. In meetings we learn that our struggles and troubles are not unique, and we gain hope and assurance that our own coupleship can recover and grow. Meetings often bring partners closer and encourage communication. Being honest and vulnerable in front of our partner is frightening but worth it. Many of us believe that our coupleships recover in direct proportion to our willingness to share at meetings.

> *"We discovered RCA through an ad, and my partner made the first call. We found our way to our first RCA meeting and have never given up since. We found an abundance of compassionate people who were willing to love us through the trying times we experienced. The process of being held by others and our inching trust with each other brought about amazing results."*

Calling a Meeting of Two

Either partner can call a Meeting of Two anytime, anywhere. If the other partner agrees, what follows is a typical RCA meeting format even though there are only two people participating. A structure of opening and closing with the Serenity Prayer, and following the Safety Guidelines guarantees being heard and often helps us regain our sense of humor.

> *"We have a Meeting of Two every Saturday morning. We pretend that all the people who attend our home group are actually there with us—this keeps us aware that we must speak respectfully. I have a tendency to 'read' and react to my partner's body language, so our chairs are facing away from each other. We use this time to talk about what is going on with us personally and in the coupleship."*

> *"When we started RCA, we always read the Safety Guidelines at the beginning of our Meeting of Two. It helped us remember the 'do's' and 'don'ts' of respectful communication! Our old habits were hard to break, but through our persistence we are winning!"*

> *"We call our couple meeting a 'knee to knee' because there is such a big difference in our sizes. We use chairs that put us on an even plane—eye to eye and knee to knee. This way we can look into each other's eyes. It's a deeper level of honesty and a symbol of our equality."*

> *"Before RCA, our 'Meetings of Two' were impromptu shouting matches. Right away we made an agreement to hold an RCA-style Meeting of Two daily, reading and discussing the Daily Reflection. The format became second-nature, and today instead of reacting, we respond by using this tool, which invites God into the equation and reminds us to use the Safety Guidelines!"*

Calling a Moratorium or "Time-Out"

When communications break down, a prior agreement to call a "time-out," also called a moratorium, for fifteen minutes, an hour, or a day can interrupt destructive interaction. We can walk away from each other without walking away from the coupleship. By stating specifically when we will be available to continue discussion, we are showing that we are not abandoning the coupleship or our partner.

> *"When things get too heated and we need to walk away, we always commit to each other that we will try again to talk about things at a specific later time, generally within forty-eight hours. This is crucial for us because otherwise we could potentially use the moratorium to justify acting out our dance of avoidance and pursuit. We've asked our sponsors, and we've made progress by seeing the problem as a separate thing; we are two on the same team working to find mutually acceptable changes to help resolve it. We've had great success bringing our issues to a therapist who specializes in communication."*

> *"When we came to RCA, we had several 'insolvable issues.' No matter how many times we'd talked about it, we hadn't found a solution. In RCA we learned that many happy couples had such issues. It was freeing to realize that not every situation had to be 'resolved.' We began to enjoy other aspects of the relationship even though some issues were unresolved, by agreeing to put an indefinite moratorium on discussing the problems. We recognized that we were powerless over the problem and that repeating the same old arguments was driving us crazy. In Step Three, we turned these problems over to our Higher Power. One day we realized that these problems had simply dissolved."*

Conflict Resolution Contracts and Written Agreements

We are learning to practice "fair fighting" by developing our own "Conflict Resolution Contract." We establish respectful conflict guidelines and boundaries that allow the healthy expression of feelings, and we work for resolution of our common problems and concerns. (For more information see Contracts and Written Agreements, Appendix, pp. 342–353)

Developing a Support System Within and Outside of RCA

To help build balance in our coupleship, each day we remember to develop personal relationships with people other than just our partner. Each day we remember to nourish our spiritual growth together, our creativity, and our playful attitudes. Reaching out to other couples outside of meetings allows us to get other perspectives on our problems.

"I" Statements

We use "I" statements such as "I feel hurt," or "I am sad," rather than "you" statements, such as "You did," "You are," "You said," to help each of us take individual responsibility for our feelings and thoughts, and to avoid blaming others. We do not globalize a conflict, as in "You always" or "You never," and we keep the focus on current issues, not past issues.

Listening and Communicating

We set aside a time each day for hearing each other's comments, feelings, and gratitude. Before accepting any major couple commitments, we consult and listen to our Higher Power for guidance.

Reading and Working the Steps

Recovering Couples Anonymous is first and foremost a Twelve-Step program. The principles and techniques that helped restore our lives to sanity and bring a measure of serenity to us as individuals can work for us as couples.

Reading Recovery Literature

Just as daily reading of literature can help keep the focus on our individual recovery, reflecting on our RCA literature can help us focus on our couple recovery. If our partner is in an individual recovery program, reading that recovery literature can help us grow in understanding and compassion for the challenges that they face.

Service

We readily extend help to other couples, knowing that assistance to others adds to the quality of our own relationship recovery. We seek out and accept joint service positions in RCA. We find that doing service together builds our sense of joint participation in our relationship and in its recovery. We get this program when we give it away. Step Twelve is about carrying the message, and the message we carry is a liberating one meant for a lifetime. The spiritual experiences that result affect all of our relationships, and, if we have children, we will be breaking the chains of addiction that have bound our families for generations.

Sponsorship

As part of the surrender process, we admit our weaknesses as individuals and as a couple. We ask others for help, especially our RCA sponsors, and other members in the RCA Program. Acting as sponsors helps bring our coupleship closer. Helping others focus on their relationships can give us perspective on our own coupleship.

Using the Safety Guidelines

By adhering to the Safety Guidelines in our meetings and in our couple communication, we receive and provide the safe environment and nurturing our coupleships need to grow and endure. We affirm our personal rights and agree to act and speak respectfully to others. (See Safety Guidelines, p. 55.)

Chapter V

Couples' Stories

The following stories are from RCA couples who are willing to share their experience, strength, and hope in printed form. They are included as examples to which the reader may relate and see an opportunity for couple recovery. Some Step One stories are at times quite vivid in describing how it was before recovery because they were written early in recovery when the pain was still fresh in mind. The stories are not given as guarantees of couple recovery, but to show how these couples obtained healing using the approach to their coupleships found in this book.

Mark and Deb

Let Us Begin Again Today!

Step One. We admitted we were powerless over our relationship—that our life together had become unmanageable.

Our story began in our families of origin. They determined whom we would look for in a partner as we began to date. We met early in that process while still in high school.

Mark

Mark was raised in a minister's home. His father was extremely strong and controlling emotionally, a very public person, admired greatly by the congregations he served. His mother was extremely passive, quiet, and shame-filled. While Mark's dad had little trouble sharing his thoughts and feelings, usually with religious interpretations and without boundaries, his mom usually talked to no one and shared almost nothing about herself.

Mark's perception of his parents is that they talked of superficial things with each other, with his dad always dominating conversations with his thoughts. The life and business of the church was the life of the family. His parents didn't seem affectionate toward one another, either emotionally or physically. They were lonely even when with each other but didn't consciously recognize or accept it.

Mark became a sexual abuse victim, some of which he remembers, some of which he "knows" took place before the age of three. He was also an emotional incest victim. His dad expected him to be his "buddy" and to be available to him for many activities and conversations. In this process his dad was grooming Mark to be just like himself—a minister—and taught Mark that people in power can bend the rules, including exploiting others. His mom let this happen—even encouraged it—as she abandoned Mark emotionally.

Mark was looking for a woman he could dominate emotionally and sexually, one who would be perfectly nurturing physically and sexually, but who would also be submissive and passive. Although he did not know it, he was lonely and longed for a deeper emotional relationship, but he didn't have any tools to ask for it. He was also afraid of a strong woman—afraid that she would leave him if she really knew him. Mark was also looking for a woman from a social and economic background that would correct his image of his family as being poor.

Deb

Deb has a twin sister and an older brother. Deb was raised in the home of an executive who is very successful and popular, a "good guy" everybody likes. With all this he is very concerned with money and security, taking care of things so that nothing "bad" will happen. He is very protective. He is a gentle man, oriented around his family to a fault. He is also generally affirming and supportive. There is, however, a loneliness about him that we sense especially now that we're in recovery. There was certainly no ability to share emotionally in Deb's family. Her parents taught her the attitude that if you worked hard everything would work out all right. There were always solutions to everything. Deb had polio at age three; she doesn't remember anyone talking to her about how painful and frightening it was.

Deb's mother was a trained professional who stopped her career when she married. She was an only child and was moved numerous times as a youth and teenager. While she played a traditional domestic female role, she was extremely strong-willed and opinionated. She learned how to control her own fears and insecurities and passed down a general inability to deal with them. She did not discuss sexual things, but she passed on clear messages, instilling in Deb a general fear of one's body and of men.

Deb's twin sister was very socially and athletically outgoing. Deb also perceived her as more physically attractive as well as more popular. Deb took a back seat in many ways while growing up. She became an exceptional student and organizer and was very successful at school in various activities. A major social victory for her was becoming a cheerleader as a junior and senior.

Although Deb's family attended church, religion was rarely discussed. Deb would often go to youth groups and church alone. When she was a senior, her family began attending the church that Mark's dad served.

Deb feels she was abandoned emotionally and spiritually, that she was taught a general workaholic lifestyle and to fear problems but not talk about them. She was also instilled with traditional sexist values and roles, with dislike of her body, and a fear of sex. Despite all of this, she brought a strong family-centered orientation to her relationship with Mark.

Deb was looking for a man who was socially outgoing and religious (when she first started dating Mark, one of her favorite songs was "Son of a Preacher Man"). She also was lonely, but didn't know anything about sharing feelings.

Mark and Deb

We started dating during the late sixties while Mark was in college and Deb was a high school senior. Previous to this we had known each other from afar. Friends of ours who were dating each other set us up. This is significant in that this couple later married, and we came to be totally enmeshed with them as a couple later in our own marriage.

We dated for four years while we pursued our education at separate campuses. Ours was a relationship of weekend visits, telephone calls, letters, and summers at home. The alone time served to heighten the "absence makes the heart grow fonder" effect. For Mark, his abandonment issues with his mother made him pursue visits, calls, and letters rather fanatically. For example, in just two years, he made over sixty six-hour round-trip visits to see Deb at her campus.

We are now conscious that we sacrificed a lot of campus social opportunities and other activities to see each other so much and to be "faithful" to each other. Deb is also aware that she sacrificed career interests she might have had in order to prepare herself adequately for the role of minister's wife. Mark had "decided" to enter the ministry (actually he was following the incest script that he had been given). The fact that Deb sacrificed her interests to support Mark's career is an ongoing source of grief for her. It also angers her to know that Mark was pursuing some of this out of obligation and not out of a sense of what he really wanted to do.

We both had been "programmed" to go to and stay in college. We were on separate campuses and felt like we "wanted" to get married as soon as possible. This led us to accelerate our pace, and we both graduated in three years. We were married during Mark's Christmas break from seminary.

While others around us participated in the sexual revolution, we had not. Though we had read Masters and Johnson and "knew" a lot, we were both virgins when we got married. Of course we each had quite different expectations regarding frequency of lovemaking after we started living together. These different expectations were a constant source of tension that we felt but never talked about. We played many silent games around these expectations.

Also, as Mark prepared to enter the ministry, both of us were growing uncomfortable with the roles we knew the ministry would bring, but we didn't know how to talk about it. Mark's solution was to enter graduate school and work towards a Ph.D. in the field of pastoral care. So we went off to a new town. Mark worked part-time at a church and Deb, who had prepared as a home economics teacher, taught for one year in a totally frustrating situation. The expectation was—again—that Deb would work while Mark pursued his career.

The frustrations in our communication, work, and sexual lives were mostly unrecognized by us and certainly unexpressed. Each of us had anger that we had learned as children to hide, so we were left with passive hostilities toward each other. Gradually, more and more, we "left" each other to take care of our individual selves in ways we had learned as children: Deb in her work and crafts projects and inhibited sexuality, and Mark in his eating, sexual fantasies, pornography, masturbation, staying up and getting up late, TV, and general silence. Deb criticized Mark's lifestyle and Mark used her criticism to go deeper into his addictions and his silences.

During this time Mark became a diabetic, which he hated but which also became a source of nurturing. We sought help in a group of very fundamentalist Christian friends. We went to Bible studies and prayer meetings. Neither of us felt quite comfortable with this, but we didn't talk together, and it seemed like the "right" thing for a minister and his wife to be doing. Mark pursued his lofty studies and Deb went off to her work supervising a dining service for one of the university dorms. Mark also preached as a supply pastor at local churches and received lots of affirmation for his abilities. While one part of Deb was proud of this, another part was resentful of the attention he got, and she found the grandiosity it seemed to create in him very difficult to live with.

Also during this time we gave in to having our first child, a girl. We were twenty-six and it seemed like the "natural" thing to do. While she was a joy, our lives became complicated by her needs, and we gave up opportunities in order to get caught up with studies, work, and survival.

Otherwise our aloneness from each other continued, as did our lifestyles. Mark's sexual fantasies and masturbation graduated to occasional visits to massage parlors. As Mark neared the completion of his Ph.D. he went to work as a pastoral counselor at a type of counseling clinic which had been pioneered by a father-type figure in the pastoral care field. We moved back to the city where our parents lived, and this placed us back in proximity to our dysfunctional families.

Mark found himself in over his head with counseling. He had been more academically than clinically trained, but he was expected to earn his own salary with counseling fees and was forced to learn by the seat of his pants. While he sought some supervision, his pride feared it. He had been raised to think that if you needed help you were an intellectual and personal failure.

Mark hated going to work, dreaded some of his counseling appointments, and silently celebrated cancellations, but he could not talk about this with his supervisor. The center he worked for was constantly in financial crisis and he was underpaid. He finished his Ph.D., but was silently so unhappy he couldn't enjoy the accomplishment. It seemed to doom him to work he hated. Mark did manage to begin building a teaching and speaking career that took him away from home many nights. This was, of course, a convenient escape from the tensions at home.

Deb was home for the first time, at first without a second car. We purchased a home, which financially strapped us, and again we fell into having a child, our first son. To save her sanity during this time, Deb began a business producing stained glass pieces, a skill that she had learned at the university. This business began to grow.

During this time we began exclusively seeing the couple who had set us up on our first date. The man seemed to have an exciting career as a lawyer and was fun to be around. He drank heavily, but while we may have noticed it, we never talked about it. Our children were the same ages and we became godparents to each others' children. We talked in enmeshed and codependent ways of our affection for each other, even to the point of planning to move to a new place, perhaps even living in a communal house.

To this end we purchased land in another state, which continued our financial pressures. The man was continually pushing us to spend money on entertainment and other things like vacations together. Deb grew more and more uncomfortable with this, but we were enmeshed. Mark was really trapped in his need for approval from the man and went along with things the man did despite not really liking many of them. Often Deb felt left out of the social activities even though she may have been there.

As we vacationed together, we often stayed in the same room or cabin. On one occasion our enmeshment and flirtatiousness with each other led to sleeping with each other's partner. Mark remembers feeling that he "had" something that "belonged" to someone he so revered. Deb remembers feeling swept up in the event, not really approving, but not knowing what else to do. Mark's demands for sex, and Deb's encounters with his pornography, had already invited her into areas of sexual compliance that she found uncomfortable.

This episode destroyed our friendship with that couple for years. The man's jealousy of what had happened opened up sexual wounds in their relationship and they backed away from us. It has been only recently that we have done a Ninth Step with them as people we've harmed as a couple. This seemed to have a healing effect, but since they are not in recovery—he is still a practicing alcoholic, and their relationship is not good—we cannot move on to another level of friendship with them.

While we lived in this city, we also experienced pressures from our families. It was particularly hard to be with Mark's family, but we tolerated the pain of our discomfort. We attended Mark's dad's church, where Deb taught Sunday school. We went out to lunch after church. While Mark never was aware of this, the pain of his incest wounds forced Mark to do these things and, when doing them, to become silent and removed. They also fueled his addictions and coping strategies. Deb resented these "escapes," but again she had no tools to express her resentment in healthy ways.

During this time Mark became sexual with several of his female clients. It is clear that these episodes were about his sexual addiction, loneliness, and anger at what he was doing. They were also about his incest and the boundaries that had been crossed with him.

Deb and those around him were oblivious to this. When an opportunity to go to a new counseling practice in a new city came up, it seemed like a good escape. To Mark it was an escape from families, from the other couple, and from the sexual relationships with clients. It was a geographic cure that would not work. To move, it seemed that we also had to sacrifice Deb's business, which was becoming more and more successful. Again we followed the pattern that what "seemed" good for Mark's career was the most important. The new job was for more money, status, and power: a bigger fish in a smaller pond (city).

In this new city we moved into a nice neighborhood, where those around us generally made more money than we did. We tried to keep up appearances; and we put ourselves in continuing financial binds. Mark was successful in his career, and Deb began to rebuild her business. She began to travel more on weekends. Mark's career made him very public in this smaller place. To test his own popularity he ran for and was elected to the local school board. Our third child, a son, was born soon after we moved.

Increasingly, both of us were away from home and from each other. We both had numerous distractions, the kids and our careers. At one point, right before our recovery started, Mark was counseling full-time, teaching college, pastoring a church on weekends, and serving on the school board. In these ways, we coped with the tensions at home. The anger and loneliness would occasionally surface, and we would have dramatic arguments. Mark would want to talk them through into the middle of the night. Deb would want to escape. Our sexual relationship was strained, infrequent, and full of dysfunction, but we were afraid to talk about it.

We went to see a counselor, but she could not help us as there were pieces of our addictions—mainly Mark's—that remained hidden from her. She was nice to talk to, and her role as a mediator helped for several days; but this passed and the tension returned. Both of us had thoughts of divorce and knew how lonely we were, and it was probably only our kids that kept us together during this time.

Mark's sexual patterns continued. A number of his work associates eventually did an intervention with him and he went into treatment.

Our recovery as a couple couldn't really start until recovery started for us individually. The main reason is that there were so many things hidden from each other (the "double life" that most addicts lead). Individual shame and addiction totally blocked any hope for intimate communication.

As Mark began to achieve sobriety, we also started to go to individual therapy, to men's and women's groups, and to a couples' group. In our first year of recovery we were gone most nights of the week to a meeting or a group. Our kids protested. Our first year was a time of painful honesty as long-buried feelings gradually surfaced. Some of the anger took months to surface. The incest memories took nine to twelve months to surface. It was still a very tenuous time, and there were occasions when we still didn't know if we were going to make it.

As we experience the peace of the program, we find many things changing. We experience healing in all aspects of our relationship. We continue to struggle with the financial hole addiction carved out for us. Mark struggles to rebuild a career. Deb's business is very successful but creates enormous demands on her time. Although our primary addictions are in check, we can still distance from each other with work, moodiness, overinvolvement in the kids' activities, and a host of other possible escapes. It is vitally important to maintain the discipline of the program. We find great strength and hope in each other, in other couples, and in the ability to share our story with others.

Mark and Deb L.'s Renewal

Let me love you without possessing you . . .

Let me share my feelings with you knowing you will handle them with care but not responsibility. . . Let me ask for my needs, knowing you can only sometimes fulfill them. . . Let my need for aloneness at times not be a rejection of you, but a time of nourishment for me . . .

Let me not depend on your affirmations of me, but live assuredly in the well-being of my own soul.

Let us be honest with each other . . .

Knowing we will not be ridiculed or threatened or ignored. . . Let us both find good friends without it being a threat to the life we share. . . Let us respond to each other without judgment or expectation, rejoicing in the moment to share intimately . . . Let us be weak sometimes or strong sometimes, knowing that both contribute to the growth of our relationship.

Let us dream together . . .

With the playfulness of a child. . . Let our love be a wellspring for the renewal of our own "little children," the safe place to nurture all of our feelings, the playground to experience God's abundant life.

Let us begin again today!

Deb L.

Dave and Mary

Meant for Each Other

We were still in our thirties and still in our first marriages, which were not very fulfilling. At that time phrases such as "family of origin" and "dysfunctional relationship" had no meaning to us, nor would they for some time to come. We were both into our work, which we used as a means to isolate from each other.

Our relationship began with a chance meeting one evening at a local bar and restaurant. We were each with friends from work and we would deny that we were looking for someone that evening. But meet we did, and we followed it up with an agreement to have lunch the next day. There was no doubt in our minds that we were meant for each other, and the lunch led us to an affair that lasted the next five years. As a result we eventually divorced our partners and got married a few months later. We were full of optimism that this time we were going to do things right.

It was almost impossible for us to see what was really going on in our lives at that time. We were addict and co-addict fulfilling each other's needs and were blind to any reality. We would reshape our lives, and others would have to fit around our plans. It is interesting that our character defects were so invisible to us during this period. We were enmeshed. Looking back, we see there were plenty of warning signs about the problems ahead, but we were oblivious to them at the time. A year after our marriage, our old behavior patterns began to surface, and the idyllic marriage began to develop "cracks." Dave had welcomed Mary's two daughters, saying that it would give him a chance to "do it right" this second time. Dave could see what he had missed with his own two daughters. Mary wanted a husband, not a father for her children. She wanted Dave to act like a friend or an "uncle" to them. He wanted to parent them with the discipline he had learned from his stepfather. It took another year for the marriage to get into really rough water; it became a destructive whirlpool that pulled everyone in.

Eventually we decided to seek counseling for step-parenting skills for the oldest girl, who was twelve and was starting to have problems of her own. Those sessions caused us to really look at our relationship and the reality it held for us.

Dave felt more out of control and confused than he could have imagined. The ideal life he had created was now coming apart. The feeling of abandonment was with him every moment. His job of some fourteen years was also in jeopardy as he had been neglecting it for some time. The "lie" he had lived with was out in the open. It was a relief, but it was also very frightening. Now he was ruled more than ever by feelings of shame and guilt and was heavily into his sexual addiction. His addiction continued the odyssey of craziness that affected the very core of our lives and the lives of those around us.

The fights, the rage, the isolation, the impotency devastated us. Dave's other life was getting harder and harder to keep secret. Four years later the "Happily Ever After" marriage was virtually at an end. Dave tried to explain his sexual addiction to Mary, who went into a state of shock for a long time. She took it upon herself to learn everything there was about sexual addiction. The "watching" consumed her.

As he started reading the books of Dr. Pat Carnes, Dave admitted that he was addicted to sex. He promised to go to SAA meetings and did so for nine months. Then for the next four and one-half years he practiced a deeper secret that he hid from Mary. She was excluded from his secret life. Each felt that life was OK during that time. Mary didn't realize that Dave had gotten back into his addiction three years earlier. He clearly had underestimated the power the addiction had over him.

There seemed to be no way to reestablish trust. The end, each agreed, had come, and they would part in a civilized manner. Now the secret was out with children and friends. Mary felt a great relief, even though the marriage had not made it. She proceeded with divorce despite feeling they really had some type of love. We both knew that the relationship would fail no matter what—or so we thought!

As Mary was waiting for the attorney, she picked up a copy of a national magazine and flipped through the pages, and there staring at her was an article on sexual addiction. It stated that whether male or female, sexual addiction could be treated successfully and the prognosis was excellent.

We met over the "last lunch." She explained what she had read, and Dave said he would find out more. His heart was finally talking. He found out that other couples were hoping to start a support group for couples in recovery. The necessary arrangements were made and we met with two other couples. This was the first RCA meeting.

The hardest part for Mary, however, had just begun. She started dealing with her responsibility in the relationship and discovered that she had brought many of her old traits, good and bad, into this relationship, as well as into her first relationship. In front of two other couples we made a six-month commitment to work on our relationship. We committed that we would not abandon each other during this time, no matter what (except for physical abuse).

Our major challenge was dealing with the underlying damage that was becoming so clear to us. This included lack of trust, couple shame, lack of intimacy, and a deep fear of abandonment. Mary was afraid of leaving Dave. She also was fearful of abandonment. We both realized we have a talent for zoning out. Now that the fear of abandonment was identified and spoken of openly, we could begin our work on our relationship and do some solid work in recovery as a couple.

Our weekly meeting helped us deal with so many crises, little and large. It was a safe place for us to open up to each other and to be honest in front of safe and caring couples. These two couples were instruments in our having a loving and gentle marriage. We thank them now and forever.

We cannot say that the hurtful words and actions are gone, but we can say we understand them and what brought us together. We realize all too well that it is an ongoing process. We still fight; however, the past hurts, mistrusts, and issues are in a clearer perspective.

Our mutual sadness about our childhood is now openly shared with each other. We understand that pain, but we do not dwell on it. We have lives to live and, most importantly, a true loving and intimate relationship to build.

Beth and Stephen

Freedom from Bondage

Beth

I am thirty-two years old, and have been in relationship with Stephen for three years. We have been attending RCA meetings together steadily for a year and one-half. Prior to meeting Stephen, I was sober in Alcoholics Anonymous for almost three years. God willing, I will soon celebrate six continuous years of sobriety in that program. Little did I know when I first got sober what other addictions awaited my discovery and my recovery from them!

I was the first of three children born to a couple who were, in my not so humble estimation, already deeply engaged in their own addictions. My mother, in my opinion, was addicted to rage and to my father; my father to alcohol, gambling, work, my mother, and enmeshment with his mother. I believe that my mother was emotionally abused by her parents from early childhood. I recall her frequently saying that she didn't feel free until her father's death. Sarcasm and name-calling were the operative means of communication in her family, and those patterns were repeated in my family. My brother was referred to consistently by his full name, with his middle name replaced by either "liar" or "whiner." Raging and screaming, including the following routine phrases, were directed at us morning, noon, and night: "Get out of my sight; I'm going to rip every g-damn hair out of your head; I'm going to brain you; I'm going to shove my fist down your throat; I'm going to break every bone in your body; I'll give you something to cry about." My mother prided herself on having a repertoire of dirty looks of the "if looks could kill" variety. These looks were not used to ensure we minded our manners in public, i.e., as a replacement for humiliating public reprimands. They were an integral part of the family communication system, as were my father's silences, which could go on for weeks or months. I learned all of these behaviors and, until sobriety, thought that practicing them was the normal way to have a relationship. Learning new ways of communication has been absolutely necessary for me in order that I might have any chance at intimacy.

My father was one of two boys who were "mommy's little angels." During my childhood, I observed my father and his brother being continually invaded emotionally by their mother. I presume this invasiveness began in their childhood and that, in response to this invasiveness, my father learned withdrawal and silence as a defense. He used "the silent treatment" as a form of punishment against my mother and, later, against us. This was the way he expressed his hurt and anger, and I learned to do the same. He also learned, in his family of origin, that children were for the use of adults, not that adults were responsible to meet the basic emotional needs of children. In both my mother's and my father's families, the children were made responsible for the parents' happiness, and this turnaround of parent/child roles was repeated in my family. My parents did not take emotional responsibility for parenting us. Instead, we were required to provide for their emotional needs. It was our job to receive their rage when it overwhelmed them, to stop our tears in order not to make them uncomfortable, and to cuddle with them when they felt the need for loving, not when we needed such attention. My two brothers and I were also made responsible for our grandparents' happiness, especially after both our grandfathers died and our grandmothers were left without partners.

I choose to share my story with you in the sincere hope that you may find some help or comfort in your own earnest search for working solutions to the problems facing you in your relationship. I include information about my addictions and the dysfunctional behavior of my family of origin because they are elements that contribute to my behavior in my relationship.

As part of being responsible for our parents' emotional needs, we had to play assigned roles and, insanely, were then shamed for doing so. This took the focus off our parents' misbehavior. I was the "smart one" with the "big mouth," and my brother was the "not so smart" one who "lied" all the time. Of course, I lied too, but they did not confront me with it in order to preserve their assigned family structure. My littlest brother was the "good" one. Interestingly, we were assigned our roles before we really had the opportunity to develop our own personalities, and the roles we were assigned closely paralleled our same-sex parent's particular dysfunctions. For example, I was known as cold, sarcastic, and unemotional, with a repertoire of dirty looks. These characteristics were my mother's, the result of her childhood abuse. My brother was cast as "not so smart," which is the role my father played, both to avoid parenting responsibility and as part of his addict dance with my mother. She was the "smart" one and patronized him, while he wielded his power under the table through the threat of silence and withdrawal.

Silence was also an integral part of the family communication system, in a different way than simply as my father's punishment of us. We had to be silent about what was happening to us. I eventually became so silent about what was happening to me that I stopped knowing what was happening to me. This created my current difficulty trusting, or even being aware of, my own perceptions. I am working to overcome the resulting hypervigilance and overdependence on "rules" to determine how things "should" be, as opposed to how I feel. I am learning to feel my own feelings and to trust my own judgment, so I can stop constantly evaluating my behavior and that of others, especially Stephen's. This does not mean, of course, that by ceasing my endless intellectual evaluation, I wish to avoid the Tenth Step, or that my goal in using my own judgment is to allow self-will to run riot. What I am striving for is balance, here, as in all areas of my life.

The requirement for silence also created immense shame in me. One way they enforced the silence was to shame me and call me names ("argumentative," "oppositional," etc.) whenever I disagreed with their assessment of me. I am not speaking here about the type of shame one appropriately feels when one has offended or done something unacceptable. I refer to deep, pathological shame, the sort that makes you feel like you are defective at your core, that you are disgusting even for existing and drawing in breath. I came to believe it when I was told that I was crazy. Since nothing was wrong with my parents, something must be wrong with me. I am healing this shame, one day at a time, and it is only by healing this shame that learning new ways of communication is possible. I realize I cannot impose a veneer of "appropriate" communication over a shame-filled spirit. I understand why my parents behaved as they did and I believe that they are shame-based as well, and could only give me what they had inside themselves.

My father gave up gambling when he lost a $40,000 loan by gambling it away in the stock market. He learned his drinking and gambling behaviors at his mother's knee. His parents owned a tavern, and one of my earliest memories of my grandmother is of the enjoyment she took from going to the "track," i.e., to the horse races. After giving up gambling, my father began to rely more heavily on his drinking to sustain him.

Physical abuse was present in my family, which leads me to believe that my parents experienced similar abuse as children. Both my brother and I were routinely beaten for simply doing what children do—crying, saying "no" when we were toddlers, etc. Although I am fiercely opposed to spanking a child of any age, for those of you who are not, I will distinguish here between my understanding of beating and spanking. Spanking, in my view, is a non-painful blow delivered with an open hand, on a well-diapered toddler bottom, by a calm parent, for the purpose of teaching. Spanking never involves the use of objects (belts, hairbrushes, etc.) to deliver blows, and never involves repeated blows. Beating is the delivery of blows to a child by parents who are in the midst of their own rage. My brother and I were beaten. I don't say "brothers," although I had two, because I have many gaps in my memory, and I don't remember what happened to my youngest brother regarding beatings. I remember feeling that my parents had let up to some degree in their treatment of my youngest brother, but I truthfully do not recall. I left home when he was six and I was sixteen.

I never knew what behavior on my part would "cause" a beating, and what would merit praise. Throughout my childhood, I had a recurring nightmare. In this dream, an unspeakable, invisible evil would be chasing me through our neighborhood. I would manage to escape into our house, and I would feel deeply relieved to have made it to the safety of the kitchen, where my mother was standing, back toward me, stirring a pot on the stove. I would begin to describe my desperate flight, and my miraculous escape. My mother would slowly turn around to face me. As she turned, I would see that her face had turned to wood, much like that of a wooden ventriloquist's dummy. She was possessed by the invisible evil that had pursued me. I would run screaming from the house to our neighbor's home, where the same thing would happen again. I had this dream repeatedly through my childhood, and sporadically into my adulthood, until I got sober. Once I realized that the dream was a true description of my life in my family of origin, I never had the dream again.

Sexual abuse was also part of my family-of-origin experience. As a toddler, I had a bladder infection for seven months, which only stopped after I was hospitalized for two days for diagnostic tests. The doctor's notations each month referred to genital redness and irritation, but no one intervened. The tests did not cure me, and the doctor did discover that there was no congenital abnormality causing the problem. Apparently, the hospitalization scared whoever was molesting me enough to make them stop. In addition to my early experience, I was also abused by my paternal grandmother. After the death of her husband, she would sometimes whine, "Make a little love to me," and then I knew I was in for it. She did not mean intercourse, but meant that we were supposed to meet her needs for physical touch, which were sometimes sexual. I was also forced to sleep with her, both when I would visit her apartment, and in a trundle bed in my bedroom when she stayed over on weekends. This was a set-up for my own abuse. She frequently sexually abused my youngest brother in front of me on the family room couch, in the guise of comforting him. This was both disgusting and exciting to me at the time. It was both relieving and painful, in that I was greatly relieved to no longer be the focus of her attentions, but I felt abandoned and jealous as well.

Emotional sexual abuse also went on in my family, in many forms, including comments made frequently about my developing breasts, and a rivalry developed between me and my mother regarding the fact that my breasts were much larger than hers. My parents expressly taught me (not just in messages and by example, but in words) that I came second to their relationship with each other.

They explained that children always grow up and leave their parents, so children come second. Someone would come along and love me one day, they explained, and then I would be first to that person. But until then, I had to wait. I learned sex/relationship addiction early on from what I was taught in my family of origin, both by example and explanation. Sex was love, as I clearly saw, both by the fact that the only touching I got that wasn't beating was from my grandmother, and from the way I saw my mother behave with my father. I got the clear impression that men were incredibly stupid and easily manipulated by sex, but also, somehow, incredibly necessary. I knew, in my child's understanding, that to be loved as an adult, you had to read the book in my mother's drawer about "how to please a man," because if you didn't, they would leave you, and then you would die.

It was with these lessons that I was armed to face the world when I left home at sixteen. I had become sexually active at age fourteen with my high school boyfriend, whom I later realized (in my sobriety) was an alcoholic. He drank prescription codeine cough medicine out of the bottle when he didn't have a cough . . . I always wondered why he didn't use a spoon, and why he took it in the absence of a cough! He went to college and broke up with me. I was devastated. I went to the same college he did, even though it was out of state, in hopes of getting him back. Immediately upon arriving, I started using drugs and alcohol. When my youngest brother was diagnosed with leukemia, I began using daily. I did hallucinogenic drugs during the week I gave him a bone marrow transplant, although good girl that I still was, I checked with the doctor first. When he died, I was expected to comfort my parents over the loss of their son. As they had learned that children were to serve the emotional needs of parents, it never even occurred to them that they were responsible to parent me through the loss of my brother.

At college, I fell into the arms of a man whom I disliked the minute we met. I ignored my first impression, which was that he was somehow oily and dishonest. Although he began cheating on me within four months of the initiation of our relationship, I stayed with him for nine years. He was the one who would finally love me first, in my addicted mind. He was educated and articulate, interested in public affairs, and compassionate. Of course, he came from an abusive family too, and learned techniques of communication from them, so his sweeter spirit was increasingly masked as his disease progressed. His family was very kind to me, and this also kept me with him. They welcomed me for two weeks at Christmas every year, and they took me on long family vacations to the lake every summer. Although his father used name-calling and raging too, since I was not a family member, it was not directed at me, and I felt safe in their home. My parents had long since stopped taking me on family vacations, saying they didn't like me. So being welcomed by his family was like heaven to me, until the end, when I started learning about alcoholism and dysfunction.

Initially, my partner and I used together; more and more our addictions drove us apart. He drank and was abusive, occasionally physically; I used and was abusive, relying on my old standbys of name-calling and raging. He threw me across the room in January of 1985. The first time of the few times he hit me, my mother said that I was so difficult to live with that I probably provoked him, and I should just try harder to be nice. I was angry, but I believed her and stayed for another eight years. This time, somehow, I knew we needed help. We went to counseling, and the doctor said we needed individual help. Since I was afraid that my partner would not go back to therapy if he was forced to change therapists, I found a different counselor for myself. She immediately required me to go to Al-Anon as a condition of seeing me. So, I went.

Within three months, he quit therapy and hid the fact from me. I found out and, after two months of hoping he would get another therapist as he promised, I asked that we separate. Not yet in recovery from my relationship addiction, I only got the strength to ask him to leave because I was carrying on an intrigue with another active alcoholic with whom I worked. I "knew" I wouldn't take the relationship further, but when this new fellow got sober the week my partner left, I became involved with him. When, after several weeks, the grief hit over my partner's departure, I attempted to break off with the new fellow and go back to my partner, but he was already involved with a young girl. We went back and forth until I collapsed and went into treatment for co-dependence. I had a dream there that I was an addict, and that if I admitted it, I would feel better. When I told the dream to the group, instead of laughing and saying, "Oh, pshaw," much to my disbelief, they all nodded their heads in agreement! I came back home, got involved with the guy newly sober in AA, got sober myself, and lived happily ever after in relationship addiction until I discovered his sex addiction. Then it was back into the fetal position for me. I got into ACA recovery. After a lovely year on my own, in which I learned, deep in my gut, that God was enough for me, and I was enough for me, I met Stephen. I was at a meeting where I was a regular, and I noticed him because he was a newcomer to that meeting. He shared about doing bodywork in therapy, which was one of the few forms of therapy I respected. I was intrigued. Then he began to talk about what he was doing in that particular day's therapy session, which was dealing with the fact that he did not want to have sex with the woman he was dating. I thought this was great! A man who also did not want to have sex sometimes; a man who felt like me! He came up to me after the meeting to chat, and he was so soft-spoken and nice. My friend Allison was standing with me, and after he left, she said she hoped he would stop dating the woman he referred to in the meeting, and start dating me, because she thought he seemed so nice. So, after the meeting the following week, we went out for coffee. I then realized that he was active in his sex/relationship addiction, and he wasn't just dating the other woman casually, he was living with her! I "knew" I wasn't going to get involved with him! Ha! Two weeks after we met, he left his relationship and started to go to SLAA. I went for it!

Getting involved with Stephen, even against my better judgment, was the clue to me that I was a sex/relationship addict. In my relationship with my partner of nine years, I thought the problem was his alcoholism, when, in fact, his alcoholism was a mirror for my own. With my first partner in sobriety, I thought the problem was his sex addiction, which, in great part, it was. But when I got involved with another sex addict—which I vowed I would not do—I realized the lesson was the same and admitted my powerlessness over my sex/relationship addiction. Initially, I liked to keep a safe intellectual distance from the "sex addict" stuff, and just say I was a relationship addict. I never did any of that disgusting promiscuity stuff, or used pornography, or . . . but, when I heard myself listing all these items in my mind; I heard the "not-yets" of AA, and remembered what denial sounds like.

Slowly, just as in my alcoholic sobriety, I have remembered things I did, and thoughts I have, that put me squarely in the sex addict class. I now realize that there is no difference between sex and relationship addiction. Just as in AA, some people drank beer, some fine wine; some were in the gutter, some were in the corporate boardroom; some had a DWI (driving while intoxicated), some didn't. So it is in SLAA—some were prostitutes, some were housewives, some used pornography, some just used seductive clothing and flirtatious behavior as their stock in trade.

But just as we all in AA are alcoholic, whatever floor of the elevator we got off on, I cannot put myself above those disgusting sex addicts whose behavior I hold in such contempt. I am one. Of course, I still struggle with my contempt and my desire to separate myself, but God provides me with plenty of reminders that whenever I have one finger pointing away from myself, I have three pointing back at me.

In spite of our addictive start, the fact that I was attracted to Stephen was a sign of my healing. He had six and one-half years of sobriety in AA when we met. This was a definite improvement over the active alcoholics I had begun relationships with before. He was already in therapy for himself, not because anyone was making him go. Also, because of my physical abuse, I had previously only sought relationships with men who were very slightly built, and not too tall, as I thought that somehow this would protect me from abuse. (Wrong!) I was also turned off by any obvious indications of masculinity, dating only men who were hairless and as close to womanly as I could find. Stephen, on the other hand, is six feet tall, very muscular and hirsute, and unmistakably male. Trusting in our commitment to nonviolence with each other was a big step for me, as he is certainly large enough and powerful enough that he could kill me if he wanted to do so.

Many of the experiences I had, and behaviors I learned in my family, affect my ability to participate in an intimate relationship today. While my problems started there, my healing and changing are my responsibility. As a child, I was a victim, and so I learned to be both victim and abuser. I cannot blame my parents, or somehow separate myself from "child abusers," and consider myself superior. I am as they are, and I can only be grateful that I have been given the opportunity to change my behavior and to break the abuse chain. My "automatic pilot" behaviors, when active, are things that damage my relationship and are problems Stephen and I have to deal with in our healing together as a couple. My propensity for violence; screaming and raging; name-calling; my post-traumatic stress disorder, which causes my "fight or flight" response to be permanently stuck in the "on" position; and my related constant anxiety, hypervigilance, and inability to relax are all things I am working on changing with the help of RCA and other Twelve-Step programs, therapy, and body work.

Regardless of our awareness of our family issues, I find that we act out aspects of both our parents' addict dances, and even mimic some of their circumstances. I guess the AA Big Book is right when it says self-knowledge availed us nothing! Some of the similarities are astounding. I have an advanced degree; my mother went to a prestigious university. Stephen and my father completed high school and did not go on to college. I patronize Stephen; my mother patronized my father. Both my mother and Stephen's mother raged; I rage at Stephen. I often struggle with the contempt for men I learned growing up in a family where the role for all the men was "stupid." I am overly responsible; Stephen uses under-responsibility as a way to withdraw, which often draws my contempt and rage, and relieves him of his responsibility to deal with his own anger, just like my father. Stephen's defense mechanisms against his invasive mother include withdrawal, which he uses in our relationship as my father used with my mother and me.

Stephen also uses crazy-making, table-turning, and subject-changing as addictive fighting tools, which parallel the crazy-making that was nonstop in my family of origin. The good news is that, thanks to the Steps and lots of help, we can see our patterns, which, while not enough in itself, opens the door to healing them.

Stephen

I am a multiply addicted person. My addictions and compulsiveness are full-blown diseases, yet, as paraphrased from the AA Big Book, they are but symptoms of deeper underlying causes. More concisely, I believe these addictions to be coping mechanisms that I adopted as a child to alleviate emotional stress. The causes of my childhood stress are numerous: ineffective or absent emotional and social skills, incidents of abuse or trauma, and so on; however, the greatest underlying source is the parenting I received. I don't mean to suggest that my parents are monstrous humans who have committed terrible personal crimes. They are simply individuals, like myself, who were damaged as children. Upon becoming parents, they passed the damage on to their children, in this case, me.

I choose to share my story with you in the sincere hope that you may find some help or comfort in your own earnest search for working solutions to the problems facing you in your relationship. I include information about my addictions and the dysfunctional behavior of my family of origin because they are elements that contribute to my behavior in my relationship.

My mother became pregnant with me when she was eighteen and still unmarried. Her mother and grandmother used this circumstance to shame her. Her grandmother told her to leave the family house, and her mother withdrew a "contract" wherein my mother would have received $4,000 had she remained "pure" until the time she married. Her parents also informed her that she could not depend on them. She had to live entirely by her own means. This was the crowning event of my grandparents' shaming and scapegoating of my mother throughout her childhood. In this spirit of shame and abandonment, my mother married my father and they moved to a tiny efficiency in the city.

In the spring of 1961 I was born, and one month later my parents moved to a small two-bedroom townhouse in the suburbs. During the following three years, we lived together as a family. My father finished his last year of college while working at night to support us. My mother prematurely ended her college career to work full-time housekeeping and childrearing. My parents had regular fraternity parties at the house (as a toddler I sometimes got drunk at these events). After my father began working days, my mother felt more and more abandoned by my father's escalating drinking. He began to miss dinners and stayed out late drinking with increasing frequency. Finally, my mother consulted a doctor who identified my father's alcoholism. He made her aware that my father might or might not quit drinking and that she could choose to stay under those circumstances or leave. She chose to leave and my parents divorced just after I was three.

That year, my mother found a job as a Girl Friday; I began daycare, and we became the best of pals. One night my father visited. He showed me how to shake hands. I felt overjoyed that daddy had found his way home. You can imagine how I felt when he left again and I realized that his absence was intentional rather than by some accident. I may have been spared from the direct effects of parental alcoholism but I did experience the absence of my father as a result of his disease.

Roughly one year after my parents' divorce, my mother began dating a man who would become my stepfather a short while later. His son was only one day older than me. Initially, we were a happy family, but as time progressed, this man became more violent. I recall one night that my mother had taken me into her room as if to protect me and clutched me while screaming hysterically in fear as my stepfather beat on the door and yelled threats.

I was terrified. Then a few months later, he brought a bowl of soup for me into my first grade classroom and tried to explain that he was taking my brother. I simply couldn't understand but I enjoyed the special attention. That afternoon, he left with my brother. My mother held me and cried as I watched them drive away.

From this point on, I began to experience grief over the absence of my family, but I didn't know how to express the pain and sadness and anger. I needed help, but as my mother's emotional needs had not been met as a child, she did not know how to help me with my needs. Instead, she used me to meet her needs. Therefore, because I could not express or release my pain, sadness, and so on, these feelings stayed inside me for many years. I had internalized them. I continued to internalize feelings when new emotional circumstances arose.

Carrying my emotional baggage was uncomfortable, so naturally I developed some tools to distract myself from these unprocessed feelings. I began to withdraw and I discovered, somewhat unconsciously, that isolating was more comfortable than socializing because I didn't create troubling emotional situations for myself. Reading lots of books disguised my withdrawal and provided me with another tool for emotional escape fantasy. Likewise, schoolwork provided intellectual pursuits, which were equally effective for shutting down my feelings.

I was six years old when my second family left. My mother and I once again became very close. We cuddled in bed on weekend mornings and I spent most of my mother's free time with her. Our neighbor's children brought their father's *Playboy* magazines to my backyard "fort." Looking at the nude women did not sexually arouse me, as I was seven years old; however, I did experience immediate and intense mood changes. I felt excitement, a quickening of my heartbeat, and shortness of breath. I felt guilt and shame and curiosity. Only two years ago, I was finally able to recognize that this was the initial stage of my addiction to pornography.

When I was eight years old, my mother met a third man whom she married after a few months. I viewed this man and his attendant son and daughter with some suspicion. I did not trust that they cared enough about my mother and me to stay with us. Also, I noticed that this man drove a real wedge between my mother and me. Gone were our cuddly mornings and extra times spent with each other. Suddenly, I found myself in the back seat with two other children who were strangers to me, with whom I was expected to share my time. I eventually began to accept these people and grew closer to them, but this marriage ended after eight months.

My mother was married and divorced one more time, for a total of four marriages and divorces before I was sixteen. Between the third and fourth marriages, she dated numerous men and had two longer relationships, each lasting about a year. In between relationships and affairs, my mother used me to meet her partnership needs. We would be close when she had no partner, and I was abandoned when the partners came along. She used me as her surrogate spouse. My mother's behavior toward me became increasingly "boundary-less" as her sexual addiction progressed. She would use the bathroom with the door open, dress in front of me, and ask me to give her body rubs while she was nude. I would be shamed while giving her these massages during my adolescence, because she would tell me not to look at her genitals, while requesting me to rub her buttocks or legs. I did not realize that this behavior on my mother's part was incest until three years ago. Prior to this time, I only felt shame that by accident or curiosity, I had seen my mother's genitals. Through these experiences, I began to equate sex with love.

When I was fourteen years old, I began to drink on weekend evenings when my mother was out dating, which was almost every weekend. I drank between half a pint and a pint of vodka each night. I also began smoking cigarettes. Here I launched my alcoholic career, with a brief interlude of social drinking the following year, when I began to attend boarding school. I survived this year with tolerable grades, even though I felt that I was near my bursting point emotionally. During the summer, I started using illegal drugs. This was also the summer that I was raped by a man when I was hitchhiking.

The following school year I came apart. My alcohol, drug, and pornography use became nearly daily activities. My grades plummeted. I met a girl at school that year and fell head over heels in love. She practiced much of the same "come here, go away" behaviors as my mother, and much of the sexual promiscuity as well. I wanted to be monogamous, but she wanted an "open" relationship, so I acquiesced. At semester break, the school asked me to leave, instead of attempting to determine the cause of the precipitous drop in my grades, or providing me with help. I was crushed. When I came home, I learned that my mother had turned my bedroom into an office even though she had promised me that I would always have a place to come home to until I came of age. I slept on a couch in the family room and was also shamed about sleeping in the morning when employees were in the house. Then my mother put me in a psychiatric daycare center where they knew nothing about addiction, sexual abuse, or family dysfunction. This treatment was ineffective.

About this time, my father, whom I had only seen or heard from a few times in fourteen years, got sober and contacted my mother. My mother seized upon this opportunity to give custody of me to my father, even though he was in his first month of sobriety, and he made it clear that he could not care for me. For the next three years, I was shuttled between my father, my grandparents, and my mother. As I had not been allowed to apply for a driver's license, I hitchhiked from my temporary homes to visit my high school girlfriend, and to go to bars. A number of times over these three years (ages sixteen through nineteen) I was picked up while hitchhiking by men who gave me alcohol and drugs in return for sex.

I had, during this time, a one-week and a three-week stay in psychiatric wards. These programs also knew nothing about sexual abuse, addiction, or family dysfunction. My shame deepened as I was treated by the psychiatric community as the "problem," rather than an indication of the problems in the family that needed to be resolved systemically. I kept dropping out of high school, as I could not handle the work, or anything else for that matter. At one point, my father even took me to court as incorrigible.

I was put in a halfway house, and the staff informed my father that I needed more help than they could provide, but he did not get it for me. He kicked me out, and I went to live in a house owned by a man I did not know, but where I heard through friends that I could stay. It turned out that I was expected to pay for my rent with my body, which I did. I was not yet eighteen. Besides being raped for rent, I was also locked in the basement with a man I did not know and raped again in that house while friends of the owner watched through the windows. I got out of that situation and briefly lived with my mother, and then with my grandparents after I turned eighteen and my mother kicked me out. While I lived with my grandparents, I went to school for one semester, dropped out, and stole beer when I could in order to drink with my alcoholic friends.

I attempted to commit suicide by drinking half a bottle of rat poison in July of the year I turned nineteen. I almost died but was miraculously saved by my grandfather, who somehow discovered the empty bottle amidst the clutter in the very cluttered garage. I spent five weeks on a psychiatric unit, and then a year in long-term residential treatment for emotionally disturbed teenagers. In this treatment program, I was reintroduced to AA. The treatment program did not understand addiction, but they had one AA meeting a week on site, and I attended (mainly because I liked a pretty girl who was going to meetings).

I attained six months of continuous sobriety, which ended when the treatment center required me to find a place to live for my outpatient treatment. The center offered me no help in finding a place and the people who attended my AA meeting lived on site, so I went to live with the only other people I knew—my drinking buddies. After thirteen months of drinking hell, I called my grandmother in desperation and asked her to take me to a meeting. She did, and I have been sober for the ten years since.

In the past three years, I have discovered and begun to recover from other addictions. I have stopped using pornography, and have begun to take a teensy look at my money issues, which were created in childhood and exacerbated by the fact that my father did not contribute child support, so my mother and I lived near poverty quite often. I have begun to work with a therapist who is familiar with Twelve-Step programs, sexual abuse, and family dysfunction. I have started to grieve the loss of a safe family and childhood, and realize that I used drugs, pornography, alcohol, and cigarettes mostly to numb my feelings.

In my early sobriety, I desperately wanted to date women who were also sober and who were available to me sexually, because, as I associated sex with love, I wanted to be loved. I dated a few women in my early sobriety but did not get into a long-term relationship until I was four years sober. I met a woman, and we had sex on our first date. I immediately leapt into the relationship with both feet. Within a month I was living with her. I assumed the role of caretaker, just as I had learned with my mother. We seemed to be doing well, but in my gut I began to recognize that I did not want to continue taking care of her financially and emotionally to my own detriment. I did not realize at the time that I was repeating the pattern I had learned with my mother. I began therapy and realized more and more that I wanted to leave. I didn't know that we could change our dynamics. I was unaware of RCA, and I didn't realize that we were acting out old family patterns that could be healed, so I left.

Just before I ended that relationship, I began to notice a woman in another Twelve-Step program who talked about ways that she was learning to take care of herself. I was impressed and I listened to her carefully in later meetings. She was also very attractive, so I really wanted to meet her and I hoped that she would like me. Beth agreed to join me for coffee at the local family restaurant. With a good deal of embarrassment, I recall that while trying to impress her, I poured my life story out to her as though I had no boundaries. I also made remarks that clearly indicated that I was in active sex addiction as well. When we parted and I asked her for a hug she replied, "I don't do men." I reeled with the realization that my behavior had been revolting and felt saddened that I had pushed Beth away. Later, I found that she only hugged men who she knew well and she hadn't found me so revolting that she wouldn't go out with me again. We seemed to be attracted to each other like sex-addicted magnets. Since I was still in a relationship, we didn't fully act on our mutual attraction, but we did engage in some inappropriate intrigue. Shortly after I ended my relationship, we were courting.

I would like to say that we were and are a picture of perfect couple health, but truly, the lack of healthy relationship models when we were young and our absence of partnering skills have often left us struggling in our relationship as we learn basic tools and behaviors.

Since we have been in RCA, we have gotten a real boost in the frequency with which we are relieved of our addictive relationship behaviors. We have learned new ways of interacting and communicating. Once we realized that we were in a relationship, we knew that we needed help. We sought help from a relationship counselor. We have been seeing this counselor almost since the beginning of our relationship. We still consider that therapy essential to our relationship recovery, but it wasn't until we added RCA to our sources of help that our efforts really started to pay off consistently. Applying the Steps to our relationship is not something we were taught how to do in our individual recovery programs. RCA has given us the tools we need to keep bringing the healing that we do in our individual recoveries back into the coupleship. We have been able to recognize the little child in each other and to remember more often that we are friends, not enemies, even in the middle of fights.

It has also been of great benefit to us to have the tools provided in the RCA literature. The reflections and the weekly inventory sheets have been very helpful, even though we have not gotten into the discipline of using them regularly.

Hearing other couples relate their problems, such as struggles with their addictive behaviors, fights, and so on, has been very healing for us. We no longer feel that we are so shameful, or unique. Likewise, sharing our difficult issues with other couples has been comforting and enlightening to us. We now know that our relationship is not hopeless. This has been a great relief to us. RCA has brought us closer; we are experiencing intimacy for the first time. We have come to believe that what is written in the AA Big Book applies to our RCA recovery; the promises can come true for us if we only work for them.

Paul and Jane

A Spiritual Awakening

Our couple recovery began the day we walked into our first RCA meeting, March 4, 1990. At that point, we had been married for eighteen years and had three children. We had each begun our own individual recoveries in 1987. However, our relationship was floundering, and we felt emotionally divorced. Even though we had been trying to use many tools from our own individual recovery programs, from counseling, and from other support groups such as Marriage Encounter, the way was not clear.

We had each made a limited commitment to try working on our relationship one day at a time, but hope for couple recovery was scary. Pain and despair were frequent companions, and yet we also had many good memories of times together to use as sources of strength. We could each admit that important parts of our story had begun long ago in our families of origin. What we had not realized was the extent of the damage from our family histories, and its impact on our relationship.

What we know today is that couple recovery does work. As we share our story with you, we owe much to the support of many loving people in RCA who made it possible to share with you today as a couple.

Jane

I'll never forget the night Paul came home from work and said he didn't know if he loved me anymore and wasn't sure he wanted to stay married. It was the day after a romantic weekend at a bed and breakfast, and I had planned a surprise fortieth birthday party with friends to coincide with our return. I thought we were really on our way to new growth, having begun our own individual recovery programs the previous year. My first reaction to his "bombshell" was to find a cure for my shock and pain! Make love, go on a vacation, make a marriage enrichment weekend, anything to make the pain stop. The day before, I had given Paul a card that said, "Thanks for standing by me at this time in my life." I had no idea what was to lie ahead.

Through my Twelve-Step support groups (Adult Children of Alcoholics and Overeaters Anonymous), I had discovered that I used many illusions and defenses as protective walls to support a very fragile, lost, frightened and wounded inner child. My most powerful visual image of this child was a fallen little girl in the middle of an empty room with black menacing hallways surrounding her. This little child had surrendered, fallen, and could not pretend to be strong anymore. I was only just beginning to explore the depth of my emptiness. The frozen tears began to fall. How did the darkness begin?

As I was growing up in my family, long before I met Paul, patterns were developing which were filled with both healthy strengths and crippling deficits. Today I am grateful for the peace I have found through recovery. I have given myself permission to feel all my feelings and accept that my parents did the best they could with the tools they had available to them.

My childhood was marked by contradictions. When I was born as the fifth of six children in my family, dysfunction was clouding our family life. Loyalty, family fun, family rituals, spirituality, support, and achievement were important values. However, alcoholism and co-dependency were also insidious poisons.

It was difficult and painful for me to relate to stories of alcoholism in my early recovery because my father stopped drinking when I was young. However, I'll never forget the two years he laid on the couch, believing, or so I was told, that he thought he had cancer. It didn't make sense. Here he was a successful doctor; why couldn't he go get help like he told other people to do? I was constantly seeking a bond with my father, to earn his love, praise, and recognition, but my brothers were his favorites. My bond with my father was incredibly important to me, especially due to my mother's emotional illness. My mother was caring, loving, and devoted. She was also a co-dependent, affected by manic depression and an eating disorder. Her life was marked by a series of "nervous breakdowns," the second of which occurred immediately after my birth. My mother was sent home to stay with my grandmother for several months. As an infant, I was cared for by my aunt, who worked full-time; by an alcoholic maid; and by my father, who had withdrawn into his own world of alcohol and depression.

When I was eight, I was left at home to be Mother's caregiver during a "breakdown." It would be thirty years before I talked about that day and its horrible memories. That night, I crept out of the house, went to my aunt's down the street, and begged to go to school the next day. She charged over to the house and confronted my father, but the damage was done. I had broken the family rule of "Don't Talk." I'll never forget the look on my father's face.

We all had nicknames. I was so proud I was named "Princess," and I did my best to live up to it. I was always placed between my brothers in the car, and told to be the "peacemaker." Later in childhood, I was devastated when my father changed my nickname to "Chatterbox." During those years, the TV, the newspaper, and what my brothers did wrong were the frequent focal points for my father. I became increasingly angry and frustrated, but had great difficulty sharing these feelings with anyone. I could never understand how the TV was more important than me. I retreated with isolation into a safe world that I could control.

During my teenage years, the whole family was "bottoming out." I received no formal sex education, which left me naturally confused and naive. When I was sexually abused by a man on a public bus, I was terrified and hurt, but trapped by my lack of healthy emotional skills. Mostly, I got my needs met through academic achievement, creative outlets, and helping others.

I had learned from my family that it was not OK to talk about feelings, especially anger, fear, loneliness, sadness. Family messages that were powerful for me included: "Trust only yourself; if you want something done right, do it yourself; put on a happy face; and if something doesn't work out right, look the other way." One family member had said to me: "The absolute worst thing that could ever happen is to feel depressed. I will never, never allow myself to be depressed." I began to believe that I could control all my feelings. I also believed that I could manipulate any situation and make it better.

Later in life as an adult, I talked with my sisters about anger and the difficulty we all experienced when sharing that feeling. I remembered making a promise to myself as a child that I would never ever lose my temper, scream, demean, or be sarcastic with anyone. My anger felt like a firecracker with a burning fuse, waiting to explode. Although progress was made in the family, the scars went deep. An important healing occurred when my father shared with me that he could never take a drink again, since he was afraid that it would kill him and destroy the entire family.

At the end of my sophomore year in college, I met Paul. Our early days together were filled with constant conversation, fun, and feelings of belonging. I remember the solemn promise we made to each other that we would do things "differently," and not make the same mistakes our parents did. I felt important and special to him. What I overlooked was the fact that he rarely talked about his family or his feelings.

Paul

Both of my parents are alcoholics and have been actively drinking since before I was born. They met at a pub in England during World War II. As it turned out, their meeting in a bar was to be prophetic, as alcoholism and the resulting consequences were to be a prominent theme for our entire family.

I am the oldest of six children, the "hero" of the family who always did everything right. On the surface I was the model child: good grades, never a behavior problem, well liked by friends and family. What my outward appearance betrayed was a lost child who had been emotionally abandoned at the age of fourteen months, when my sister was born to an overwhelmed mother who drank to forget her homesickness. Emotional trauma gave way to sexual trauma, as I was sexually abused by two teenage boys when I was four or five years old. I never dared tell my parents because "good boys" don't let things like that happen to them. The memories were buried for nearly forty years.

In grade school, I was quiet but studious. At home, the violent anger of my mother terrified me as I watched my brothers and sister run from her unpredictable attacks. My father was traveling all week and drinking all weekend. There was little help from relatives, although I did learn how to mix alcoholic drinks for my grandfather as I listened to his wonderful stories of World War I and early motor cars. Life was becoming more dangerous at home, so I learned to spend hours playing at a local park where a creek offered hours of solitude. It was here that I was sexually abused a second time by an older boy or teenager (memories are incomplete here). Even my sanctuaries were turning into war zones.

At the end of grade school, I began to consider entering a seminary to become a Catholic priest. At the time, I thought it was just another "wonderful" thing to do; as the Family Hero, I could make everyone very proud of my vocational choice. In retrospect, I was trying to get away from home as soon as possible in another effort to save my sanity. Get away from crazy parents and have salvation guaranteed. What a deal!

Just about the same time I entered the seminary, I also discovered that sex was a very powerful way to escape from my family and my own feelings. Pornographic books, "girlie" magazines, X-rated movies, and erotic fantasy became my favorite diversions. There were dangers, of course, threats of damnation, burning in hell for all eternity, that sort of thing, but the power of sex for a fourteen-year-old makes hell sound like recess. I was hooked. For the next twenty-five years, obsessing, being compulsive, and feeling shamed around sex were to consume much of my available energy in life.

Paul and Jane

I (Paul) met Jane exactly five days after I had mustered the courage to leave the seminary at the end of my junior year of college. I make this point about the "five days after I left" because Jane would later defend herself in a teasing, yet fearful manner, lest someone accuse her of "stealing" a potential priest away from the Church. I had indeed left on my own to pursue "other interests" as I so formally indicated to the rector of the seminary. In truth, I had found out that leaving home didn't cure my spiritual and emotional hurts and sex couldn't fix them either. I had decided to try other people and the "R" word, relationships, as the answer to the loneliness and depression that had marked my life for the first twenty-one years.

Jane and I met at a summer camp working with handicapped children. She first saw me performing in a small but fun rock band called the "Origin of the Species." I was drawn to her smile and her warm manner. She took my hand on a walk and I was in love. I hadn't been touched by a girl since playing Red Rover in third grade, but suddenly I knew what I had been missing during all those years of pre-celibacy: friendship, caring, fun, sharing with another person who cared, and closeness that was nurturing, not abusive. I had finally found a person I could trust.

Jane and I were married in 1971 and began our journey together. What we did well, we did very well. We played and had fun together. We talked, and created three beautiful children. We shared many common interests. We built on each other's strengths. However, our marriage began to unravel as the stresses of life crept in and the seeds planted in our families of origin came to bloom.

I really had no idea about how to do a healthy marriage, since all I ever saw at home was my mom's anger, my dad's avoidance, more anger, more avoidance . . . an endless circle of futility tempered with liberal amounts of alcohol. At first I tried to be close to Jane, but all I really knew how to do was act like we were on a date, have a good time, be together for a couple of hours, don't get too serious, and maybe have sex at the end. What I didn't understand was how to talk about feelings, how to ask for help, how to be supportive, how to argue in a healthy way, or how to talk about my needs. I had all of the responsibilities of a husband, and later a father, but none of the tools to do the job.

I began to distance myself from Jane as I felt increasingly trapped, lonely, bored, frustrated, and scared about the future. As I began to withdraw, many of my old escapes from childhood and adolescence began to re-emerge. Fantasy consumed much of my waking moments. I returned to school and became absorbed in a master's degree. Sexual acting out with myself and other women became more frequent. I was on a downward spiral and heading for destruction. Fortunately for me, my Higher Power intervened by finding me a job as a consultant for a chemical dependency treatment center. Although I am not an alcoholic or drug addict, I am addicted to sex, fantasy, unhealthy relationships, and intellectualizing. My addictions began to control my life.

The more I (Jane) tried to reach Paul, the more he withdrew. When Paul would try to reach me, I would be confused by what I saw as mixed messages. Our lovemaking had always been very special to me, and Paul made me feel important, unique, and special. As the years went by, though, I noticed that Paul seemed less interested. When I asked what we could do differently, he seemed confused and sad, but never really made any concrete suggestions. I often asked myself, what was I doing wrong.

Despite our growing problems, the good times were always there, and our family life was very special. It was the contradictions that were bewildering. I would recoil from teasing and sarcasm or any form of anger, as I was playing out the scripts I had learned early in my life. Escapes were safe and frequent. Parenting, busyness, control, co-dependency, compulsive eating, and romantic fantasy novels were a big part of my coping. My bottom came at a time when we had a four-year-old daughter, we were both out of work, and I was eight months pregnant with a baby I was scared would have problems after the previous miscarriage. As my situation became more insane, so did my behavior. I began shoplifting. Fortunately, I was caught rather quickly, since it's hard to be sneaky when you are that pregnant. I really thought I had destroyed our marriage. Paul was surprisingly supportive, but still incredibly distant. I attributed it to my problems, graduate school, and the loss of jobs. What I did not know at the time, and he didn't share, was that his behavior was just as insane as mine, since he was having an affair with another graduate student up until a week before our second baby was born.

A significant step in our growth occurred when we made a Marriage Encounter weekend. We joined an ongoing support group of other couples who were also encountered and began talking about feelings. That process opened the doors to deeper communication and sharing, but the addictions were still there.

Recovery

As I (Paul) began working in a recovery-oriented environment, I gradually became aware of how much pain I was in and the impact of my abuse history on my personal life. Most importantly, though, I learned how to begin my healing process through the Twelve-Step and recovery fellowships, where everyone wanted to be free from their individual, family, and relationship pains. For the first time in my life, I began to feel some sense of hope instead of despair, peace instead of fear.

However, my relationship with Jane was still confused and dark. I began to wonder what "love" was, and if I had any left for her. I chose to begin sharing my pain with Jane the day after my surprise fortieth birthday party. The black crepe was more fitting than my friends ever knew.

During the summer of 1988, Paul introduced me (Jane) to the Twelve Steps of Alcoholics Anonymous. I had known about them intellectually, but never embraced them on a personal level. During the next year, I continued to focus on my individual recovery by entering a co-dependency treatment program.

I grew as a person, letting go of the old tapes that had been strangling me, stifling our relationship, and Paul. My family of origin and the healing of my inner child were the primary focus. Later, Paul told me that he thought about sharing his sexual addiction with me that same night after the birthday party when he talked about his confusion and despair about love and our relationship. However, it had been recommended that it would be helpful for him to look at his motivation and at Step Nine. I believe accidents do not happen in recovery and that our Higher Power was definitely with us each Step of the way. If Paul had shared everything then, our course of recovery might have been different. The pain would have been more devastating, and my own individual recovery would have been severely challenged even more. As I grew in recovery, the imagery of the fallen child surrounded by dark menacing hallways gradually transformed into a garden of trees. The child began to blossom under the shining light of the sun, a powerful spiritual image of my Higher Power. The circle of trees at first was still very closed, and only gradually were other people allowed to enter safely.

As we developed separate recovery networks, however, our coupleship grew further apart. It was an incredible relief when I decided to surrender our relationship to my Higher Power and accepted my powerlessness to fix anything. But what then? How were we to work through the resentments, barriers, and broken trust? At this point in our journey, Paul shared the full story. Shock, despair, anger, rage, confusion, and depression were feelings that I now allowed myself to feel. There was also insight and understanding of the overwhelming degree of pain that Paul had been experiencing in his secret addictive lifestyle, and his history of abuse. Our First Step as a couple now began anew. I committed to staying in the relationship one day at a time, to share my feelings, but also to use other resources for support systems to work through my rage and my co-addict issues. We turned our relationship over to the care of our Higher Power. It would only be through a power greater than us that trust could be rebuilt.

Couple therapy did much to help us sort out our most painful issues, but it was through the fellowship of RCA that the shame and isolation of two abused and lost children would finally begin to be healed. We walked into our first RCA meeting filled with couple shame, questioning if there would be a future for us together. Gradually, Step by Step, our sharing of experience, strength, and hope with other couples helped our trust to be healed. Participation in the "We Came To Believe" program also did wonders for our shame and couple pain.

Together, we experienced a spiritual awakening that showed that the "Promises" were working, and that Step Two was happening. On a guided imagery, separate, but together, we each experienced our inner child meeting our partner's inner child at the same lake and on the same rock in Colorado. They took us to the adults, us, and hand in hand, we stood together, embracing all that life has to offer us in recovery with our Higher Power, and with you.

As a direct result of our couple recovery, we were able to recommit ourselves to each other on our twentieth wedding anniversary, August 7, 1991.

What we know now is that we have the tools and the support to use as a couple as we face the many challenges ahead. We know it is safe to share with the many people in RCA fellowships across the nation, and that we share a common dream: to grow in our commitment, communication, and caring as a couple, one day at a time.

Ann and Chuck

The Search for Intimacy

Ann

Chuck and I met on a blind date for a fraternity party. I was instantly attracted. I guess it was mutual, as we started dating.

I was in nursing school; Chuck was in college. He went home for summer break. I stayed and pined for a letter or a phone call, all to no avail. By the end of summer, I had finally given up any hope of hearing from him again, when a letter came a week or so before school was to start. I was instantly hooked once more.

Heavy drinking was an accepted part of the college scene in the 1960s. Neither of us thought much about it. This was either naiveté or denial. We married and eventually had four children.

Over the years, there were times when I'd become angry about the drinking. After softball games, Chuck would stay out and come home fairly drunk. Friday evenings were "stop with the guys after work." Again it didn't seem too unusual, as all his friends did the same.

After twenty years of gradually more and more drinking and then lapsing into a maintenance mode, Chuck decided he was a problem drinker and was going to give up alcohol.

Abstinence seemed to be going fairly well. Like many others, I thought since he wasn't drinking any more, all our problems would be solved. Take away the alcohol and everything seemed just fine. Chuck undertook a new high-pressure job. Of course we hadn't heard about avoiding big changes during the first year of recovery. For that matter, we hadn't even heard of recovery!

Chuck's alcohol therapy group fell through. He was on Antabuse, but AA wasn't in the picture. His cravings weren't talked about. Day by day, depression started to creep in for him. But

I didn't notice the slow decline in Chuck's energy or his low feelings.

In early January, now six months since his last drink, Chuck suddenly quit his four-month-old job. The next day his depression and suicidal thoughts were our main focus. We spent a terrifying day in the emergency room. The psychiatrist on duty felt it was inappropriate to treat Chuck because the psychiatrist had been and still was my own therapist at the time. We limped home. Chuck was put on antidepressants.

We saw another therapist early the next week. She said unless we went to AA and Al-Anon, she couldn't treat us. It hadn't crossed our minds that his depression might be alcohol-related. We didn't know that Twelve-Step programs were necessary in our lives. Looking back, I feel the therapist was too hasty. She needed to talk to us once or twice more to help us acknowledge and accept the role alcohol had played and was insidiously still playing in our lives. At that time I was totally devastated. I felt I had reached out for help and it wasn't given. I was overwhelmed.

As a "good co-dependent," I stayed home and tried to do a suicide watch. I read about depression, noting the craziness in Chuck's frightening attitudes toward our youngest child, and toward life in general. I tried to control things and make them better—"fix it." I had reached my bottom.

Finally, I just couldn't do it myself anymore. I phoned the hospital for the weekend therapist who was on call. Luckily, when I got through, I reached another therapist we had seen as a couple years earlier. I knew, liked, and respected her and her judgment.

I remember saying about AA and Al-Anon that we didn't want alcohol to be the focus of our lives. Wisely she asked, "What is the focus now?" Of course it was the alcoholic and alcohol, plus the resulting depression. A light went on for me.

I was getting emotionally more and more sick, being dragged down by my worry about Chuck. It was time to "Detach Lovingly," time to "Let Go and Let God." And I did it!

I went to Al-Anon and started taking care of myself. I learned more about alcohol, addiction, and co-dependency at a local treatment facility.

When my stomach was in knots, I'd go for a walk outside the house. I realized I couldn't control anything but myself and my attitudes. I learned not only "One Day at a Time"—sometimes even that was too long— but one hour or even one minute at a time. This was pointed out to me by a true story on TV about a man sailing alone around the world.

Sometimes he had to break a day down into minutes or seconds not to give up. A month, six months, or a year into the future looked too bleak for me, but an hour or a day could be gotten through.

Meetings gave me support and encouragement, and of course a place to share my pain. I came away each time with hope, peace, love, and growth.

After about five months, Chuck decided he wanted to get better too. An alcohol education and support group was available through our HMO. We started to attend together.

One of their premises, which I thoroughly agree with, is that the whole family is affected.

If one person is to recover, the family needs to recover, too. The alcoholic or addict and the co-dependent both need education and support about their roles in the dysfunction or disease. Recovery changes the couple dynamic. When one person is recovering, the other must change also, if they are to stay together and be happy together.

After "Family Night" we would go out for pizza or Chinese food with other couples from the HMO support group. This was one element of the fledgling start for RCA in our community. We could share with other couples who were working to change themselves in order to stay together.

In September of 1988, a Twelve-Step "Couples in Recovery" meeting was started in Berkeley, California. We debated about affiliating with Al-Anon or AA. Al-Anon was chosen in hopes of widening the group's appeal. There were just four of us at the first meeting, but the group soon outgrew our small room and moved to larger quarters in nearby Oakland. A second meeting was started.

Couples who survived active addiction and still felt there was good in their relationship were drawn to the meetings, as were couples struggling to recapture lost trust. Stories were told, and members shared how they dealt with painful issues from in-laws to rearranging the household furniture to buying a car together. Clean and sober couple friendships were started.

After the "Couples in Recovery" meeting had been growing in size for about nine months, a member shared about a new fellowship she had noticed in a recovery magazine. It was called Recovering Couples Anonymous (RCA). The California meeting contacted RCA headquarters in Minneapolis for information.

After much debate, our group decided to affiliate with RCA. It seemed to more closely address what we couples were looking for than did Al-Anon or AA. The Steps of RCA said just what we were hoping to attain: more commitment and more intimacy.

It's easier to share feelings and thoughts about couples' issues around addiction and recovery with someone who is gaining acceptance, understanding, and recovery from personal experience. Even though each person has to put his or her primary program first in order to maintain health, the coupleship needs to be strengthened and nurtured too.

Our coupleship is stronger since sharing our experience, strength, and hope through RCA meetings. We value the love and friendship we have found in our recovering community. Each meeting is a reaffirmation of our commitment to each other and to growing healthier in a clean and sober relationship.

Chuck

The support of RCA is warm and enriching. There's usually a special tone in RCA meetings, a vivid spirit of fellowship, sometimes a quality of awe.

Two years into recovery I started going to Couples meetings. Before these groups, I'd heard a lot of good advice and stories in other Twelve-Step programs but little about relationships, struggles with intimacy, sex in sobriety, and commitment to a partnership. I heard pained and angry complaining about members' partners, and for sure I was one of the blaming malcontents myself. Often it felt like "us versus them," and at other times as if relationship and commitment topics were bad form.

Ann and I, with our separate meetings, resented the other's "selfish" time apart. I know I'd grill her afterward about who had been at her meeting and what she had said or hadn't said.

I gloated about her going to fewer meetings than I did and also what I decreed were her less visible efforts and less driven resolve to work the program of my understanding (!). I identified with people in my own meetings and began to dis-identify with my partner. I started to feel "better than," superior, more informed, more aware.

Plus, with my long-standing fantasies of being rescued by females, I was especially drawn to certain program women; we would share long phone calls in the evenings, or strolls in the park, lunches, almost dates. Tension between Ann and me grew. Were our individual recoveries to take place in separation, and maybe generate even more strain between us?

Both of us felt this tension and sometimes were able to discuss it, Ann defensively and with hurt, it seemed, and me with haughtiness, badgering, and harsh anger. Looking back now, I believe we both sought more intimacy but feared greater closeness, both of us longing and resisting at the same time.

The Couples meetings helped right away. The group met first in a day-care nursery. (Today this seems highly appropriate!)

We had been to Marriage Encounter years earlier, before our recovery had started. We remembered how we'd cherished the closeness we'd felt and declared we'd wanted. It was painful and distressing that this welcome connectedness didn't endure. In the Couples meetings, we felt others' awkwardness and defensiveness, longings and hurts. With hesitation, we started to talk of our own distress.

After a while, I was able to share about my sexual impotence during my depression in early recovery, about my guilt in coming to the painful belief and understanding that while a practicing addict I had loved work and alcohol more than I did my partner, about my anger when we'd be driving through a ritzy neighborhood and Ann would exclaim, "Wow! Look at that big house!" I'd take this as a veiled, justified, and mean exposing of my deep secret inadequacy as a partner and provider.

Gradually, I was able to share my confusion and bewilderment, groping to understand how I'd fallen into the months of extreme depression half a year after my last drink. Was it the collapse of a sobriety without a firm program? Was it my bottom around compulsive working and compulsive activity? Was it deflation and implosion, after years of growing rage and impotence being unable to control my partner, our finances, and our children?

Some of these things I'd been able to explore in my ACA support group, or in AA or Workaholics Anonymous meetings. But wasn't it dangerous and shaming to tell this in a Couples meeting, with Ann present? Wouldn't other couples take sides and judge me? Wasn't I inviting ridicule from members who could see falling-apart me next to detaching and accepting Ann? Wouldn't other couples turn to each other knowingly and cluck their tongues and nod their heads, smirking as if to say, "Yes! Just as we thought! Another pretend husband! There is something phony and deranged about them!"

So my admission of powerlessness over our relationship was painful and difficult. And my group-level acceptance of that powerlessness was at first unimaginable. This despite having thought I'd done the First Step in three other programs.

I began to hear in other programs about practicing these principles in all my affairs, and began to hear members tell me of the progress they saw in me that I had not seen for myself, and later I started pinching myself and recognizing some changes, noticing my relief and diminished fears, the absence of panic attacks, night sweats, occasional dizziness in crowds, my initial alarm at being called on to talk in recovery meetings—all this good material, and then the jarring contrast of feeling like a critical, impatient, sarcastic, despotic, withholding ogre at home with my partner and kids. My sense of shame was scalding and acute.

Talking in meetings with one's partner right there adds a special dimension to relationship recovery, and also listening without interruption or cross-talk when my partner is sharing. Or noticing that another member has said something striking, and telling myself what a wonderful insight that person's just had, and what a beautiful gift I've just received to be able to make that insight my own and later, to realize suddenly that in last month's meeting, or last week, or fifteen minutes ago, my partner had said the exact same thing, and I'd mentally rolled my eyes and had secretly wished she had said something more profound and riveting—"My partner, my spouse, who can make me and make us look good, or make us look bad," I'd tell myself.

As I write here, much of this sounds nasty, harsh, and unrecovered. And so it's a good reminder that lots of that has gone away, that I've been relieved of much of that automatic lashing-out and habitual contempt, the judging and loathing which served ever too well to keep my partner safely at a distance for ever so long.

For what RCA has helped me see is that my routine, instinctive behaviors and thoughts are both my rock-solid defenses and also the obstacles that keep me imprisoned in myself when more closeness is desirable, when deeper sharing without guardedness or fear of ridicule is urgent, when the yearning to break down "The Wall" is intense.

There are still many institutionalized opportunities for painful stress and fear-generated hurtfulness, like April tax season, Christmas, in-law visits, or awkward dinner parties. But we don't get nearly so crazy. When Ann does something less than perfectly (to my eye), I'm not as harshly quick to "clarify" her behavior for her or "offer helpful solutions" as to what she obviously should have done. All of that was poorly disguised abusive superiority to cover up feeling "less than" or excluded, or hurt about something I experienced long ago which my partner had nothing at all to do with. Thankfully, we're more able to accept weakness and vulnerability and confusion. We're healthier in conveying what we want from our pleasurable "couplings in recovery." We're more able to say "No!" with less fear of being withered in retaliation or igniting a two-week conflagration. We don't as frequently play master and slave, trading off occasionally for variety. As a couple, we're not so often paralyzed or angrily silent as before. Something amazing: we no longer have raging conflicts with our children or nasty fights about them.

A warmer and more loving relationship is actually being granted us. To paraphrase some program stuff, what we've received is a free gift, and yet in some small part we've made ourselves ready as a couple to receive this gift.

All of this helps a lot as I recover from two primary addictions, compulsive working and excessive activity plus alcoholism. In my recovery I get a lot of support from WA and AA, which in and of themselves are certainly bases for a more joyous partnership. RCA helps me to be sober and more content in my two primary programs; the relief and hope I receive in RCA are an additional insurance policy for my recovery around work and drink.

So, in a way, RCA is something other than my primary program, but it definitely is a glue or catalyst or strong supplement that serves to sustain my WA and AA recoveries. RCA helps me become available to receive some of the promises of the program.

Today, I'm glad Ann and I are the couple we are. We're able to let go of many of our crazy-making expectations. It's easier to have and state our desires, hopes, and goals. For both of us, our fear of being blind-sided by relapse or one of us recovering and leaving the other behind is diminishing. Our capacity for enjoying our lives has flourished.

Ann has inspired me through some of her changes, and also I've been grateful to see her lay down some of her burdens. Also, though perhaps selfishly for me, she's been able to be more there for me, and in being there, support me to be me.

Our more intimate life together has supported me as I've sagged through dry drunks, or gotten crazy around jobs, or struggled in recovery with long stretches between jobs. One terribly upsetting event was when our sixteen-year-old son horribly broke his arm, a grotesque and nauseating sight, and all his awful suffering. Right afterward at the hospital, I had a strong, clear vision that if he were put under general anesthesia he wouldn't come out of it. I'd had compelling visions and dreams before; I knew that it paid to heed the messages.

Well, I stonewalled the intake doctors, and the anesthesiologist. I insisted on a local anesthetic only, while we all waited for the other doctor who'd perform the five-hour surgery. I was grim in my determination not to sign the consent form. I resolved to protect my child by honoring the warning I'd received. You can imagine how Ann felt during all this!

The surgeon arrived. He explained why a local anesthetic just wouldn't help. Gently he asked for our consent. Ann and I left to another room and I told her of my vision. Finally we decided anyway to give our consent. Ann was wonderful and supportive and considerate, but I'm so grateful that she was able to take full care of herself as well.

Chris was wheeled away. Perhaps it was one of those occasions when I really surrendered, not quit, just surrendered.

Chris made it through the operation, plates and screws, gross incisions and general anesthesia and all. Soon I was able to accept that I'd been overtaken by normal terror, or perhaps that the outcome was different in a parallel universe or something. Ann and I were both able to be really there for Chris, for each other, for ourselves, and for our coupleship. Ann says she gets a kick now out of telling at meetings, "And Chuck was able to say afterward, 'Thank God it wasn't something to drink over!'"

Where are we now with RCA? We got a sponsor couple way back. We'll be doing our Fifth Step with them soon, so we're writing our Fourth Step now. We started two new RCA groups in the past sixteen months, and we go to two or three RCA meetings a week. Of course, we need our other programs as well. Ann is serving on the RCA Intergroup that's just been formed to support the five RCA recovery groups in our area and carry the message.

We've experienced a lot of our own euphoria in RCA meetings, plus the obvious excitement and hopefulness of most newcomers and regulars. In the last few months I've felt somewhat different in the meetings; maybe it's the end of the RCA pink cloud, or taking for granted the gift of the initial relief, or my stumbling around and in the Steps of RCA (how do you work the Steps as a couple??!!). Or the fact that there are no couples with twenty or ten or five years of RCA recovery we can look to and say, "There's what the future for us can be. They've got what we want."

Maybe it's the healthy release of an early illusion that Ann and I would finally, fully merge into one harmonious entity, no disagreements or disappointments, no drudge work left. Maybe it's a gradual withdrawal from co-dependency, while we grow and learn more about healthy interdependence, healthy caring between us. Maybe it's the Dreaded Fourth Step!

Today it feels more comfortable to be in a close, committed relationship with my partner, with our many different preferences and beliefs. The old habits die hard, but they are diminishing, little by little. Our wonderful times together are more common and less remarkable, while our average times together seem no longer mostly hollow or cold or distasteful and tense, lives of quiet desperation, but instead OK, pleasant, non-anxious. I don't feel "alone and lonely inside a relationship" anymore. No longer do I feel I could get healthier and better and get exactly what I wanted if only I were somewhere, anywhere, else.

In our meetings we've felt and seen our own progress and also the striking changes in others. Two couples who are friends of ours have gotten married in RCA. One pair has moved back in together. Two partnerships have had first babies. One couple got engaged. Some members have used RCA to help them reach the decision to separate or to end their relationship.

For myself, I'm grateful that these RCA meetings came into being. I no longer feel we're a defective couple or bad people trying to get good. The Fellowship has helped a troubled coupleship that longed to be healthier. Thanks, RCA!

Gabrielle and Cheryl

Free To Love

Gabrielle

When I met Cheryl, I was not looking for the big "R." I was involved with a variety of women at the time and so was Cheryl. We were open about our non-monogamy and comfortable with it. On top of that, I lived in Los Angeles and Cheryl lived in San Jose (about four hundred miles apart). I had no expectations of anything serious coming out of our relationship. After hundreds of dollars in phone calls and plane fares, I started to feel a twinge in my heart, and I promptly ignored it by dating someone new.

At the time, I'd been in many Twelve-Step programs for thirteen years and knew how to protect myself from harm, real and perceived. Cheryl respected my boundary of no chemical use while we were together, and smoked her cigarettes outside. I had no idea she had any addiction problems other than the obvious (nicotine), until she called me from a hospital to tell me she had been injured and a week later admitted she had a drinking problem. My first reaction was, "Oh no, I'm involved with a newcomer!" Apparently all the sharing I had done about how the Steps and the fellowships had specifically helped me opened the door to Cheryl's acceptance of the Twelve-Step approach for herself.

During this time I had been battling against an abusive supervisor at work and all the employees decided to walk out on the job in protest. This meant Cheryl was on injury leave for three months and I was unemployed. We spent most of that time together. We were no longer just lovers, we were becoming friends. The thing I liked about us was our cooperative tendencies. We traveled well together, with each helping the other with the mundane tasks. It was a real pleasure not to be competitive.

We noticed we were losing interest in dating other women. We both admitted we felt monogamous and freaked out for two days. When we finally calmed down we started to feel more comfortable in what was for both of us a new experience. Our only explanation for this strange occurrence was a Higher Power; it certainly didn't come from us. I think this was our first inkling that there was a Higher Power involved in our relationship.

The time was getting close for Cheryl to have to go back to work, and I had to start looking for work. Something in me (or something Higher) decided that I would never know if this relationship could go anywhere if we stayed in separate cities. I decided to move to San Jose. Thank Higher Power for the Twelve Steps. I knew I needed to develop my own support network. I found my own place to live, looked for work, discovered my own meetings, and began to make my own friends. I really liked my independence and it felt good to know myself and to know how I wanted my life to be. The thirteen years in Twelve-Step programs had given me deep knowledge of myself and courage to go forward in my life. However, as soon as I moved to San Jose, Cheryl withdrew emotionally and sexually, and I panicked and raged. All my thirteen years of the program went down the tubes. I had never worked the program to deal with being in and staying in a relationship before. I usually left when it hurt too much, believing it was either that or stay with a hopeless situation. This time a part of me said, "We are not leaving!" I felt trapped by my own inner conflict and raged at Cheryl, blaming her for my pain. We spiraled into a pit of awful arguments, painful feelings, and an inability to leave the relationship.

I interpreted her withdrawal as her wanting to leave me but not having the courage to leave. I felt I was invited into a big beautiful house and Cheryl ran into a room and shut the door in my face. I felt trapped inside and alone. This was my biggest nightmare, my core issue from my family of origin. I had the fear of abandonment and Cheryl had a fear of enmeshment; we were the perfect couple!

Cheryl

Gabrielle moved to San Jose the weekend before I went back to work. I was just over two months clean and sober. To deal with my anxiety about returning to a stressful work environment, I put up my protective shield. I didn't recognize this behavior as shutting down; I was reacting to my fears the only way I knew how. With Gabrielle in the same city, I no longer had the cushion of miles to keep my distance. With daily contact, I was no longer able to disappear into my shell; I was in a monogamous (gasp), committed (gasp, gasp) relationship.

I was able to communicate with Gabrielle about physical aspects of life, but it was very difficult for me to talk about the emotional aspects. In my family I did not learn to express my feelings. All negative feelings (sadness, loneliness, frustration, anger) were either fixed or discounted. I learned to disengage from my feelings at an early age. Even when I could acknowledge a feeling, I did not have a vocabulary to describe it. My catch phrase seemed to be, "Hey, I'm a newcomer, I don't even know what a feeling is yet!" I was able to ask Gabrielle to point out to me when she felt I was withdrawing. I would then stop and examine what it felt like physically; it felt like my chest was in a blender. This was the only way I could learn when I was withdrawing. I also discovered that this was the feeling I drank over, smoked over, overate over, and was compulsive over. Through participation in the ACA program, I knew I needed professional help to assist me. I found a Twelve-Step therapist. Not long after, Gabrielle began to see the same therapist.

Gabrielle

I didn't know about the hypnotic family state I get into when I'm vulnerable and intimate and sexual with someone. I always interpreted the discomfort as external factors. I had never thought that I invited my whole family into the relationship, or that I started to react to Cheryl as if she were my family. So by seeing the same therapist, I would have to begin owning my own projections. However, knowing this didn't stop me from going into my crazy thinking. I knew I was powerless over my interpretation of Cheryl's withdrawing, yet still continued to rage and say crazy things that I later regretted saying. I felt like I was two separate people, and they didn't like each other.

Cheryl

Then one of many miracles happened. I read about Recovering Couples Anonymous in a local recovery newspaper. We both jumped at the concept immediately. In the classified section of the same newspaper, I saw a notice for a Lesbian RCA meeting in San Francisco (fifty miles north of San Jose). We took this as a sure sign from our Higher Power. In the RCA meetings, we were amazed to hear that other couples experienced similar problems. We were not the only couple who had a complimentary dysfunction, where one partner's dysfunction triggered a diseased reaction in the other partner. When I withdrew, Gabrielle raged; when Gabrielle raged, I withdrew.

Gabrielle

Cheryl worked on her tendency to withdraw and didn't always succeed. I worked on my tendency to rage, and didn't always succeed. I at first thought everything would be OK but I continued to rage. I got frustrated with myself and our continual participation in our complementary dysfunction. It did get better and then we'd slip. Sometimes we didn't slip so far down. Sometimes, it was worse than ever. Cheryl finally got sick of me thinking she didn't want me. She told me she would release me from our monogamy. I knew then that she was sincere, and I believed that she did want to be in this relationship but she was powerless over her tendency to withdraw. I no longer took it personally. I began to see she was struggling with a lifelong pattern which started as a defense to help her survive her family of origin. This was a major breakthrough for me. This new way of perceiving

Cheryl's withdrawal gave me new insights into Cheryl. I could see and feel her struggle and even feel compassion for her. I began to have the ability to let go of her withdrawal.

I discovered that instead of expressing what I was angry or upset about, I would store it up. I would obsess about it, interpret its meaning according to my way of seeing the world, and create a mass scenario in my head. It ended with me exploding into an insane rage. Cheryl, who was new to recovery, didn't know herself or how she felt well enough to know whether I was right or not. When she knew I was wrong, she wasn't able to articulate the correct interpretation.

Gabrielle and Cheryl

We started to work the RCA program. We set up a Fair Fighting contract entitled "When We Funk Out . . . " Even though we didn't always follow the contract, it made us more and more aware of when we were in our couple disease. By acknowledging our communications breakdown, we discovered that some of it was due to our cultural differences (Australian English versus American English). But much of it was due to the different emotional languages of our families of origin. We found that we could occasionally stop the disease in mid-air. We found that if we said, "We're doing it again," we could create distance from the disease. What often helped was back-tracking our arguments to find the exact point at which we began to react. Sometimes we were able to pinpoint what one said to trigger the other. We discovered that we have trigger words, phrases, tones in voices, and facial expressions. We gave each other permission to ask the other to rephrase something or to not use certain words. We then took time to find out what we meant by certain words. We gave each other the space to articulate what we really wanted to say. We no longer had to be perfect the first time around.

Cheryl came home from a CoDA meeting one night excited about an RCA meeting in San Jose. It was wonderful having a local meeting. It didn't matter to us that we were the only gay couple there. In fact, it was amazing how much we identified with other couples regardless of sexual orientation. The first meeting that we attended was on the Second Step: perfect! We realized that our commitment and intimacy were in God's hands and not ours. Although our commitment was given to us (neither of us manipulated the other into it), we both did a dance around the intimacy issue. I (Gabrielle) felt Cheryl was actively running away from the intimacy, and I was trying (unconsciously) to control it with my rage. Knowing that the intimacy was in God's hands meant that all we had to do was work on the barriers that each of us put up against it. We learned more communication skills in RCA. We learned that it was OK to point out to each other what upset us about the other, as long as it was respectful, non-accusatory, and was said without directing anger at each other or intending to hurt each other. We also tried to explain why we were upset, "It pushed an old family button," for instance.

The other helpful aspect of the RCA program was discovering that we have a Higher Power looking over our relationship. We wrote a prayer, which we recited every night before going to sleep. We've started to say the Serenity Prayer together every day and before any discussions that may be "trigger subjects" for us. Reading the Reflections got us talking about how we felt about various couples' issues. We began to acknowledge our Higher Power, and started to see where we've had Divine Intervention in our relationship several times already. We started to take walks, do outdoor activities, and experiment with new adventures together. We are coming to believe more and more in Our Higher Power. We sometimes feel as if our Guardian Angels are guiding us and our relationship. Other times it feels as if there is a cosmic force that visits both our hearts and joins us together. We sometimes feel that the universe sends special power to shoot into both our hearts when we are open and loving toward each other.

Despite the fact that our complementary dysfunction wasn't yet eliminated, our commitment to each other deepened. We decided we were ready to live together. Moving in together triggered another level of my (Cheryl's) fear of intimacy. The first night in our new house we got into an argument. I felt I had recreated my family of origin and this confirmed my fear of intimacy, so I shut down even further. I felt totally enmeshed with Gabrielle because I interpreted her actions as if I were interacting with my enmeshed family. When Gabrielle would specifically ask for my attention, I would go into emotional overload and push her away. Gabrielle did not know I felt enmeshed with her. This triggered her abandonment issues. Our relationship was still on an emotional roller coaster. I felt I was at the end of my rope.

It was tough times for us both. It got so bad that I (Gabrielle) started to lash out at objects, like smashing a window and breaking furniture. I felt I was hitting rock bottom around my rage. I started to feel my rage was not just about Cheryl, but was also becoming a channel through which I expressed all other angers, hurts, and fears. I had never wanted to become one of those people who was friendly to everyone and took everything out on their partner at home. Both of us independently were starting to doubt whether this relationship would make it. One night I gave myself permission to think about leaving the relationship. I cried for hours and went to bed exhausted and traumatized. The next day I woke up feeling great. I later realized that by feeling free to leave, I was free to stay.

Cheryl finally quit smoking, and I gave up my rage two weeks before our second Christmas together. What a miracle this has been for us. We disagree about this, but I feel I was able to give up the rage because she quit smoking and thus quit using nicotine to suppress her feelings. I find my life with Cheryl is so much easier when she expresses her feelings, even when she's grumpy. I am learning to hear her without interrupting her and without reacting to what she is saying before she is finished. Cheryl is learning not to instantly shut down when I do interrupt her. I know that when she expresses how she feels (even if I hate what she's telling me), it means she doesn't have to shut down or suppress her feelings. When she does occasionally shut down, I don't panic and go into my hypnotic abandonment issues. I'm amazed that I haven't raged, even though some of our problems still exist. We have been experiencing more intimacy and enjoying it.

I (Cheryl) no longer need to play the victim role, and I am discovering my many forms of co-dependence. I am learning to ask for space for myself (without feeling guilty). I am learning that I can be with myself even when I am in a relationship; I do not need to lose myself. I can take time away from the relationship, even if Gabrielle does not have other plans. I am developing an independent support network and learning to meditate with my Higher Power. By working my own programs, I am able to be present in the coupleship; by being present in the coupleship, I am able to grow in my own programs. This is the upward spiral our coupleship has been blessed with. I believe that being in this committed relationship has accelerated my growth in my individual recovery.

We have discussed doing a commitment ceremony, but we don't know how to include our families. My (Gabrielle's) parents hate the fact that I am a lesbian. When I'm single, they can live in the hope that I will meet a man and become heterosexual. So we don't usually talk about my sexual orientation. But being in a committed, monogamous relationship makes it impossible to ignore the fact that I am in a lesbian relationship. It is sad to think that the very people who should be my biggest cheerleaders at my marriage have such mixed feelings about it.

I have a brother who supports me 100 percent, and an extended family my mother refuses to tell. I (Cheryl) have a large extended family and I am in a dilemma about what to do about wedding or ceremony invitations. My immediate family has grown to accept me and us, but it is still difficult to deal with what is traditionally a large family affair. It is difficult to decide whether to send out invitations with no explanation, or personally contact every aunt, uncle, cousin, second cousin, etc., to discuss my orientation with them individually. Am I setting myself up for rejection? How do I deal with this dilemma? This is one example of how gay relationships do have unique issues.

To acknowledge and nurture ourselves as a lesbian couple, we recently started a lesbian RCA meeting. We have a standing joke at the meeting, from the Characteristics of Functional Couples: "We don't have to be socially acceptable." We still go to other RCA meetings because we have a lot in common with all recovering couples struggling to restore their relationships to commitment and intimacy. We attended the National Conference last year and had a wonderfully affirming time. When we arrived, we realized we were the only gay couple attending the conference. We wondered whether we should ignore it or say something in our introduction. We "came out" to break the ice in case people didn't know what to say or not to say to us. We were met with acceptance.

Our Higher Power keeps pushing us deeper into our commitment with each other. After several bad experiences around our rental house, we decided we wanted to buy a house together. This is now bringing up all our money issues. We have been able to discuss very difficult aspects without too much trauma. We believe it is because we are now better practiced at the communication tools we have learned through RCA. We listen to what the other has to say and not react. We check to see if we've heard correctly, then say what we have to say and the other checks to see if they heard correctly. We allow each other to have their feelings. When I (Gabrielle) react to Cheryl, I am distracting her from her feelings and injecting mine. When Cheryl is reacting to me, it disturbs my whole inner process and brings Cheryl into my focus instead of my feelings. We discovered this is a way enmeshment develops. Allowing each other to have our feelings is healthy individuation.

We have been in RCA and therapy for most of our two-year committed relationship. We have been through a lot together. Since I gave up the rage, I have slowly become more comfortable expressing my anger without fearing it will trigger my rage. I've actually found the opposite. The more I express my negative feelings at work, meetings, home, etc., the less likely it builds up into a rage. I can no longer fill up the rage sack with all the unexpressed feelings and eliminate them all when I explode. I have to deal with all my feelings each day now that the trap door to raging has been removed. I have become more real. Cheryl says it is like being with an entirely new person. I am no longer afraid that Cheryl wants to leave me. I am more able to let Cheryl be Cheryl and truly observe, discover and appreciate her for who she is. I (Cheryl) feel safer to come out of my shell. I am more trusting that the other shoe is not going to drop. I am more confident in my feelings and am able to express them without fear of ridicule or shame. I am feeling freer to express my sense of humor.

Being two separate human beings feels liberating. Being intimate feels liberating too—we are free to love.

We have to keep remembering we have a Higher Power taking care of our relationship. Nothing bad is going to happen just because we are having feelings about something, or disagree about something, or have a seemingly unsolvable problem. There is nothing that can hurt our relationship if we are working our own and the RCA programs to take care of business, and allow Divine Intervention to take care of the impossible.

Pat and Gene

Reliving Their Parents' Relationships

Pat

Pat came from a large family of nine children. Her dad owned his own business and was a chronic alcoholic until he died at age fifty-two. Since Pat was second oldest, she had become a good caretaker, not only of brothers and sisters, but of her dad too. Dad could only have emotions while drunk, which was daily. Pat's mom would leave nightly to escape confrontations with her drunken husband, who was physically abusive with one of his two sons. Pat's parents had a very passive-aggressive relationship, which the children learned, along with blame, dishonesty, denial, and hopelessness.

At age seventeen, Pat's mom kicked her out of the house in anger one night when Pat hadn't done all the dishes. Pat decided to move in with her sister. A year later she went to Europe for two years while her parents separated. Her dad went to a halfway house. Pat was always in the middle of her parents' marriage. The night her dad died, she was at the hospital with her mom, whom Pat had called to come.

"Why?" they each asked her privately.

"Because you love each other," she said. No one had told her they didn't or that it was not her job to keep them together. (This triangle pattern has been an important issue for Pat in her recovery.)

Pat spent the next five years working on her individual recovery in Twelve-Step programs while also attending the University of Minnesota.

Gene

Gene's dad was a survivor of the Holocaust. Only a few family members lived to tell about it, although things were kept pretty secretive. His dad turned against God in anger over this tragedy and became an atheist/agnostic. His dad's profession took Gene's family all over the world. They moved on a regular basis.

Gene's mom was emotionally and physically abusive to him from the age of three. His dad was not present much, either physically or emotionally.

Gene became chemically dependent in his early teens and was capable of violence in his disease. After eight years of destructive behavior, Gene finally entered detox and began his recovery. Gene's family (one sister) chose not to participate or support him in his recovery. There was also a hopeless theme in his family.

Gene and Pat

We had some parallel experiences: each of us had come from a dysfunctional family, each had been in our individual recovery for five years, and neither of us had been in a serious relationship since we'd moved out from our significant others five years earlier. We were ready to give things a try between ourselves.

Because we attended a support group together, we quickly became aware of some of the issues we had as a couple. Anger was a major problem. Although Pat was attracted to the way Gene could express his anger so easily, it soon became difficult for both of us when Pat expressed hers. Gene was attracted to Pat's ability to express her other feelings, except when she got angry; then he would shut down completely.

Something was feeling very familiar. We were reliving our parents' relationships of rage and emotional withdrawal. Both of us felt trapped and neither of us knew how to break the cycle that seemed to overwhelm us. Pat was into smoking and food addiction and could not figure out what was wrong even though we both were in counseling on and off for several years.

Since things didn't seem to be getting better, Pat thought being a mother would help fulfill her needs. Getting pregnant was a power struggle. In fact, life for us was one power struggle after another for a long time. We were both good reactors.

In five years, we had gotten married, had two babies (major surgery), bought a house, maintained our jobs, and attended individual recovery programs as well as kept up friendships. Life was busy and our focus was on the external rather than on our marriage.

We hit bottom the year following our second child's birth. Either we wouldn't talk to each other at all, or there was lots of sarcasm. Pat had quit smoking before getting pregnant but was just beginning to deal with her food addiction. As the months went by we were spending less time together and becoming more distant. We finally ended up in separate bedrooms.

The tension level was always high; there was no laughter, no time for family activities, and no peace. The screaming and shouting got out of control. We quit our long-time therapist and saw a crisis counselor, who helped mediate all the anger. By this time, Pat was in a Twelve-Step program for her food addiction. We continued seeing this counselor for a year. Then Pat realized that this counselor could not hear her when she got underneath the anger to the other emotions. Gene was ready to leave.

We had left therapy for four months and still felt stuck. Neither one of us was interested in further therapy. We had learned about a couples' Twelve-Step group a few years before. We went one night while Gene was on vacation just to check it out. That was our first RCA meeting. Immediately, we felt at home; we were terrified of what would happen, yet knew we too belonged.

Things have changed a lot since that first meeting. We have realized how difficult it was to try to resolve some of Pat's "triangle issues" because the therapists reactivated the pattern in an unhealthy way.

It has been a gift to have other couples be so honest and share their struggles with us. We have been much more respectful of each other and can let go of our "unsolvable issues," knowing that God is with us. Even though both of us had been in individual recovery programs for fifteen years, we had not learned to "let go and let God" as a couple. It was a big step to release ourselves from the blame and the need to have all the answers.

Now we can bring our strength and experience to the group and support others like ourselves. The shame is still there at times, but we can release it and heal from the past. "You will know a new freedom . . . Keep coming back; it's working . . . " Things may not be perfect, but we're learning to accept ourselves for who we are, individually and as a couple.

Jack and Deb

Cosmic Mates

We have been married for four years and can say that we are really doing well as a couple for the first time. It has been a long and very painful road to where we are now, but it has been worth it.

We both come from alcoholic families. One is a survivor of incest (possibly both of us are), and both of us have had to endure the brutality of being raised in our out-of-control homes. We are in recovery for our individual addictions and attended the first RCA meeting in 1988. This is our story.

We met in the lobby of the apartment building where we both lived. Our first date was a boat trip on a popular lake in the Minneapolis area. We sat in a quiet bay and ate bread and cheese and talked. It seemed as if we could share for hours and never get tired of talking. We had an immediate "bond" and seemed to know what the other was thinking and feeling.

We continued to date each other, and the next few weeks we spent in each other's company most of the time. We talked until the wee hours of the night and hated to say good night and return to our apartments. We wrote love letters to each other and put "love messages" under each other's door. We were sure that we had found a "cosmic mate," someone who understood us like no one else could. Three months after our first date we were engaged, and eight months after that we were married.

All had gone well during the first few months of our courtship, as we were sure that we had found that once-in-a-lifetime partner. But after we got engaged, the reality of what it might be like to spend the rest of our lives together became clear, and things started to change.

We began to doubt our ability to survive the mounting obstacles as the wedding drew near. Could we reconcile our spiritual/religious differences? Would we handle a blended family situation with a child from a previous marriage? Would the pressure of our disapproving families get to us and tear us apart? Would the nine-year difference in our ages make it impossible for us to relate to each other? Were we making a mistake, as our families kept saying? Following much pain, confusion, and deliberation, we decided to go through with the wedding.

After a small, private wedding (which none of our families attended), we moved to an apartment and set up house for the first time. What a shock! Neither of us was prepared for the feelings that were to come. Our sense of ourselves all but disappeared when we moved in together. We were unable to express our needs, both afraid of what might happen to our "perfect relationship" if we did.

Our blended family was the source of the most pain for us. Jack had a five-year-old son from a previous marriage, and Deb had no children. What at first appeared to be an issue of little concern quickly became the "elephant in the room." Deb had feelings of resentment toward Jack and his son because of the special relationship that they seemed to have, and often she felt "on the outside." Jack was aware of this and began to distance himself from his son so Deb wouldn't leave him. Jack had a severe fear of abandonment. Deb tried harder to accept the relationship between Jack and his son. This brought about great feelings of resentment from both, and arguments became a regular occurrence.

As the weeks went by we stuffed more feelings and built more resentments toward each other. Our addictions were in high gear; we were both co-dependent, one bulimic/anorexic and the other a workaholic and relationship addict. We began to use food and alcohol more frequently to numb our pain and resentments. Soon we were blaming each other for our misery and often talked of divorce.

We separated in the summer of 1988, unsure of our ability to make our marriage work. Our pain was immense, and no amount of talking, individual Twelve-Step meetings, or counseling seemed to help. The only thing that seemed to kill the pain was to not be together. We were truly on the brink of divorce.

Our Higher Power had a plan, unknown to us. We enrolled in a weekend retreat for dysfunctional couples called "We Came to Believe." This was the first retreat of its kind to be held and was an experiment of sorts. It showed us how to practice the Twelve Steps as a couple and gave us tools to repair our broken relationship.

After the retreat was over, we knew we needed to continue the healing that had begun. Two other couples from that first retreat agreed to meet with us at a nearby church to talk about our issues as couples in recovery. We all felt a great sense of relief in talking with other couples who had the same kinds of problems we did. Our shame as a couple had been so great that we never talked with other couples about our problems. We had assumed that our inability to "be like other people" was a problem that no one else would understand.

That small church room was a haven for us. We were able to be honest in revealing our shame and powerlessness in our relationship and felt that someone understood what we were going through.

We are truly grateful to our Higher Power for our new life as a couple. We hope that other couples will find as much comfort and healing as we have.

Joy and David

A Reality Tale

1. A Fairy Tale

Once upon a time, there was a little girl named Joy and a little boy named David. Both of them came from families that were not quite like other families. When they grew up big enough to get away from home, they went off to college.

David and Joy met each other, fell in love, and got married. They were going to have a wonderful marriage, and for a while it was. They were very much in love and they were going to have a child of their own and have their own wonderful family. Things would be different in their own wonderful family, not like their childhoods.

But the evils of fortune struck them and the baby girl never breathed the air. They were both devastated. But David did not know how to grieve and he shut off all the feelings he could. Joy couldn't stop grieving and couldn't get help from David because he was shut down. Joy was put in a horrible hospital to make her stop grieving. David began to feel only through things that fed his ego, like sex and achievement.

They eventually had more children, but that did not right their loss or help them regain their feelings. They pretended to have this wonderful, happy family, but they fought a lot about things that didn't seem to be as big as the fights. No matter how hard they tried, something was missing.

Now David could only get feelings through sex and work and he saw many other women to try to feel the feelings. Joy's feelings were mixed up. She wanted to believe that David loved her and the children. Just when she started to believe and think things were OK, David would be shut down and unavailable again. So, they separated from each other for two years and tried to figure things out alone.

Both of them were very lonely. David was mean and angry. Joy was sad and depressed and had to be both mother and father to their children. Each of them was determined to live as best they could. Then David found drugs and a whole new way to hide the real feelings and pretend to feel. Joy was angry that she was abandoned with two little children. She kept thinking that David would come to his senses and realize how much he loved her and their beautiful children.

After a while David and Joy began to live together again. But now David was high on drugs all the time and Joy was trying to figure out all his moods and there was no real intimacy or sharing.

Then David lost his job because he was either angry all the time or happy on drugs. So they moved to a big, fast, busy city where David found more drugs, more achievement, and more women. David traveled a lot to other cities in his new job and he found women in these cities to try to make him feel better. But still there was no intimacy and Joy was still being mother and father to their children, even though David lived at home.

They were like two strangers in the same house. David's drug use got worse and Joy got help in Al-Anon. David was very angry when he was down and happy when he was high. When he was angry, he sometimes took it out by physically abusing Joy and the children. But one day Joy invited him to an AA meeting. After a while, he learned to live without drugs. But being in AA and NA and Al-Anon did not fix the lack of intimacy and communication between them.

David did not know it, but he became a love addict and he fell in love very easily with other women. Joy kept hoping that NA and AA and Al-Anon would somehow fix all the problems between them. Under the guise of detachment, she shut down to all the painful things between them. She thought that one more group, one more therapy session, or joining a church would make everything all right again. She hoped and waited and denied and triangulated with work and kids and pretending and isolating.

David tried to stay out of other relationships, but he could not. He was a sex and love addict, but he didn't know it. He really loved Joy, but still there were only separation and blocks between them.

David tried to stay faithful, but he could not. And after he had nine years drug-free, he began to sponsor a lady in NA. He really thought he could do that without falling in love, but he could not. He never should have been her sponsor. After a while he found that when he had no contact with his sponsee, he got depressed. He tried to stay away from her, but he was powerless.

Now Joy realized what was going on with this NA relationship and confronted David about the violation of the integrity of their marriage. David agreed to get help and entered SLAA But Joy could not stop obsessing about David's sex and love addiction. She was very angry that David was throwing away their twenty-seven-year marriage. She felt betrayed by David and betrayed by this woman, who was associated with one of her work projects. Joy felt shame and depression and hopelessness. She went to COSA, but while she was obsessing, she lost her job.

So Joy went to a treatment center for co-sex and love addicts. David came to family week and they learned about their core beliefs. There, they found out about RCA and the "We Came To Believe" seminars. When Joy got out of the treatment center, it was close to Christmas time. Joy and David were so angry and shut down to each other that it took a meeting with both their sponsors to plan the Christmas season. They were both ready to call it quits and get a divorce. But they remembered what they learned about RCA, that "the only requirement for membership is a desire to be in a committed relationship."

David was sick and tired of hurting Joy and the children and Joy was sick and tired of being hurt. They decided to start an RCA meeting and found two other couples for the first RCA meeting in their area. A month later they went to their first "We Came To Believe" weekend.

2. A Reality Tale

Both Joy and David had a desire to be in a committed relationship. By using the tools of RCA, which they learned in "We Came To Believe," they began recovery together. They learned about the baggage they each brought into their marriage and about how to recognize when they were "powerless."

They learned that David's father abandoned him with traveling jobs, controlled alcoholism, and gambling. David never really had a healthy male role model. David's mother was dominating, controlling, arrogant, cold, matter-of-fact, and did not show or honor feelings. She was not nurturing. David was often shamed in his family. He was never enough or as good as his brother.

Both of Joy's grandfathers died of alcoholism. Her mother was an abused adult child of an alcoholic who modeled the victim role: passivity, submission to anger, fear of authority figures, low self-worth, people pleasing, other-centeredness, and toxic shame. ("I am not enough—I am somehow defective as a person.") Joy's father was an adult child of an alcoholic who brought abandonment issues (from his own father's alcoholism and death), controlling over-responsibility for others (he was the only one who could do anything "right" and "if something was worth doing at all, it was worth doing right"), perfectionism, authoritarianism, low self-worth, rageaholic, and toxic shame. ("I am defective and not enough.") Thus, Joy and David had a lot of heavy family-of-origin baggage to interfere with their fairy tale.

Joy and David learned about "coupleship" and how, as a couple, they were powerless over things which they used to blame on each other. They learned about making and taking time together in reflection and study. They learned to schedule time together. They learned about their Fourth Step as a couple and admitted it to God, to each other, and to another couple. They learned about dysfunctional intimacy and dependency and about healthy intimacy and dependency, and they learned about healthy conflict and how to fight fairly. Now they have a fighting contract and although they don't always use it, when they do, the real underlying core issues surface and can be dealt with, with understanding, compassion, validation, and commitment. They took the Eighth Step, listing the people they had harmed together and became willing, together, to make amends to them all.

Joy and David have learned that "living happily ever after" means living with presence in the today. They have learned that when they blame each other, that blame dynamic is really about each partner's core issues, baggage, and wounded inner child. They can stop blaming and look at the real underlying issues. They have learned about the safety to feel and to express feelings. They have boundaries, express differences, and negotiate comfortable compromise and agreement. They have learned to honor and respect each other. They are grateful to RCA and the spiritual awakening of their coupleship as a result of working the Twelve Steps together.

Jason and Christi

The Courage to Open Up

Jason

A fellow at my individual meeting told me about RCA's program of recovery for coupleships. It seemed like it could be a way of healing the wounds of the past and restoring communication, trust, and intimacy to my relationship with Christi, but I was nervous about suggesting the idea to her. I thought she had lost hope; however, I found myself finally feeling hopeful for our relationship. I was finally honest, and although I was scared to open up, I was finally willing, and it felt good. Through RCA, I was able to see other couples being honest with one another. I saw other addicts modeling openness to hear the pain and anger their partners have felt, and really being honest with their partners about themselves. I could see that when these other addicts were able to open up and share of themselves honestly, they weren't abandoned by their partners—in fact, they became closer through the process of sharing and honesty. This helped me find the courage to open up myself and share with Christi some of the parts of me that I was so afraid to share. This, in turn, helped me to examine my own feelings and share more honestly and openly at my individual program, and release yet more shame.

In letting go of that shame, I could become more and more open and available to really hear Christi's pain. I also became more willing to be open to hear Christi's side through first hearing another co-dependent share at our RCA meetings. I hadn't caused that other person's pain, therefore I didn't get defensive or feel the need to justify my behavior when I heard them share. This empathy for another person could then carry over to Christi. I could be more open to hearing what feelings she experienced in our relationship. I could let them in then.

Christi

I have found that the gifts I've gotten in the RCA program have not only enhanced our coupleship program of recovery, it has enhanced and brought gifts to my individual program. As the co-dependent in our relationship, I had a difficult time relating to my husband when he tried to share about his own pain. I found, however, that I could hear an addict who was not my own husband speak about their woundedness, their pain, their struggles in their coupleships, and allow it in. I didn't have the "filters" of anger, hurt, and betrayal with these other addicts, so when they shared about themselves, it didn't bring up my own pain or anger nearly as much. I could then "translate" this insight to what Jason had to share with me.

Christi and Jason

We believe that the three legs of our stools of recovery are incredibly interdependent. Our individual programs support and nourish our individual souls, which in turn supports and nourishes our coupleship. Our work on our coupleship healing and growth supports and nourishes the coupleship, and in turn supports and nourishes our individual programs. It's all interwoven, all interdependent. Each leg is individually important to the whole. Without any one leg, our life together would lose its balance. We need all three legs to have stability.

Elena and Andres

Addicted to Fighting

Elena

I'm from Texas, from an alcoholic home with my father being a full-blown alcoholic: dominant, silent, and very powerful. He beat my mother up every Saturday night when he was drunk and in his macho pride. He had a motive for everything he did and he built a home for my mother and grandmother—his mother, who was mean and controlled everything he did. I didn't fit in anywhere in my family. My brother was mom's favorite, and my oldest sister was my father's favorite. My brother got in trouble a lot and there would be silence around this while all the rest of us had to kneel down to confess for as long as two hours at a time.

From the age of seven on, I was the one who took over the parenting. When I was twelve we did a geographic move to California and then things got really devastating. I had always been taught, especially in our Hispanic culture, that women did not drink. But after our move, not only did my mother start drinking, but she started bringing home some sleazy companions after work.

My brother found gangs and our house became their headquarters. With our parents working nights, I would lock my sister and baby brother in our room as I didn't trust this group of boys. I didn't date, didn't play outside. I was isolated in my own bubble world. I tried to reach out to my mother's family, even though my father put them down, called them "ghetto poor" and "dirty tramps." I wasn't allowed to talk to anyone. There was lots of violence, being hit with belts and isolated; this continued until I was married. I did graduate from high school even though I was nearly illiterate. I am in school now and loving it—recovering from being taught that I was stupid.

After graduating from high school, I got my first job and was able to purchase a car and clothes. Then I met my first husband. I thought I'd met "the love of my life." I couldn't recognize it at the time, but he was identical to my father. And, unknowingly, I became my mother. With a circus wedding arranged, my husband passed out and I drove myself there. I did as Mexican women are told, "be a shadow, never question where your husband goes or who he's with." I went on in this abusive relationship, having three daughters. When I was eight and a half months pregnant, he beat me not only drunk but even when he was sober. After many blackouts and being beat up more, his work sent him to treatment and THIS IS THE MOST IMPORTANT PART: they confronted me, noting that I'd been molested, had survived verbal and physical abuse. They tried to pierce my denial—confronting me with "What are you going to do?" insisting that I have my own plan; it didn't matter what his plans were.

I went to Al-Anon—just to get them off my back—and with a black eye. They told me, "Honey, no one's ever going to touch your body anymore." And that was the last time anyone did. I left that abusive relationship. And after one year of the program (no major decision in the first year) my sponsor became my mother-in-law. But prior to that I had learned how to date, and was initially attracted to my old pattern of macho men who wanted to take care of me. When I did marry I married an entire family and a husband who was silent and couldn't or wouldn't talk. He was violent but he never stood up for me with his mother (my dad again). In Al-Anon I learned I had to be strong and to care for myself. At one point I left him for three weeks and when I returned I started as a new woman, to have rules and set boundaries. My husband was told, "You better work the Steps or she's not coming back." In January of 1999 I was speaking at an Al-Anon gathering and afterward at coffee I heard about RCA. I came home and told my husband, "We're going to go to RCA, I'm sick of you" and he responded, "I'm sick of you too." We grabbed the first couple sponsors we could, learned more about communication, and have built a strong marriage today.

Andres

My name is Andres and I am glad I can share my story with you. I am grateful to RCA, and know I need to show gratitude. I can do that by being of service. Taking time to tell you my story in writing is not easy for me, but I made a commitment to do this and here it is.

When my partner and I came to RCA in mid-January of 1999, I had been in the program of AA, sober for nine years. I had worked the Steps. Because of the strong program my home group passed on to me, I had faith in the Steps. I knew they could be helpful for any addiction. I didn't at that time know about my addiction to fights and arguments—fights that were ripping my guts out day after day. I didn't know that I just couldn't handle a healthy relationship.

My partner was in the program of Al-Anon; my mother was her sponsor at the time we met. My mother was living with me, helping me with my kids because my second wife had committed suicide in 1985. I was trying to raise my two natural daughters and two stepdaughters from my second marriage. I was a bad drunk at the time. Being a drunk is another story, but it is mentioned here to let you know where I came from. Elena would visit my home to do sponsor stuff with my mom. She had her three daughters living with her and she had been divorced for about eight years. We got to be friends at first. After a while, we dated, we fell in love, we broke up, we got back together, I got sober, and we fell in love again. We got married and hell broke loose.

My two daughters, Elena's three daughters, Elena, and I tried to make it as a blended family. My older stepdaughters decided they couldn't stay because of new rules in the home Elena and I were putting down. We were not very successful at setting rules and structure. Because I was just sober, and had a passive behavior, I was not much of a parent or stepparent. In the time before the marriage I was really a pushover to my kids, a family-of-origin trait that I picked up from my mom, and I was always tying to be the nice dad so that I would be able to keep drinking. When Elena tried to set some rules and structure in the home I had problems supporting her. I thought she was too mean. I was sure she was wrong and I was right. I thought the kids would hate me if I was too strict. That was one of our unresolved issues. The kids started to act out by getting into drugs, getting pregnant, and running away from home. The kids, I believe, were doing their best to break up the marriage. Elena and I had so many fights over that. We had much heartbreak over that. Time passed and the kids grew and moved out. But even with the kids gone we still had fights over issues about them.

We still worked our individual programs, went to meetings, still stayed in love. I really didn't get a lot of help for the relationship from my individual program. I can recall sharing my troubles. I would get advice like, "Just keep your side of the street clean;" "All you have to say is, 'Yes, dear, I was wrong.'" Then I asked what to do when she wanted to talk about feelings. I was told, "Forget about feelings, they'll change all the time . . . " Of course that advice wasn't much help to me in dealing with the relationship.

We managed to have some good times and bad times, but the times when we fought badly negated the good times. Our fights sometimes got violent. There was so much broken furniture. Many times we took a piece of paper, drew a line in the middle and divided the bills, and talked about moving out. I never struck Elena but would not hesitate to pound on things and throw things to get my point across. I could raise my voice louder than Elena could any time. I could get right in her face, sometimes pushing my finger inches from her nose. We broke furniture and doors. The fights could last till two or three in the morning; we would rest and then continue the next day.

Sometimes we thought we had the problem solved but it would crop up later, like a weed. We never got to the root. We had an addiction to fighting. Once we started, we could not stop, but each time we thought that maybe this time things would end differently. They never did. The fear of those fights and that we were going to fight would tear my guts out.

There were so many unresolved issues, mistrust, hurt feelings, and bad behaviors. I can share the major issues; to share everything would probably take the whole book. The biggest issue was around my second wife—the one who committed suicide.

I had caused Elena much pain and doubt because I refused to see that I did not have a healthy relationship in any of my past marriages. Heck, I was too sick. I had family-of-origin issues. I had trust issues. I could never give my complete self. I was not capable of intimacy—you know, like "into me see." I did not have the ability to see my part. When Elena wanted to talk about the past marriages I would get defensive. I did not want to admit that I had not had a good relationship. So when I defended my past, Elena believed that I was placing the past wives, even the one that committed suicide, above her. That was the "killer issue," the "white elephant," one of the big roots in our past. Thank God we got that out of our relationship.

Communication was not a problem! I communicated to Elena that she was wrong and the cause of most of our troubles. She just did not want to see that! We could have really used the Safety Guidelines then. We really could never hear what the other was saying. As soon as Elena would touch on issues that reached into my tender self, I shut down. I would start to think of how to stage my defense quicker than the words could come out of Elena's mouth. I got frustrated when I got advice and my inventory was taken. The best I could do was to shut down and refuse to talk. I would back that up with "Why should we talk about it? You never listen anyway." I could escape the issue for a while, but not for long. Elena was dogmatic about "prying open the Iron Gate to the inner me" that I had to keep shut. I really did need to open up, but I was afraid to, so I felt isolated. I was like the giant who lived alone in his castle: huge walls surrounded the castle; a moat filled with crocodiles ran around the castle. The windows were always shut. Yet, the giant would weep and was so lonely because no one would ever visit him. I am grateful that I have finally become free of that bondage.

Our Recovery

When we walked into our first RCA meeting we were both ready to give up and end the marriage. We could no longer go on. Elena had spoken at an Al-Anon meeting the day before and met a woman who had been attending RCA for a few years. Elena heard that RCA was a program where couples could work the Twelve Steps as a couple and learn to restore their relationship. She told me about going to a meeting and I was all for it. On the way we got lost, had a fight, and almost went home. God was working in our lives because we immediately found the meeting place. We were late but got to hear couples share about their struggles and using the tools and Steps to get over them. I believed that this could work for us. We shared at the end of the meeting and both admitted that we were at the end of the line, but saw hope here. At the end of the meeting Elena said, "We need to get sponsors." I wanted to wait for a while but Elena said "No" and grabbed one of our sponsors-to-be. Back then there were few couples available as couple sponsors. When the leaders asked, "Will all available sponsors pleases raise their hands?" no hands were raised. Still, Elena was sure that we needed to get sponsors that night. That couple said they would get back to us, and later said they would be our sponsors.

It would be great to say we got immediately fixed. The truth is we both had a lot of fight left. I still had to grow to trust in Elena. I had to really look at my part, my fears, and the way I protect the tender me. I had to see that sometimes I play the role of my passive mom, sometimes I play the part of my dad. My dad rarely showed affection, he only showed emotions that put him above and apart.

He was an alcoholic who grew up homeless in the streets of El Paso, Texas, from the age of ten until he joined the army. He could scare me with just a stare. I learned through the Steps in RCA how my family-of-origin traits reacted with Elena's. When we were fighting or in disagreement we played out those roles because that's all we knew.

We did not get into the Steps right away. I wanted to finish the Steps in a year or less. But guess what, we weren't ready for that. When we tried to work on a Step it seemed like we were dragging huge boulders uphill. I would get frustrated because Elena gave too much detail and she got frustrated because I gave too little. I would see that a question in the Step asked this and Elena was sure that it asked that. You can see we still had communication problems. Making "outreach calls" to couples who had worked the Steps helped. Some other things that helped us were going to Step Studies, hearing from other couples that we had to stop reacting to body language, using the Tools of RCA, and understanding the Safety Guidelines. We learned that it's OK to have conflict, make mistakes, have needs, and walk away from the argument, not the relationship. We started having a "Meeting of Two" regularly. We got to feel safe, at first working with our couple sponsors, and later, working out our problems ourselves using the Tools.

When I saw that Elena was willing to give in to the Steps and admit her part, I started to be more honest. Before, we seemed to be at a standoff. Each was waiting for the other to move towards the center. That center was where we were no longer individuals but a couple. That is where our Higher Power exists. As we progressed through the Steps we slowly gained trust. I was soon able to be more open and vulnerable, more intimate. The fear of fights and of disagreeing slipped away. I learned to look at our "dances" objectively. I found that I have a responsibility to not take the dysfunctional role that I always did before. I know I can do and say stuff that will trouble or hurt Elena. When I think that my tender self is getting violated or I am not getting what I deserve, I act out—we sometimes can get into those old behaviors. But because we have inventoried them and admitted them to our Higher Power, our couple sponsors, and to ourselves, we know that each has certain responsibilities to not take part in those "dances." We still have those meaningful discussions but they no longer last all night. Today I have hopes that we will resolve our disagreements if we apply the Steps and Tools. Today we can live in the Promises if we work for them.

There is so much more to say. I need to wrap this up, so here it goes. At the end of each RCA meeting someone will usually read the Promises. There's this part at the end that goes something like, "Are these extravagant promises?" The rest of the couples in the meeting answer along with the reader, "We think not." I'll chant, "I think so." You see, what the Steps, Tools, Safety Guidelines, and Fellowship of RCA have given me is something beyond my wildest dreams. Those Promises are an extravagant luxury that I need to work for on a daily basis and that isn't easy, for me anyway. But it does work when I work for it.

We have gone though the Steps of RCA. We use the Tools, work with others, and do what we can to give back to the Fellowship of RCA, though we can never fully repay what RCA has given us. We share our story, what it was like, what happened, and what it is like today. Though we realize we know only a little, we hope that what we share with you will be helpful in some way.

JoAnn and Carl

A Twelve-Step Story

JoAnn

Do you believe in miracles? Carl and I are a miracle. Our couple story started in 1966 in Phoenix, Arizona. Carl was an intern at the hospital and I had my first job as a medical technologist. I was attracted to Carl because of his intelligence, his patience, and his generous attention with the patients. I wanted some of that attention also. I hadn't had that attention as a child. My family history is that I was educated in the Catholic school system by priests and nuns. There was no nonsense, mortal sin, and God was watching. My Catholic religion is important to me and has carried me through the many crises we have had. Sexual education consisted of a big, dark secret. Knowing what I know now, I believe my mother felt shame about sexuality. I was sexually molested by a cousin—an older male cousin. I felt shame and guilt. I also felt betrayal as he talked to many of my classmates. Mother wasn't helpful. I was told to stay away from those boys and to deny everything. Being a child I couldn't make sense of all that. I developed safety issues, particularly around men. I also developed an exaggerated need to control my environment and my emotions. I hear sex addicts desire sex more than anything. Well, my greatest fear was of sex. Sex and my codependency caused a great deal of problems with my husband. It wasn't any coincidence that food became my comforter. It became my way of acting out and continues to be my way of acting out. If I felt anxious, guilty, or fearful, I would want to eat compulsively. Then I would feel shame, shut down, and then repeat the cycle. I hated myself. Responsibility and motivation were not my strong suits. Fast forward to our relationship. Carl was a perfect choice for me. At a party in Phoenix he threw his champagne glass into the swimming pool. He was in no shape to drive. I asked him for his keys and he gently gave them to me. At that moment I knew I could marry him and change him. We were married in 1967 and Carl left for Vietnam shortly thereafter. We have been blessed with two wonderful children—Randal and Vanna. The early years were busy with work and raising the children and Carl came last in our relationship. Then things started to change. Carl, drunk, drove into the back of a truck and went to jail. I was not so angry with him, but embarrassed and humiliated—I had to borrow money from my boss to bail him out.

At that time, life was still exciting for me. I was a small-town girl and here I was traveling the world enjoying Carl's academic accomplishments. New Orleans has great parties. Tulane had many outlets for our entire family. My esteem came from Carl's accomplishments. Carl took care of all the finances, travel arrangements, and many other things. I didn't have to do anything outside the home. Our sex life was a struggle. I had a headache. If that didn't work I could use fantasy and disassociation. To escape housework and volunteering I decided to go back to work. I didn't know how to say no. One night late I got a phone call from Carl who was incoherent and didn't know where he was. Finally an airport official came on the phone and told me they had escorted him off the plane and were letting him sleep it off. I panicked. "JoAnn power" wasn't working. Our business dinners came to a halt. Carl could be alive and charming one moment and fall asleep the next. I would make excuses for him. I tried drinking more but that didn't work for me. We lost our friends. We stopped going out. Our home became a tomb. Our son, who was in medical school at the time, living in an apartment, said that Dad occasionally drank too much. Our daughter, who was living at home, was more affected. After a fight about a boyfriend of hers, she moved to California to escape from us. In 1992 we had our twenty-fifth wedding anniversary. Carl planned a wonderful surprise for me. We hadn't had a big ceremony when we got married. For our twenty-fifth anniversary, we had a room on the Gulf, twenty-five long-stemmed roses were waiting on me at dinner, we had a photographer, we renewed our vows, I got a new ring, but I had to suppress a little voice. Every night a hotel employee had to drive us in a golf cart back to our room. I was the queen of denial.

During a rare dinner with old friends Carl got out of control with his drinking and rage. I learned the power of prayer and my powerlessness. I called my friend to apologize and she started us on the road to recovery. She sent us to a psychologist, who validated my fears—my husband was an alcoholic. She introduced me to Al-Anon. Carl was in denial but eventually asked for help. I didn't think it was possible. He had a few relapses, but his bottom came in 1996 when he was in a car wreck. Carl embraced sobriety and now has ten years of continuous sobriety. I think he would have died if he hadn't found sobriety.

As Carl got better, I got worse. I was suspended from my job, I had a stomach ulcer, and our relationship was dissolving. We had sold the wine collection so we had the money for me to go to The Meadows for co-dependency. Family week was a disaster. In a safe place my sexual abuse came out and my food addiction was revealed. We decided to separate for four months, as we couldn't live together. We were too raw. We then decided to live together with the agreement we would be honest with each other, we would have our own therapists, a couple's therapist, and start an RCA Meeting. I was introduced to RCA in The Meadows. I was handed a starter packet and told if there wasn't a meeting in New Orleans to start one. As I progressed in recovery I learned I suppressed my anger as I projected it on Carl. I wasn't angry; he had enough anger for both of us. Carl became less responsive to my tears and dysfunctional actions. He became less domineering and I became more assertive. In working my own program, and together working the RCA program, we became more accepting of each other. I learned to face my fears.

We made a conscious decision to act in loving ways; it doesn't always happen. Pain was a great motivator for me. It was no coincidence that I was introduced to meditation while working the Eleventh Step. I do Centering Prayer, a twenty-minute morning meditation, which is maintenance, and twenty minutes in the afternoon, which is my divine education. Through my Twelve-Step work and my meditation I have learned I have energy centers which give me trouble: I need security, I need approval, and I want control. When one of these centers is frustrated it's like starting a fire. I get upset and start making unhealthy choices.

One of the best gifts we ever received was a Valentine gift from our daughter—two Harville Hendrix books on getting the love you want. We also have an Imago therapist. We learned we needed to close our exits, renew our commitments to each other, and provide a healing environment for our relationship. At the Convention in Hawaii, we climbed the extinct volcano Diamondhead. This seemed to me like the journey of recovery. It starts off flat, but then starts winding around. There is someone there to sell you water and flashlights. You wonder why you need them, sort of like the Tools. Then the trail starts with switchbacks. As you climb a little there is a plateau where you can see the ocean. It's beautiful. Then you climb a set of one hundred stairs. Then there is a tunnel that is really dark. There are people there and you trust and follow them, holding hands with your flashlight showing the way. At the end of the tunnel there is a circular staircase, which leads to a bunker. As you come out you can see 360 degrees. You can see the sparkling ocean and the beautiful city of Honolulu. It's worth the trip, and so is recovery. Both of our children are now living in California and we are spending a lot of time there. Recovery has changed our relationship with our children and we are truly grateful.

Carl

I won't talk a lot about my pre-recovery past, but will tell you one episode similar to many others. I lived in a house with forty other guys in college. One day my folks came to visit, knocked at the door, and asked if Carl lived there. It was a spring day, the windows were open, and one fellow in the second story yelled down, "Just drop him on the steps. We'll be down to get him in a while." After that I had an absolutely average life. I wasn't arrested any more often than usual. I have had the usual number of wrecks, been in jail about average, and been thrown out of places just like everyone else.

Before I came into recovery, I thought I had to feel like doing something before I could do it; recovery has taught me that if I just do the right thing, sooner or later it will feel like the right thing and I'll be glad I did it. What feels like the right thing to do is not necessarily the right thing to do; I need to ignore my feelings frequently and do the right thing. This is how we have done the RCA program, and the emphasis is on the doing. RCA is a program of action; if you continue to do the right things, right things will come your way. For instance, previous to RCA we had ignored our friends. In Step One we learned our powerlessness and joined RCA for recovery. We met many couples and associated with many couples. Almost all our friends now are couples we have met through RCA. Pre-recovery, we blamed each other for how we felt: I am angry because of what you did; I am sad because you didn't take out the trash. As part of Step Two we learned we needed a Higher Power responsible for our feelings and not our spouse.

If we had the right relationship with our Higher Power, it didn't matter much what our spouse did; we could feel OK as long as we had that right relationship with our Higher Power. If I have unpleasant emotions, I can't blame JoAnn, I'm responsible and I need to turn to my Higher Power to change those emotions. Then I can have a pleasant relationship with JoAnn.

I isolate when I am challenged. Pre-recovery I could be silent for days or weeks with no intimacy possible. Now, with the help of my Higher Power, I still can isolate but it usually only lasts for minutes or hours. As part of our Step Two we do nightly prayers together. I go to bed with JoAnn, we talk a little, and then we say the Serenity Prayer together. I frequently can't sleep so I then get up and work for a while, but we have had that spiritual time together. We go to church together. We baby-sit our grandson together, which is a beautiful spiritual experience for us. Seeing the generations of my daughter and grandson reminds me and us that we are not the center of the world; we are just one generation of countless generations and this keeps us right-sized. We go to RCA meetings together wherever we are. We do not have an identical Higher Power, but we do share a Higher Power who has an energy source not available to us otherwise that can help us.

Notice the action items here. We did Step Two once before and didn't change our actions much and we didn't benefit much. Before we did Step Three we tried to control the future. We had the idea if we couldn't have our way we would not be OK. We were reasonably intelligent, vigorous, and focused people and frequently it seemed we could control the outcome of things. That required a great deal of work, more worry, and great frustration when things didn't go our way. As part of Step Three we learned to do the best we could about whatever needed doing at the time and let go of the outcome with acceptance of however things are. That has saved us a great deal of work and worry, and allowed us to be contented with however things are. For instance, we were living in New Orleans and our children were living in California because they wanted to get away from me when I was still drinking. We had repaired our relationships and were spending a fair amount of time in California. We didn't rush to any judgment about making a move, letting things develop as our Higher Power wanted. Then came Hurricane Katrina. We took that as a not-so-subtle hint it was time to move to California, which we did.

Step Four was a real challenge for us. It was not so much the problems between us, as we had worked that out as part of our individual recoveries. It was the relationship between our coupleship and the world we had problems with. I found RCA to be less helpful with this problem than between us. It was clear we had not been good parents with our children. I won't give the details of that, as that is part of their story. I can tell you before we did Step Four we did not have a unified front with the children. They could play us against one another and get what they felt they wanted or needed. As we recognized that as part of Step Four, we decided we should now work together and provide a unified response. We feel this has led to much healthier behavior on their part. We also had lost contact with our friends. One thing we hadn't corrected was our intimacy. We didn't have sexual intimacy or any other intimacy. We now have some degree of sexual intimacy and many other kinds of intimacy. We have dog intimacy; we do canine Frisbee both for fun and for competition. We try to be open about our actions and feelings so we don't hide things from each other. What you see is what you get.

For Step Five, we've used our sponsor couple. We've had the same sponsor couple for almost as long as we have been in RCA. We didn't complete Step Five at a single sitting; we did it as we went along. We talk on the phone every two weeks and meet with them usually several times a year. We're open about what we have done and how we feel and they know all about us. I don't advocate that as the right way to do Step Five, but it seems to have worked for us. For Step Six, that was easy. We were entirely ready to give up the way we were relating with each other and the world. For Step Seven, we have worked the RCA program to have our Higher Power help our character defects. However, in my individual program and in our coupleship our character defects were never removed. They could be helped a great deal and life certainly made easier, but if we slowed down in working the program, those defects started to flare up again. We haven't worked formal contracts, but we have come to understandings about many things that have simplified matters between us.

For Step Eight we may have a great deal of denial still. We didn't identify a lot of problems with the world. We had been honest, and kept our end of agreements, and were good role models except when we were acting out, of course. We did recognize we had problems with being there for our parents and children. We were physically present, but were not available for intimacy. We know our children have felt the effects of that. For Step Nine, we needed to make amends to ourselves, particularly for not living a spiritual life. We have made those amends. We needed to make amends to our children. We did that and they did not want to hear it. We made those amends, taking care of ourselves. That was all we could do. We now live those amends, leading a much more spiritual life to model for them. We are much more available to the other family as well. We're much more in touch and more supportive than before. I wasn't sober and we weren't in RCA when Mother died so we couldn't make direct amends to her. We did some graveside work with all our parents and were able to be there for my father during the final few months of his life, which meant a great deal to him. For Step Ten we review our status every two weeks with our sponsor couple, we regularly attend our RCA meeting and review our status, and we continue to keep our own inventory. For Step Eleven we pray together, go to church together, and meditate regularly as individuals and occasionally together.

For Step Twelve, we feel we have done a lot. Again we believe the Steps are action Steps and we have taken actions. We were on the RCA Board previously; JoAnn was Secretary for two years and I was Literature Chair for two years. We are back on the Board again and I am Literature Chair again, rewriting the Blue Book. We started an RCA meeting that was working well from 1997 until Hurricane Katrina. We have been to every Convention since 1998 and take the results back to our group. We have been and are couple sponsors. We attend RCA meetings and openly share at such meetings.

We do not hold out this way as THE way to do the Steps and the RCA program. We have found it a better way to live for us. Our lives have improved so much since we started RCA. We now know what intimacy is. We have joy in our lives. We can relate to our children in positive ways and be good role models for them and have fun times together. We are back in the world leading useful and satisfying lives. If you have problems anything like ours, you might want to try the RCA program. We hope it helps you as much as it has helped us.

Dianne and Nelson

Matchmaker—Make Me a Match

1. Blame, Attack, Defend

Dianne

I looked at the dining table in disgust. It was a mess. There were stacks of papers and machines all over the place. There was no way a meal could be served on it AGAIN. I started to state my complaint—AGAIN. I realized that the words that were coming were words I had said before. I knew what he would say in response, and what I would say next, and what his rebuttal would be. We were in the full flowering of our blame-attack-defend syndrome.

How did it get to that point? How could something that had started out so right have ended up so wrong? What happened to our dream of living our golden years together?

Nelson

We are from distinctly different heritages: I was born in New York City of Jewish parents; Dianne, my wife, was born in Virginia of Southern Baptist parents. Talk about differences: Mason & Dixon knew what they were doing when they drew that line in the sand. Yet there are a lot of similarities in our behaviors, as we both suffer from extreme "family-of-origin" syndrome. Neither of us has fully recovered from the negative messages we received from one or both of our parents. This is not a genetic defect; it is the direct result of the sad emotional environments in which we were raised.

Both my parents came from Nazi Germany before World War II. Their ancestors had escaped the Spanish Inquisition in 1492 and got to Deutschland by crossing the Pyrenees. And in the 1930s, my family escaped the Third Reich and certain extinction again. My father was trained as a butcher in Germany, and had no problem immigrating to the USA, as men of his ability were in great demand in this country in the early 1930s. My mother, while studying for the opera in Vienna, had fallen in love with a goy—unforgivable!—and was consequently shanghaied by her mother and put aboard a steamer to NYC, where she had her sister arrange a marriage between my parents. This was a customary procedure at the time. I was the first (and almost immediate) offspring of that ill-fated match. My parents were destined to "act out" the rest of their lives: My father became a rageaholic, settling arguments with a meat hook, while my mother morphed into a world-class guilt-thrower and *qvetch*. Happiness eluded them 'til death.

My parents' marriage quickly disintegrated into what my father called "a shouting match." The only time they seemed to mellow out was when they had a "highball." By the time I was eight years of age, I had decided to mellow out also. On New Year's Eve, while my parents were out doing their thing, I got into the liquor cabinet and became royally smashed.

I was a practicing—but somewhat functioning—alcoholic for almost forty-four years. During that time, I got a BE degree (with almost thirty fraternities on the campus where I received my undergraduate degree, beer-drinking was considered to be part of the curriculum) as well as an MBA. Prior to receiving my BE degree, one company made me an offer . . . to become a rocket scientist (really) in Cleveland. While working in Cleveland, I went out on a double date. The other fellow's date smiled at me; I married her. We had two children and struggled along together until a career change took me to a new venue, where I fell in lust, and my first wife, in disgust, agreed that we should divorce. Those forty-four years included a long-term live-in relationship, children coming and going, more career changes as I stumbled up the ladder of success and staggered into marriage number two with another practicing alcoholic.

I found AA, and wife number two was disgusted with a non-drinking alcoholic husband. We spent several years in spending wars before she left and ultimately divorced me. But AA turned my life around in spite of all the hardships, because I finally had a relationship with a God of my understanding, who I knew really cared about me.

Subsequently, a robust yenta, who was my friend, suggested that I contact Dianna for a date. I had finally realized that my "picker" was broken, so I took her sage advice. Dianna and I met in 1996 and were married in 1998. Things went along fairly well while I was working and she accompanied me on my numerous business and fishing trips out of town. However, in March of 2000, it became obvious that I was seriously ill, and there was some fear that I would die as no one could diagnose what was ailing me. Nevertheless, my tenacious wife took on the medical community, and finally she got me to a hospital that could help. I recovered in July of 2001. Unfortunately, by then I was about to become unemployed . . . and unemployable.

2. The Courtship

Dianne

When I was forty-six, and twelve years sober, I divorced Husband Number Two, implemented my will, gave away what my children didn't want, and left for California with what personal things I needed in my car. I spent the next fourteen years as a traveling priest and practitioner of a transformational breathing practice for mental, emotional, and spiritual healing. During those fourteen years, I had chosen to remain single, but as the big 6-Oh! Loomed on the horizon I realized I was ready to settle down. I didn't want to spend my golden years alone. As my previous choices had indicated, I did not know what I wanted or needed, or how to choose a mate. I asked three women whose opinion I respected and who had known me for many years to write out what they would suggest for a mate for me, then gave the list to a matchmaker and determined to handle this courtship in a reasonable manner.

When Nelson called after his yenta gave him my brochure, he told me that he had my brochure, that he would like to meet me, and that he spent every weekday making decisions so he did not like to make them on the weekends. He asked me to make reservations at the restaurant of my choice, and call him with the address and time, and he would show up. It was so romantic! And then he said, "And before we meet, you should know that I am bald, and I am rotund." Neither a full head of hair nor a buff body were on my list, so I told him that neither of those things were a problem for me.

Our first date (or perhaps I should say "interview") was at a lovely Hawaiian restaurant overlooking the bay. We determined we had enough of a match to continue, and on our second date he brought me a copy of *Men are from Mars, Women are from Venus,* saying that what he had learned about relationships from his parents had not been useful, that what this book said about men was true for him, and he asked me to read it and tell him if what the book said about women was true for me. This was important in our relationship because Southern girls are encouraged to allude to things very diplomatically rather than state them straightforwardly. And Nelson didn't know how to listen like a Southern man. Saying, "I think women like, or want, or need ____," was easier than telling him what I wanted or liked, or needed. On our third date, we went to a Twelve-Step meeting called "CoDA Couples," and we attended that meeting regularly until we learned about RCA many years later. I was determined to "stay with it" this time.

3. The Honeymoon

Dianne

The first few years we were together went by in a whirlwind of airports, hotels, and restaurants. Nelson introduced me to cheesecake and I graduated from "choice" to "prime." Despite the fun of the travel, the world of a financial analyst is a very high-stress environment. And then Nelson stopped sleeping. At a conference, he mentioned it at lunch, and the other analysts said they had the same problem, that it was an occupational hazard. They suggested a few drinks after dinner—not an option for a Twelve-Stepping man. He had tried all the home remedies that are shared in Twelve-Step meetings, then all the common-sense advice of the holistic health community. Finally he sought the professional help of a sleep clinic and various other professionals: neurologists, psychologists, and psychiatrists, all to no avail. The sleep deprivation seriously impaired his ability to function, the medications seriously impaired his ability to function, and many medicines made him much worse. Nelson had entered a twilight world where nothing could reach him. The honeymoon was over.

4. The Days of Darkness

Dianne

During Phase Two of our marriage I morphed from his little cutie into his caretaker. I missed my husband terribly and was desperate in my search to find help for him. Within weeks, he was on full disability. In all, there were five hospitalizations, four different diagnoses, and seventeen medications that failed to work. I carried the folders with the medical tests and treatments and a list of the drugs that had been tried and his reaction to each in my car, along with all the insurance paperwork. I spoke with insurance representatives daily, and learned to keep a record of each conversation: name of person, date and time, what was said. By July of 2001 my rotund husband weighed 160 pounds. He refused to eat or to do anything. His brother and I talked daily about what our next move might be, and decided on Cedars-Sinai, where they recommended ECT (electro-convulsive shock therapy). For those readers who are going into shock at the very thought of it, the procedure is nothing like what is portrayed in the movies. The doctors said they could not explain how or why it worked, but every other alternative had been tried, and it was our last option. From the first treatment, Nelson began to improve; and from my perspective it was like what happens when you press Ctrl-Esc-Delete and reboot your computer.

Six weeks after he entered Cedars-Sinai, Nelson came home. In his reality, the world had suddenly shifted into a completely different place, as if he had slipped through a wrinkle in time. He had no memories from the last year and a half and was baffled by the changed circumstances of his life. I was exhausted from the constant caretaking and hurt that he had so little appreciation for my efforts while he was ill. We had a rocky road ahead of us.

5. How We Came to RCA & Learned to Get Along (Most of the Time)

Nelson

Our relationship was now in its third phase (the first phase was pre-illness, the second was during-illness, and now we were in post-illness). Conditions were obviously different. We started to get in each other's face.

Dianne

Before Nelson's illness, unless we were traveling, he had been gone for twelve hours a day, working. And while he was ill he was either in the hospital or on the couch. Now he was underfoot sixteen hours a day. I was used to running the house as I pleased, and making all the decisions. He was used to having a personal assistant. I wasn't used to being one. He was accustomed to a technical assistance department . . . I couldn't fulfill that role either. He was accustomed to a private office, but the dining room would have to do. My prayers had been answered, my husband was back, or was he? There were times I looked at him and wanted to ask, "Who are you and what have you done with Nelson?" We did not have the skills to deal with this unplanned and unexpected retirement. At a weekend conference, a friend who had asked to sit with us left after a few moments, asking, "Do you always argue and bicker like this?" Embarrassing!!! We enrolled in Imago counseling and began to uncover the deep childhood wounds that were reawakened and/or revealed in our relationship. We learned valuable skills then that would later help us transform our relationship into a coupleship. But it was not enough. As soon as one issue was resolved, others would pop up like dandelions in spring. *We were ready to give up.*

Nelson

But as usual, God had other plans. A couple we had known before my illness—who we thought had long-since divorced or simply killed each other, given the intense arguments that had occurred between them—came back into our lives. They were transformed, literally so different that we thought we should fire our counselor and go to theirs, but when we asked what they were doing they said, "RCA. We work the Steps together." So the following Saturday, December 15, 2001, we went to our first RCA meeting. The result has been nothing short of another Twelve-Step miracle! RCA had changed our lives and our marriage. RCA has become our pathway to happiness, which is all we ever wanted.

Dianne

We argued all the way to our first meeting, which was held in a city thirty-five miles away. At that meeting, we were given a copy of the Safety Guidelines. We took them home and made copies for each of our cars; our first agreement was that if an argument started in the car, the passenger would read the Safety Guidelines aloud before the conversation continued. These may have been written as meeting guidelines, but they have been an integral part of our couple recovery, too. It was amazing how reading those guidelines took the spontaneous, self-righteous joy out of those tiffs. And yes, we still have copies of the Safety Guidelines in both cars.

In the format at that first meeting, all available sponsors were asked to raise their hands. One couple raised their hands. This made it easy; we asked them to be our sponsors. We began writing on Step One immediately, but the daily stress of life together sent us to the phone to call our sponsors pretty regularly. They taught us to use written agreements to solve our problems instead of bickering and arguing over them. (Our first agreement was about the dining-room table, of course.) They guided us to call a moratorium when a solution was not being reached, and to turn things over to our coupleship Higher Power for resolution, so we could keep the focus on our love. I remember one phone call where they listened to each of us build a case against the other, and when we were done with stating our cases, there was a long silence, and then he said, "I think you really do love each other." And everything snapped into perspective again. We regularly attended the area monthly Step Study meeting and continued working the Steps with our sponsor couple.

We had some losses in RCA. We had to give up the skill of delivering the quick, unexpected barb. We had to forego the put-downs, and the sarcastic one-liner zingers. We nicknamed these behaviors "jackals"—a name much less acceptable to us than "barbed wit." We agreed to not use them—and found it was easier said than done. It was this contract that led us to "the game." We needed an agreement to keep our agreements! The game gave us a lighthearted way to monitor our progress in making changes. Each time one of us broke an agreement, the partner got a point. A partner who has broken three agreements within one week makes amends by giving the offended partner thirty minutes of pleasure of the offended partner's choice. Once the penalty is paid, amends have been made, and that game is over. Today, years later, our Tenth Step is usually sufficient and we rarely have to play the game to support changing old habits in a new agreement.

Nelson

One of the greatest gifts we have received from RCA is we have begun to understand each other. Through writing our Steps together, we learned to really listen and then to check back to be sure we understood. We still use this process when we unexpectedly hit a roadblock. We learned to say what was on our minds and in our hearts. We learned to look past the current upset for the family-of-origin issue that is almost always there. We have compassion for each other. In our Step-work folder we have pictures of each of us taken when we were about three years old. It reminds us to cherish the little child within our partner. We thought our matchmakers had arranged our match. Now we know that our Higher Power arranged our match so we could have the gift of working through underlying problems we had previously managed to avoid.

As we worked through Step One together, we grew in compassion and began to see that our real enemy wasn't our partner, but our past. Instead of fighting each other, we became allies working together to heal these old wounds by bringing them to the surface and letting our Higher Power heal them. Before we start writing on a Step, we say aloud this affirmation we learned from the couple who introduced us to RCA: "We are on the same team." I found a framed "Marriage Prayer" in a bookstore and keep it on the wall just above my sock drawer, where I see it every day. Although the personal interactive aspect of God in my heritage is called "Adonai," most people would say "Lord," as in this prayer:

Lord, help us to remember when we first met and the strong love that grew between us. Help us to work that love into practical things so that nothing can divide us. We ask for words both kind and loving and hearts always ready to ask forgiveness as well as to forgive. Dear Lord, we put our marriage into your hands. Amen.

Dianne

It is easy to focus on the practical everyday Tools for getting along together that we have learned in RCA. It's harder to convey the spiritual journey that we took together as we worked Steps Two and Three. For both of us, there had to be a lot of letting go of old ideas that were our inheritances. We had to get down to the bedrock of what we believed together before we could confidently invite a power greater than ourselves to do for us what we had not been able to do ourselves. Working together to select items for our Second Step collage was a wonderful exercise in opening our hearts to the flow of divine wisdom. We each selected pictures, words, and phrases that intuitively attracted us. When we spread it all out at the Step Study workshop it looked like a mess and we had no idea how it could "gel" into anything meaningful or beautiful, like the collages others had shared with us. But we turned it over and did the next indicated thing. We kept the things we both wanted and put the others in an envelope. And somehow by the end of the afternoon our Higher Power helped us create a poster to share that was colorful, beautiful, and meaningful. We call this Higher Power God. There must be hundreds of thousands of words written in the Jewish and Christian faiths; these are the words we kept:

We believe there is one God, working for good in our lives—through us, through others, and through direct action. We believe that God responds to us personally—that we can speak to God in prayer and listen to God in meditation. Once we receive guidance, we can live our lives accordingly, or not, if we so choose. God does not punish us; rather, consequences, and challenges are events from which we can learn and grow with God's help. God has put teachers in our lives; it is up to us to recognize them (that is, everyone) and learn from them. We do not have to live in fear; we can choose to live in love. We believe miracles can happen. We believe our purpose as individuals and as a couple is to seek and express God-consciousness in our personal lives, our coupleship, and our community.

Nelson

Today, Dianne and I are lovers, partners, and friends. Our relationship has become a coupleship. Thank you God!

New Hope of RCA

Having met in AA circles and having some significant time (twelve-plus years each) and an active and structured sobriety, our marriage of three years was facing an obstacle that was rapidly and fearfully becoming insurmountable. Our obstacle was whether or not to become parents.

While attending the AA World Convention in Toronto we went to the couples speakers meeting where several couples shared their stories, mostly of what seemed the drudgery of tolerance, patience, forgiveness, gratitude, and good companionship, but not much on adoration, devotion, passion, and inseparability that we had seen in a rare few throughout our lives' experience. It was probably there. We just didn't recognize it, perhaps because it was just fading from us. We knew we wanted to be together, but were falling apart due to our issue and our inability to communicate. One of these speaker couples caught our ears and we wanted to personally thank them. So, we stood in a ten- to fifteen-minute line to do so, and after switching from the longer to the shorter line, out of the blue we began to talk to a couple right next to us in line.

In no time at all we were on fire, for there was no doubt we were placed next to them and that this was to be the most memorable moment of our convention pilgrimage. It happened so fast and was so remarkable that we can hardly recall the details, only the principle of the interlude. Their situation was the same as ours except roles were reversed as far as who wanted children. Right down to the yellow lab dog being a factor in keeping us together for the time being, we were looking into a mirror but they had overcome their difficulties and had gone to any length to do so.

We briefly thanked the speakers but wanted more of what this young couple had. After carrying on the spontaneous and electric conversation for an hour and a half in the lobby, not one of the four of us had a dry eye. "Recovering Couples Anonymous," they said several times. We were high on the idea because of our faith in the Twelve Steps as a result of working them in our personal lives. All along we knew there was more, and this courageous couple was the proof. We hugged and parted only to run into them once again not long after. This only reaffirmed some additional information and confirmed God's handiwork as He has so often done in our recovery. Remember, the convention in Toronto had 50,000 plus attending and there were many we knew were there that we never saw the entire weekend.

So they returned to the West and we returned to upstate New York and looked up the meeting info on the Internet and voila, we were just fifteen minutes from one of only three meetings being held in New York State or City combined, and forty-five minutes from the second. We went to the first possible meeting and the couple there was very glad to see us. It would be just the four of us that night, and that was enough, thank you God. A bit later we went to the closer meeting and met another couple that later became our RCA sponsors. I could feel the grass roots of this program and felt like one of the first one hundred of the original Twelve-Step program.

Though it has only been ten months since we joined this fellowship, our lives have greatly reflected the Promises of the Program. We first walked away from that young couple at the convention with the priceless gift of hope. For after all, loss of hope = desperation. Suddenly we had new hope!

We attended several meetings, mostly general discussions, and every fourth meeting was a Step meeting where we began to formally work the Steps together as a couple with other couples. Of course we were introduced to just how powerless and unmanageable our lives had become early in RCA by an ever-increasing awareness of our family-of-origin tactics. We were impressed at the courage and fiber of the couples we met and the obstacles that they were attempting to overcome. And we were given the greatest gift of watching them transform these obstacles into assets a day at a time. We learned a new language with terms like "button pushing" and "baiting." We took moratoriums, among other suggestions, and admitted we wanted to stay committed to one another more than ever. We learned to hear and listen to what the other person in our coupleship had been trying to say. We didn't have to agree, hallelujah! We tapped into the value of acknowledging the other's feelings and saw their pain and even watched some of it transform into strength and wisdom.

Confidence is being restored in one another as we watch each other learn to value our coupleship, accept our parts, and develop our relationship with our Higher Power. We haven't had children yet, but we understand ourselves, our struggles, and the solutions to them better now. We have decided to begin a family soon, if it be His will, and this has come through the pains of growth and even some precious laughter. Laughter that we didn't have before RCA because we lived in the fear that struggle, strife, power, and domination was all there was to marriage. As we discover what a loving commitment is, fears slip away and we are no longer under the control of our own wills.

Through RCA we discovered what potential we have and how to draw from that, together with our Higher Power. Both of us were afraid we couldn't stay in the relationship for different reasons; one would've been denying their true relationship and understanding of God's will for the marriage, and the other couldn't live with the harm that they felt they were inflicting on the other. This was the result of not facing or understanding our family-of-origin issues and not seeing ourselves as capable and loving parents. Already today, though we are some ways from completing the Steps, we are determined to finish them. Our marriage has become like the three-legged stool we learned about in RCA, only we are two of the legs and the third is God, without whom we were doomed, and with whom we now have the unlimited strength of new hope to support us, whatever may come our way.

Geri and Peter

Some Miracles Take Time

We met in AA. Since we had a couple of years' sobriety before we started dating, we assumed that we were healthy individuals at that time. Both of us had compassion for the dysfunctional childhood we each had lived. We were sure we would have a healthier relationship than our parents with the principles of AA in our lives. We talked for hours and fell in love.

1. Babes in the Woods

We jumped into living together after one month of dating. After a year, Geri found out she was pregnant. And Peter said, "I guess we should get married . . . shouldn't we?" It was not very romantic. There was no more discussion on the topic and before we knew it we were getting married. We took our marriage vows in 1988 with faith that our years of recovery in AA would be a firm foundation. We wove ideas and principles from AA throughout our wedding vows. Within nine months, we had become parents . . . and the world as we knew it was over.

Little did we know what baggage we both brought to the coupleship . . . or how our family of origin would affect our interactions and parenting. All we knew was we were not going to be the same as our parents! And yet, as if on autopilot, we became them in so many ways. In our families of origin, Geri was neglected and Peter had been enmeshed. We were flip sides of the same coin, and this set a precedent for how we interacted. Geri used guilt trips, criticism, and control just as her mother had done. Peter used anger and avoidance as his father had done. Obviously, it did not help that neither of us had had healthy family relationships in which to learn positive ways of interacting.

And in the romance department, we didn't score any better. Peter had had mostly one-night stands and one committed relationship. Geri had spent most of her adolescence in an enmeshed relationship with a childhood sweetheart while simultaneously flitting to other boys who provided the love she so craved. Neither of us had skills or experience on how to maintain a healthy relationship. We were lost in the woods.

Our marriage went through years of addictions and co-addictions, mental illness, and infidelity. After the first child, we had a gap of seven years before having another child, because we were not sure that we were going to stay together. Each time we would hit a new bottom we would seek counseling. Then we would enter another Twelve-Step program to find recovery for the current issue. We tried it all. We now know we were essentially looking for something like our individual programs for our marriage, but the closest thing we could find at that time was a marriage encounter weekend. We tried to follow their program, and it was a good start at looking at our marriage as a couple needing nurturing, but it was not enough. Every time when some trust was beginning to be restored, a relapse or a new addiction would rip us apart again. The insanity would return. So much rage and resentment developed over time and it took its toll. We were placing Band-Aids on gaping wounds, and they couldn't begin to hold up.

2. Trying Without Hope

We came to RCA as a last-gasp effort. Finally, here was a place we could go that incorporated the principles we wanted. We believed in the Twelve Steps and knew first-hand about the healing they granted us individually. But by now, we were emotionally exhausted and empty inside. We did not have much hope that it could help us.

There were times when the drive to the meeting was unbearable. We had a difficult time sharing at meetings in the beginning. It seemed impossible not to trigger and blame each other. The idea of staying in the marriage seemed almost insane. Thank God for other people in the fellowship! Many had gone to the same depths we did. They seemed to have reached some peace and/or healing. In meetings, people shared openly from their heart and sometimes even laughed. We found hope. Often the fellowship would continue after meetings at dinner, and we looked forward to those times. It was amazing how the meeting gave us the healing we needed for a happier and more peaceful ride home.

There was a monthly Step Meeting. We started working the Steps and found we had so many issues that we could not get past the First Step. It got much worse before it got better. Everything seemed to generate more suffering. Peter struggled with bipolar disorder. He fluctuated between two extremes: he was paralyzed with depression or irresponsible with mania. The mania fueled his addiction and his clandestine behaviors. When manic he believed that consequences for any thrill-seeking, risk-taking behavior did not apply to him. Dishonesty ran rampant. We were constantly struggling with trust issues. Peter would be more honest in sharing at RCA meetings than in our home life, and each time, as one more secret was revealed, it would bring up more feelings of betrayal in Geri. We were still immersed in addiction and co-addiction. One was the victim and one the perpetrator.

The concept of each taking 100 percent of the responsibility for the health of the relationship was foreign; the deep-seated emotions within us generated impulses to blame and shame. But we tried as best we could. Peter used the accountability of RCA to finally overcome his addiction and come to grips with his bipolar disorder.

Eventually the consistent dishonesty broke us down, and after two years in RCA, we had finally reached the point where we decided to divorce. We had each hit an individual bottom that needed time to heal. For a year we lived in the same house as roommates. During that period we made arrangements to separate and dealt with lawyers. At times fur flew! The reality of divorce was here. We needed to go through the process of letting our marriage die.

It was then that our individual programs were critical. We went to separate meetings in different counties. This helped to give us space to share our issues and receive support without people taking sides.

At work, Geri put in for a transfer to a different location and found a new place to live near where she went to her meetings. Peter decided that if he was going to be alone now he really did want sobriety. Peter continued to gain time in sobriety since his last relapse and incorporated healthy changes for himself. We accepted that we were getting divorced.

3. The Magic of Letting Go

Then Geri needed surgery that required three months in a cast with six months' recovery time. It would be hard enough to care for herself, much less two children. Peter kindly suggested they live together for a little while longer. He said that if she still wanted to leave afterwards, that would be fine. For six months, he cared for her with compassion while she recuperated. Geri was touched by his unselfishness and genuine consideration. During that time we unexpectedly noticed that neither of us was doing the destructive behaviors that had driven us to that point of divorce. We hadn't . . . for over a year.

4. Safe Haven

So, we decided to give it one last effort. This time we entered RCA knowing we would have to let go of the past in order to have a marriage and grow. RCA taught us to put the good of the relationship above the wants and the needs of the individual. It was not easy to get so close to divorce and then choose to shut the anger off, but to heal we had to be willing to let go of the anger and the need to be right.

When we keep that in mind and ask our Higher Power to keep us willing to "own our own side of the street," we have more intimacy than we ever had before. Today we can be human and vulnerable with each other, and we have an emotional bond as well as a physical one. There is a deeper trust in our commitment to each other. In fact the word "commitment" has a whole new meaning.

As life goes on, it can be hard to take time out for each other in the hustle and bustle. We have had to incorporate ways to put our coupleship as a priority. We go to two or three RCA meetings a week to keep our focus on our coupleship. For the first five years, we drove an hour to the nearest RCA meeting. Today, we have brought RCA into our area and are responsible to open a meeting each week. Our marriage counselor also has been a wonderful tool. She has witnessed our contracts. She has given us necessary "extra" accountability to help us overcome our struggles. We still have several irresolvable issues, but because we face them in bits and pieces as they come up, they lack the power and intensity they used to have. When they get too heated, we use the Moratorium Tool. We "table" the issue until a time when we are safe with support from either the Fellowship or our counselor.

There is an intense intimacy that develops from our sharing at meetings. We are more open to admitting our childlike behaviors and laughing about them. The honest sharing and willingness to be vulnerable with each other is very potent. We share in front of other couples with sincerity about the reality of our coupleship—the good, the bad, and the ugly. We can never know what we would say in the safety of the meeting versus going it alone.

The miracle is, this teaches us and other couples that we are not alone in our humanness and in our strengths. Our RCA program both enhances and strengthens our individual programs. In fact, the accountability of RCA adds depth and a new dimension to our individual programs. Working with a sponsee couple has made us aware of what we are and are not doing in our coupleship. It is a little hard to tell another couple to use the Tools and the program when we are not doing it ourselves! And through working with them, we are reminded of ourselves at various stages of our recovery. One couple we sponsor had been extremely active in AA and Al-Anon before coming to RCA. They have a profound aspiration to repair their coupleship, and continue to surprise us with the lengths to which they will go to use the Tools of this program. Their diligence has inspired us and enhanced our recovery immeasurably. We get excited to see them grow closer as we witness the miracles of the program in their relationship. Now another meeting has emerged in our area with a regular Step meeting. We have no doubt that God made this happen and that God is doing for us what we could not do for ourselves.

Today, the quality of our marriage and coupleship is directly proportionate to the work we are putting into our program. RCA has taught us that it is OK to make mistakes and that change takes time; we do not have to be perfect. Our coupleship had been neglected for way too long. And how long did it take us to get this far in the woods? So why are we surprised that it takes time and nurturing to get back out of the woods . . . or more accurately, to build a safe haven within the same woods?

It is actually a relief to know that we can only get though the woods one day at a time. We are a work in progress. RCA gave us vital Tools to help us have a healthier coupleship. We have choices today as to whether we want to have destructive or constructive interactions. We have a pledge today to work our couple program to the best of our ability.

We had a hard time doing a Third Step. We each trusted God as individuals, but did not trust each other's ability to trust in God. That made it hard to trust our partner to turn his or her side of our coupleship over to God. We have placed God into our coupleship, and we trust in His will for us as a couple. It was not until we trusted each other that God was able to truly help us.

In closing, we would like to share one small but important miracle we have received in this program:

Peter

I surprised Geri on our seventeenth wedding anniversary by making a long-overdue amends. I had never actually asked Geri to marry me in the sense of a wedding proposal. And back then there was no money for an engagement ring either. I wanted to ask her to marry me "properly" and give her an exceptional engagement ring worthy of her love, but through the years, money was tight and it never seemed the right time. This year, I decided if I waited for finances to get better, it would never happen. The ring did not have to be perfect or huge, but I needed to get one and give it to her. This was one amend in particular that I had always wanted to do.

We went to the same restaurant where we had our wedding night dinner. We sat outside on the porch with a beautiful view of the Catskill Mountains behind us. After dinner, I proceeded to take Geri aside to the adjacent garden for privacy, knowing she might say "no" after all I'd said and done.

Geri

He began a little nervous and teary-eyed. He shared that he had so many things he wished he could make amends for that he had done to harm me in the past. Next, he got down on one knee and asked me if I would marry him again. If I said yes, all I would have to do was name the date and time. And I did say "yes" with full knowledge of what I was getting into this time. I did not need a date or time. This was a perfect amends just as it was. It was generated from Peter's heart with no prompting from counselors or sponsors. Now, whenever I look at that ring on my hand it brings me a smile. I think to myself . . . yes, miracles do happen!

May you stay until *your* miracle happens!

How Quickly Love Returns

Email "check-in" from a new (two months) RCA couple to their sponsor couple. They were all amazed at how quickly love returned.

We are having a lot of little victories. We have had a really good week so far and I am starting to understand what you (and the RCA Blue Book) mean when you say that respectful conflict can deepen your love for someone. When we have a disagreement that would previously have caused us harm (and still may at less happy times) and we settle it in a better way, I really feel his love. I feel his love because I see the effort and know how easy it would have been to have made a different choice . . . and yet he didn't and he decided to try. It's amazing how deeply that touches me.

I was sitting in the park the other day learning words (memorizing an opera) and there was a couple having a fight very similar to the fights we have when we aren't careful. I couldn't help but see just how useless it is to play the game. The lady was insisting that he listen to her and saying the same thing over and over. Every time she repeated herself he shut down more and side-stepped her issue by bringing up something else she did to upset him. I felt sorry for them. I also felt sorry for us and felt more love for the inner children in us that so need love that we will do anything to get it.

We have both been somewhat stupid at times this week; made less than positive choices . . . I was a total three-year-old on Saturday for a few seconds . . . but we have really worked with one another throughout them and tried to give space where needed, talk where needed, and listen where needed.

I am enjoying not having to be, and not expecting him to be, perfect. It helps a lot when he says to me that I don't have to be perfect; I can relax.

I know now that I have to remember that we are not perfect and that something (anything really, under poor conditions) can lead right back to where we came from. I try now to remind myself that it will be a slip and not a declaration of "unlove." I also try really hard not to live in fear of it—living in fear of the next fight just makes me feel unbalanced and brings it on so much more quickly. Ah, yes, the mind is a terrible and wonderful thing!

Chapter VI

52 Daily Reflections for Couple Recovery

1. Making Time For Intimacy

We live in a culture in which the average couple spends less than twenty-seven and a half minutes engaged in direct conversation together per week. Recovering people, however, know the price of neglected relationships. The old compulsions and obsessions drained our energy and occupied our time. In our pain and anger, we probably communicated even less than the meager national average. One of the gifts of recovery is the knowledge that what we wanted all along was intimacy. We were seduced into taking care of our pain in unhealthy ways, as opposed to the closeness we could offer each other.

Our commitment today

Today we will schedule intimate time. We will remember from our past experiences that intimacy is an accumulation of little moments as well as large blocks of time.

My commitment today

Today I will remember that my past obsessions were a way to avoid my feelings and life choices and that what I really needed was support and nurturing.

2. Need For Community

Couples experience more stress now than perhaps at any other time in history. For example, this is the first time in history that humankind has expected just two people to raise children. Parents in the eighteenth century typically had more childcare options than we have now. In earlier times, extended family and friends were available for help. Now, we live in neighborhoods and apartments in which we largely do not know others. Further, on average, we move every three years, which is about the time it takes to become rooted in a community. Clearly, our culture does not support those of us in recovery who come from families already isolated and incapable of asking for help.

Our commitment today

Today we will acknowledge to each other our need for others to support our life as relationship partners. We need that support and community so that we do not return to being isolated from each other and the rest of the world. We will seek ways to add to our community.

My commitment today

Today I will remember that there are my partner's friends, there are my friends, and there are our friends together. All three are indispensable for recovery.

3. Couple Shame

Many of us experience shame about our coupleships. We think others will not want to be with us as couples. We may be embarrassed about past behaviors. We may still distrust being with others because we fear old behaviors might return. Or we may feel so shameful, we cannot believe that "good" people would enjoy us, accept our struggles, and share themselves with us. Sometimes we fear others will see realities about ourselves which we either do not perceive, or do not wish to admit to ourselves. Sometimes we fail to share these feelings with others.

Our commitment today

Today we will reflect on how we feel about being with others. Do we have shame about our coupleship? What strengths do we have to offer others? What agreements or boundaries do we need to feel safe in public? Would it help for us to talk to other couples about our feelings?

My commitment today

Today I will work on accepting our progress as sufficient and focus on our strengths. I will comment aloud to my partner during the day about positive aspects of our being together.

4. Couple Self-Concept

As individuals have self-concepts, couples have an "us" concept. How couples perceive their coupleships will profoundly affect their well-being. In our individual recoveries, we learned that how we talked about ourselves or to ourselves had a direct impact on our self-worth. Self-pity, self-blame, and self-judgment always added to the burden and worsened the situation. The same principle applies to coupleships. When we judge each other or the coupleship harshly, or indulge in another round of "ain't it awful being together," we remain stuck in the old patterns. Our recovery demands that we extend to our coupleship that essential gentleness which was fundamental to forgiving ourselves.

Our commitment today

Today we will seek to treat gently our time together. We will accept the fact that intimacy is difficult, especially for recovering people. We will be forgiving of "us," and easy with one another. We will allow our sense of humor to be our guide.

My commitment today

Today I will not take myself too seriously. Rather I will look for ways to be good to myself and my partner. I will remind myself that I do not have the power necessary to fix the things about which I am obsessive, especially those things I see as "faults" in my partner.

5. Family of Origin

A coupleship is a "blending of epics." Both partners carry within them the story of the previous generations. Recovering people coming from dysfunctional families often have bitter histories. Part of powerlessness is growing up in relationships where seemingly the only options were avoidance, addiction, or codependency. As we grow in recovery, we understand more fully the impact of our families on how we relate to others. Sadly, we also have to recognize how our distrust, fear, and anger can easily be misplaced on our current partners, who do not deserve it. Part of our progress is to recognize that although we can no longer alter old family ties, we can do something about our current coupleship.

Our commitment today

Today we will remind ourselves how far we have come from the old family pains. We will refuse to allow our addictive inheritances to interfere with how we interact with each other. One step we can take is to ask ourselves if we are upset about family-of-origin issues.

My commitment today

Today I will be conscious of patterns from my addictive past.

6. Spirituality and Vulnerability

Many people experience their spirituality as individuals in solitude. Still others experience spiritual connection in community—a church or Twelve-Step group, for example. We may find one-to-one spirituality more frightening because sharing our conscious contact is one of the most intimate things we can do. The risk of being spiritually vulnerable to our partner, who knows us, is profoundly different from solitude. As with so many other risks in our recoveries, the greater our vulnerability, the deeper our potential growth. Remember, we "came to believe that a power greater than ourselves could restore us to commitment and intimacy."

Our commitment today

Today we will explore what risks we are willing to take with each other spiritually. How do we use the Second and Third Steps in our daily lives together? How prepared are we to turn our coupleship over to a power greater than ourselves?

My commitment today

Today I will ask myself what spiritual risk I am willing to take with my partner.

7. Support

One of the most difficult times in a coupleship occurs when both partners are depleted and "over the edge." Traditional wisdom has it that if we cannot get support from our partners, we should seek it from others individually. Another option exists. Part of recovery for coupleships is to develop a network of *other couples* who can be there for us during tough moments. Having such friendships in our lives will enhance our recovery if we develop them and call on our friends when we need them.

Our commitment today

Today we will talk about who in our network we can call when we are both overwhelmed. What kinds of excuses would we use to avoid calling them?

My commitment today

Today I will remember that building support for my coupleship is another way of taking care of myself.

8. Partner-Blame

Blaming our partners is probably the worst thing we can do in our relationship. The dynamic becomes so familiar that we are unaware when we do it. Clues exist, however, to indicate when we are blaming. When we make absolute statements about the person such as, "You always do this" or "You are so . . . " or "You are such . . . " we are making blaming statements. If we critique the behavior ("I don't like this behavior") and not the person, we will be taking responsibility for what concerns us—and not pushing all the responsibility to our partners.

Our commitment today

Today we will agree to talk about our concerns respectfully. We will discuss how we can affirm each other and still have our issues heard.

My commitment today

Today I will take responsibility for what concerns me, instead of blaming my partner.

9. Unsolvable Issues

Every couple has an issue that appears unsolvable. No matter how often it is discussed, or what solutions are tried, the problem does not go away. Here is where the program can really help. In our addiction and codependency, we try harder to solve a problem only to have the situation worsen. However, when we admit our powerlessness and seek help, we may be able to make progress or at least come to acceptance of the issue. Similarly, part of a First Step as a couple is to recognize powerlessness over that "unsolvable issue." By admitting the issue, a couple gains support from others who have experienced similar patterns in their recoveries.

Our commitment today

Today we will discuss one of our unsolvable issues and commit to seeking support. We will remind each other that we are not alone in having difficult issues that refuse to go away.

My commitment today

Today I will be patient with my partner, and remember that we are powerless over certain issues.

10. Stress

Family researchers have long noted that marital satisfaction declines markedly in most couples when their children become teenagers and returns when those adolescents become adults. The lesson to be learned is that stress takes a toll on the quality of coupleships. Most couples will face stress over finances, moving to a new location, loss of a job, and so forth. Many stressors are unavoidable. We cannot change, for example, the turmoil that adolescence brings to our children. What we can do is seek support from other couples who experience similar stress to try to minimize its impact.

Our commitment today

Today, following "The Serenity Prayer," we will try to recognize those "things over which we have no power," and try "to change the things we can." We will pray for "the wisdom to know the difference."

My commitment today

Today I will support my partner by recognizing our limits and reaching out for couple support. I will try to be gentle with my partner and myself.

11. Struggles and Understanding

A child takes her mother's shoes off and plays with them. She struggles to get them back on her mom's feet. She experiments, testing various ways to get them to fit. What started as play evolves into a challenge and a struggle. She works hard to master how shoes and feet fit together. Her parent, being wise about learning, resists the impulse to show her how they fit. She knows that it is more important for the child to develop the capability to make sense out of her world than to know about shoes. So she watches patiently with care and, at times, amusement. She reflects that perhaps this is how God watches over our coupleships—as we try to make things "fit"—patient, wise, caring, and perhaps sometimes amused.

Our commitment today

Today we will meditate on the reality that our struggle should not only be to solve any given problem, but also to add to our understanding of the world. Today we will share how being with each other has expanded our perceptions.

My commitment today

Today I will ask for the wisdom to appreciate my coupleship and all its accompanying struggles as central to my ability to see purpose in my life.

12. Interdependency

Nature teaches about growth in many ways. We need only walk through a forest or desert to see the interdependency of creatures, plants, and environment. We can gaze at a body of water from ocean to small pond and marvel at the complex relationships that make for thriving growth. The urge to be together for safety, comfort, reproduction, and play is one of the fundamental driving forces of the universe. We might reflect on how a couple is part of a total ecology and grand design. It helps us keep perspective on overwhelming issues when we see we are simply a small part of the ecology of creation.

Our commitment today

Today we will make an effort to connect with nature. We will arrange to be in an environment where we can see the interdependent relationships and sense the renewing energy of nature.

My commitment today

Today I will focus on my senses and how I experience nature.

13. Despair

We all can reflect on moments of despair when our lives seemed to have totally unraveled. Our life seemed hopeless. Our pain could have come from either circumstances beyond our control or our own choices. Either way, recovery teaches us that these low points can actually serve as gifts in our lives. Without the pain, we would not have the motivation to change for the better. The losses can actually give us new life, with new wisdom. As couples we demonstrate to one another our capacity to transform despair into individual growth.

Our commitment today

Today we will share with each other a moment of despair that spurred us to develop as more mature persons. We will remind ourselves that extreme difficulty is part of the renewing process, and that we shall have such moments again. We can prepare by strengthening our coupleship so we can draw strength from each other when facing despair.

My commitment today

Today I will share a memory of how my partner supported me when I was despairing.

14. Sensuality

Sensuality is fundamental. How we notice our environment—how we see, hear, touch, smell, and taste it—is vital to our total experience of life. Our appreciation of sensuality will give basic vitality to our sexual relationship. But if we do not attend to our senses, our sexuality is diminished. As recovering persons, we know that we need to stay in the present as opposed to the tormented past or the uncertain future. Living in awareness of our senses is the gateway to living in the present. More than stopping to smell the roses, sensuality is a direct path to "spirituality." Being in touch with our senses will help us to be present for each other both spiritually and sexually.

Our commitment today

Today we will talk about how sensually aware we are. We will focus on simple ways to be sensually present for each other. For example, we can notice the food we eat, the beauty of a tree, the grace of a bird's flight, the light of a full moon, or the color of our partner's eyes.

My commitment today

Today I will be present by heeding my senses. I will make a special effort to notice what is attractive about my partner.

15. Accepting Help

Recovering people have difficulty accepting help. Our reluctance likely stems from early life experiences. We may have been disappointed and hurt when help was necessary but not given. We may grieve promises of help that never materialized. We may resent having a sense of obligation. For whatever reason, we decided to go it alone and not rely on others. But in such a commitment we become vulnerable to addiction and codependency. What we needed was *help,* but the only *relief* we found was in our *obsessions.* Couple recovery needs acceptance of help from each other and from other couples.

Our commitment today

Today we will ask ourselves how well we accept help from each other and how well we accept help as a couple. What specific needs do we have at this moment for which we resist asking for help?

My commitment today

Today I will remember to ask for help from my partner and others in recovery.

16. Healthy Lifestyle

Food, exercise, and rest all enhance healthy living. Sometimes the choices present significant issues for couples, as when a partner smokes or decides to become vegetarian. We can't control what our partner does, but we can usually discuss our lifestyle choices with our partner. Comfortable resolution of these issues is one of the basic elements of recovery, but sadly, many of us simply let our lifestyles happen. Making healthy lifestyle choices will have greater success if we have our partner's support. Physical well-being has a profound impact on emotional well-being.

Our commitment today

Today we will ask each other how comfortable we are with our physical well-being. Do we need to set aside time to really talk through some changes? What pride can we take in how our lifestyle supports recovery?

My commitment today

Today I will think about my role as a "lifestyle" partner. As part of my inventory, I will meditate on the ways I currently do not contribute to a healthy lifestyle, and also on what gifts of health my partner has given me.

17. Perspective

When a child is ten years old, the passage of a year seems an eternity; yet for an adult a year seems very short. The percentages explain this difference in perception. One year equals 10 percent of the child's life yet it is only 2.5 percent of a forty-year-old's life. The adult's perception not only shifts because the time is less by comparison, it also shifts because we typically become inundated with the minutiae of daily life, and seem unable to take the time to "smell the roses." Couples can also experience a diminished sense of time the longer they are together if they don't focus on their intimate moments together. As recovering couples, we need to regain the perspective of a ten-year-old, when the world was fresh and full of wonder. This can start a day at a time by focusing on the wonder of our lives.

Our commitment today

Today we will talk about how we would spend the day if we were both ten years old. Then we will reflect on what that means for us in living the RCA program today. We will commit to a time to be carefree ten-year-olds together.

My commitment today

Today I will connect with the child within me so that I am able to reclaim my enthusiasm, earnestness, and playfulness. I will focus on being as open to the world as a ten-year-old.

18. Openness and Acceptance

In our coupleships there are situations and behaviors that are difficult to disclose and discuss with our partner. The raw exposure of being fully known can be a very frightening experience. If we choose to disclose behaviors and situations to our partner today, there is always a possibility that these disclosures will be used against us in the future. Instead of the dance of mistrust and fear, we can choose to look at our willingness to be open as an invitation to a renewed life in recovery. Remembering first to do no harm, admitting something to our partner does not have to be graceful, articulate, or fully thought out. Even the half-understood and the elusive perception can be clarified simply by sharing.

Our commitment today

Today we will reflect on how open we are to admitting to each other the difficult things about ourselves. Have we created an accepting climate in which we feel safe to admit to our partner our most secret fears and thoughts?

My commitment today

Today I will reflect on what I have been unwilling to share with my partner. If I am unsure about sharing, I will check it out with my sponsor or others in my fellowship.

19. Intimacy and Risk-Taking

Intimacy is an internal adventure complete with high risk, excitement, and discovery. Many people want the excitement and the discovery without taking the risk. Recovery forces us to take risks when we choose to be intimate with our partner. We are not talking about the Indiana Jones style of addictive life in which we took risks to stave off one disaster after another. Rather, we are talking about the frontiers of ourselves and of each other in which there are real rewards for exploring new territory. There are the risks of new levels of honesty, of learning to play together, of reaching out for new sexual intimacy, or of sharing creativity with each other. If we are willing to take risks and be truly intimate, then we will know a new freedom and new happiness.

Our commitment today

Today we will have a candid discussion about what new risks we are willing to take together.

My commitment today

Today I will reflect on my spiritual quest, taking risks to be intimate with my partner. How can I use risk-taking as part of a Third Step in which I trust my Higher Power?

20. Witnessing our Partner's Struggles

Many of us have experienced hardships in our lives. Unfortunately, recovery does not ensure that difficult times will not recur. In that sense the First Step is an introductory course to the wisdom of the Serenity Prayer; we must understand that there is much in our lives over which we will *remain powerless*. We must incorporate that understanding into our coupleships. For every couple there will be moments when one partner will flounder and experience deep pain while all the other can do is witness the suffering. At that point, the Steps become vital guides to how to be respectful toward each other. First, there is a deep acknowledgment of personal powerlessness and admitting the limits of our help. Next is an act of faith that a Higher Power is at work for our partner and for ourselves. Finally, the fellowship can support us.

Our commitment today

Today we will share a memory of when each could only witness the other's struggle. We will recommit to enduring those difficult transactions.

My commitment today

Today I will remember how the Steps can be guidelines in respecting my partner.

21. Keeping Our Reality

Coupleship partners can share in delusion. When neither partner faces reality, we are vulnerable to the old obsessions. Healthy coupleship means deep dedication to reality, whatever the cost. Twelve-Step wisdom has always urged us to go to "any lengths" to stay real. So when faced with possible problems—such as aging parents, addicted teenagers, limited finances, or unhealthy lifestyles—we need to be willing to discuss them with our partner, and then take the action to confirm or deny the existence of these problems. One of the last things we need in recovery is shared denial.

Our commitment today

Today we will share questions and worries about problems we may not have acknowledged. To what lengths will we go to stay real?

My commitment today

Today I will share my concerns with my partner. Facing denial starts with listening to my inner voice that tells me something is uncomfortable or not right.

22. Conflict

If we love our partners and wish to be intimate with them, we have to be prepared to disagree with them. Arguing may be one of the most positive forms of intimacy, and as we practice being informed by our emotions, anger may be one of the most significant of the coupleship gifts. To quarrel confidently with our partner indicates that we value and respect our partner as an adult who can handle it. To avoid conflict is to diminish our partner, leave issues unresolved, and constrict all feelings, including joy, tenderness, and care. Before recovery, we had battles over right and wrong. We escalated issues into crises during which our obsessions would thrive. We preferred dramatic exits to being clear about our feelings. Now we try to avoid self-righteousness and blame, and we strive for honesty and accuracy. We work for resolution, not crisis. We try to not damage each other, leave out extraneous issues, not abandon each other, and remember our partner could be right.

Our commitment today

Today we will share our insecurities about anger and how we will respect each other in conflict.

My commitment today

Today I am not going to avoid conflict. I will be real with people and set aside my fears about the reactions of others, especially my partner.

23. Tolerating Pain

Because of our histories we have learned to tolerate pain. Most people who experience pain make changes to reduce or eliminate it. A basic principle of self-care and self-respect demands that we take action. For those of us who relied on addictive obsessions to cope with pain, confronting our tolerance of pain becomes difficult. We are used to hurting. Physically, we ignore tiredness, full bladders, soreness, and discomfort. We sustain personal emptiness and shame. In our coupleships, we bury our feelings, allowing disrespect to continue. As couples, we "adjust" to pain. Intolerable situations exist in which both partners simply try harder. Recovery means both partners working together to develop intolerance of pain.

Our commitment today

Today we will talk of ways we hurt together. We will decide on which steps to take action, and when we will take those steps.

My commitment today

Today I will tune in to any pain to which I may have become accustomed. I will make an effort to report this to my partner.

24. Committing to Physical Health

Recovery requires a commitment to physical health. For years, many of us ignored our bodies and nearly destroyed one of our best bridges to emotional well-being. Solid exercise and eating well are proven contributors to psychological health. We need to be good consumers of health information. We can make changes that would improve our quality of life. The cooperation and support of our partners, however, is key. In our co-dependency we had an investment in our partner's illness(es). Now, in recovery, we invest in our partner's health and our own health. Couples can do much together to mutually support each other in physical training programs for recovery.

Our commitment today

Today we will talk about what we can do together to improve our physical health. Do we need more information? How can we support each other?

My commitment today

Today I will think about how I feel about my body and how I can live my commitment to physical health.

25. Acceptance and Healing

In many ways, an intimate coupleship parallels a Fifth Step. Part of the healing of a Fifth Step is to be fully known—both strengths and liabilities—and accepted. Coupleships heal when we accept our partner's strengths and liabilities. Problems emerge when we control, shame, limit, or abandon our partners because we find they have either threatening strengths or disappointing liabilities. Honesty between two people does not mean that one or the other is diminished. Rather, honesty reflects a fundamental acceptance of our limitations and support for our humanness.

Our commitment today

Today we will share our acceptance of each other and commitment to healing by being honest with each other.

My commitment today

Today I will be gentle with myself by accepting my imperfections. I will challenge that part of myself which says nothing I do is good enough.

26. Faithfulness

Faithfulness is much more than sexual fidelity. Faithfulness starts with fidelity to ourselves. We can rely upon those who know what they want, say what they mean, and do what they say. People who are true to themselves make trustworthy commitments. Those who make decisions on the basis of what would look good, or what the other person wants, lose themselves in the process. As couples, we need to understand that being faithful means being clear about who we are. We are faithful to others when we are true to ourselves.

Our commitment today

Today we will share with each other an example of something we trust about the other.

My commitment today

Today I will notice when I am not being true to myself. Am I trying to please others at the expense of who I am?

27. Powerlessness

Most of us remember times we were upset and in turmoil. With the passage of time, however, we can put these periods in perspective, realizing that the pain we experienced was necessary for us to grow. Or we might recognize that our self-righteousness and indignation were exercises in blaming others for what we had brought on ourselves. We spent needless emotional energy feeling shame. The program of recovery reminds us that much exists over which we have no power, that we need to take personal responsibility for ourselves, and that there is a Higher Power we can trust. As partners committed to a Twelve-Step process together, we can support each other to take those lessons about our painful past and apply them to create a more balanced and serene present.

Our commitment today

Today we can make a pact with each other about how to support each other when we get upset.

My commitment today

Today I will focus on a painful situation and reflect on what I learned from the experience.

28. Mutual Respect

When disagreements arise, both partners are likely to say, "I don't feel respected." Two very significant questions are often overlooked. First, did I act respectably and respectfully? Were my behaviors and attitudes consistently straightforward and respectable? And second, was I respectful? Did I avoid shaming, abusive, and inappropriate treatment of my partner? Was my anger constructive or destructive? When issues existed, did I work to ensure that my partner did not feel diminished by our process? Acting respectably and being respectful creates an integrity that commands respect.

Our commitment today

Today we will recommit to mutual respect.

My commitment today

Today I commit to being respectable and respectful in my relationship.

29. Equality

Most addicted or dysfunctional couples do not have equality in their coupleship before recovery. Usually one partner is considered less responsible than the other, and treated more as a child, while the other assumes the role of the adult. The search for equality starts with making individual amends to each other, and with forgiveness. Next, we separate our partner's happiness from our own. No longer do we accept that our current emotional state is dependent on what our partner is thinking or doing. Our goal is for a happiness dependent on our own internal values such as those learned in individual recovery, not in enmeshment with our partners. Once we both understand this principle, we can distinguish what we have in common from what is enmeshment.

Another focus might be on our differences. Differences can expand our available options, making our coupleships stronger. Equality emerges when differences become assets and sources of new options versus irritants and sources of shame. Equality rests on respect for the strengths in the other's differences.

Our commitment today

Today we share a difference we respect in each other.

My commitment today

Today I will acknowledge to myself a difference in my partner that I find irritating and work to see how that difference might be seen as a strength.

30. Renewal and Risk-Taking

Coupleships grow through risk-taking. We find new perspectives on each other as we take risks. Recovery presents many opportunities to take risks: new ways of being together, new strategies for sharing, new levels of honesty, new people, and new ways to support each other. Among the risks, the greatest is for partners to share vulnerability with each other. Risk always feels new and unsettling. By sharing with each other the vulnerability we feel about our risk-taking, our opportunities for intimacy and support grow.

Our commitment today

Today we will assess our current level of risk-taking. Are we doing enough to keep the process of renewal alive?

My commitment today

Today I will share with my partner my vulnerability around risks I am now taking.

31. Twelve-Step Work Is Spiritual Work

RCA Twelve-Step work offers valuable opportunities to heal deep spiritual wounds. A spiritual relationship is one that challenges us to grow. The function of a spiritual relationship is to provide opportunities to heal. In this sense, our partner presents us with opportunities to grow spiritually by learning to practice forgiveness, acceptance, trust, tolerance, patience, and compassion. There may well be people who would be easier to get along with, but would they help us grow spiritually? We heal as we grow spiritually. Seeing our coupleships as opportunities to grow and heal can strengthen our commitment to stay together until the miracle happens.

Our commitment today

Today we will try to appreciate the opportunities for healing we present to each other. We will agree to view these challenges as opportunities to find the spiritual principles needed to heal each situation. We will try to practice forgiveness, acceptance, trust, tolerance, patience, and compassion.

My commitment today

Today I will be grateful each time my partner provides me an opportunity to express forgiveness, patience, trust, tolerance, and compassion. I will see these as gifts from my partner.

32. Living in Serenity

Acceptance is essential to serenity in our coupleship. Within that simple word lies the key to happiness. When we first come into RCA, the word "acceptance" most likely means that we need to tolerate the situation in which we find ourselves to begin to grow together. As we begin to tolerate our partners (in spite of the many things we find wrong with them), we slowly come to find out they were tolerating *us*—and the many things they also found wrong with us!

To develop tolerance, we need to call a truce in the war raging in our relationship. In RCA we refer to this as "Calling a Moratorium." Once we decide to do this, we can begin to use the Twelve Steps and Tools of RCA to develop acceptance of ourselves and each other. When we can accept ourselves and our partner, we are on the road to recovery.

Our commitment today

Today when we quarrel, we will use the tools we have learned. We can call a moratorium or use a Fair Fighting Contract. We will pray for guidance to achieve acceptance of ourselves and of our partner.

My commitment today

Today if I am upset, I will ask myself, "Do I want discontent, or do I want peace?" If I want peace, I will list my complaints, ask my Higher Power to handle them, and declare a moratorium on thinking about them. I will enjoy my day.

33. Accepting Responsibility vs. Blame

Both partners must accept responsibility for the health or dysfunction of their coupleship. All of us bring our own addictions, personalities, family-of-origin messages, and various individual dysfunctions into the relationship. The coupleship does not create the dysfunctions. Both partners contribute to the nature of the coupleship.

This does not mean that we are responsible for any addictive or dysfunctional behavior on our partners' parts. Those behaviors are their responsibility and reflect choices that they make in order to cope with feelings. Both of us are responsible for the presence or absence of intimacy. As soon as each of us accepts responsibility, we are ready for the First Step of RCA: "We admitted we were powerless over our relationship—that our life together had become unmanageable."

A paradox in Twelve-Step work is that we surrender to win. When we surrender and admit that we are powerless over our coupleship, we can begin to detach from it. As we examine our coupleship in the Step One questions, we begin to see our own part, and our partner's part, with more compassion. We start to listen—really listen—to each other. We see that responsibility is not blame, but rather a foundation for change. As our coupleship transforms, we increasingly embrace responsibility as the door to freedom from the bondage of the past.

Our commitment today

Today we will each share one thing we did that contributed to the dysfunction of our coupleship. We will strive to hear each other with openness and compassion.

My commitment today

Today I will search for the truth about my behavior. I will acknowledge my part without shaming myself. I will ask myself what I can do differently in the future, and then ask for help in changing my behavior.

34. Baiting and Button-Pushing

A fisherman baits his hook—choosing the lure that will be irresistible—a lure big enough to command interest, yet not be obvious. He knows that the hidden hook, once taken, will ensure control of the fish. Similarly, an individual who chooses to make statements to trigger a particular response is also using a lure to fish for a reaction. The purpose is to ensure control of the partner. For example: a wife (with no intention of tearing out wallpaper) may ask her partner if he will be gone all day by stating, "That should be long enough for me to take down the cabinets and remove the wall paper," (just to see her partner's reaction). She hopes that he will be reminded to focus on her and return sooner, worried that she is destroying the kitchen while he is gone.

Baiting and "button-pushing" statements reward us with attention and control of our partner. Triggering buttons can be a look, gesture, or words that cause shame, fear, or anger in our partner. Our "buttons" are wired to wounds or memories from the past—some so long ago that their origin is forgotten. By refraining from button-pushing and baiting statements, we act to preserve the safety of our coupleships. In the "blame" game, we need to win at any cost. Manipulative behaviors create an ongoing battle for control. The goal of a healthy coupleship is winning *with* our partner, not winning *at the expense of* our partner. Respecting our partner's vulnerability is an act of maturity, and allows a partnership of greater trust and love to develop.

Our commitment today

Today we will reaffirm that we are on the same team, trying to work as equal partners to solve our problems.

My commitment today

Today I will restrain my desire to use baiting or button-pushing statements. I will discuss ways that we can deal with our touchy topics using healthy communication tools. If I think I am being baited, I will ask what my partner is feeling and needs, instead of reacting by taking the bait.

35. Gratitude

In a world that bombards us with visions of what we have yet to "get," we may fail to be fully aware of the goodness we already have. Many of us experienced a sense of relief after our first few RCA meetings, when we realized that other couples knew what we were going through. We began to sense that others in the group shared our most ominous problems, and had resolved them and moved on to happier lives. We were finally with people who understood us. We learned to call this feeling that we were home "couple gratitude."

Many of us had tried all manner of treatments to get our coupleships on track. Some of us had read self-help books. Some of us had gone to therapists and counselors. Yet it wasn't until we found the RCA program that we had the tools we needed. Though Twelve-Step programs for individuals had been around since AA started, before RCA there had been no attempts to adapt these Steps for couples.

When we look into the faces of our children and no longer see the fear that went with membership in our dysfunctional family relationships, we are grateful. When we can disagree with our partners and yet continue our lives together in love, trust, and respect, we are grateful. When we are together and feel just wonderful and proud of our relationships, we have gratitude. When we can nurture and be nurtured without fear of "who's giving the most," we are grateful. We can express our gratitude by sharing our joy and by helping others find their way to and in RCA through our words, deeds, and resources.

Our commitment today

Today we will think about the gifts of our coupleship. We will acknowledge ourselves—as a couple—for taking the actions required for these gifts to materialize. We will each express appreciation for something our partner has done for our well-being.

My commitment today

Today I will commit to having "less attitude and more gratitude." I will share my joy by helping others.

36. A Program of Action

Twelve-Step programs call the process "work." We *work* our program. We *work* the Steps. We *work* with our sponsor couple. Work involves action.

Reading about couple recovery is very good and is necessary. Studying the materials is beneficial. But nothing is accomplished until we put this knowledge into action. All the Steps require us *to act* with our partners.

Action is both internal and external. Action provides the experience that makes new knowledge and behavior "stick," becoming our new, positive belief system. Many of us came to RCA with "frozen" relationship skills—repeated unsuccessful relationship behaviors. Yet over and over we expected and hoped for a different result. Now, we see that *new* action is required. We see from other, more experienced RCA couples the attitudes that new actions bring. By going to meetings and working with our sponsor couples we become more confident in our new skills. The more we act in a manner consistent with the principles of the program, the more we will experience healing in our coupleships and ourselves. Actions with positive results generate new enthusiasm for more new action. All the good *intentions* in the world are not worth the results of just one positive *action*. Action is the proof of our new thought and beliefs. Action is how we express our love to each other. Action is how we provide role models for our children. We return our coupleships to commitment and intimacy through action.

Our commitment today

Today we will celebrate one action we have taken that has had positive results. We will examine our life together to find another action we can take in recovery, and consider what positive results would follow.

My commitment today

Today I will look within myself for an individual action that should have a positive influence on my coupleship. I will take this action, keep it secret in my heart, and leave the results up to my Higher Power.

37. Out of Denial

It is not uncommon for two people, each with excellent individual recovery, to be together and yet find themselves in the most conflicted and dysfunctional relationship imaginable! We may have worked hard on our character defects but find the fur is flying in our life together.

A major gift of working the RCA program is that we have the opportunity to fully see and experience those parts of our personality that need healing. Coupleship is the proving ground in which we try to resolve our conflicting character defects.

Individually we work on our own healing, and our partners work on theirs. We should know by now that "it takes two to tango" (or "tangle"). Where we find problems with our partner, we find our own issues. We remember RCA's Step Ten, "We continued to take personal inventory and when we were wrong, promptly admitted it to our partner and to others we had harmed." So now when issues come up, we see that they are probably just a new coat of paint on an old whipping post.

Having experienced great healing through working RCA's Twelve Steps, we know the solution does not come from reacting in the same old ways. If we do things the way we've always done them, we can expect the same results.

Our awareness now gives us the courage to give the gift of owning up to our mistakes. When we say, "I'm sorry, I was mistaken" to our partners and then make every effort to refrain from that mistake again, we give the loving gift that breaks the cycle. It gives our partner the opportunity to act differently too—to respond with love and forgiveness. And there can be no greater gift.

Our commitment today

Today we will embrace awareness of the conflicts within our coupleship, knowing that acknowledging them without shame and blame is the first step in our transformational process in RCA.

My commitment today

Today I dare to admit my mistakes, first to myself, and then to my partner, in language that honors me, my partner, and the possibility of progress in our program.

38. The RCA Paradox: Commitment Brings Freedom

Oh no! It's the "big C" word. It's the dreaded bane of all things that we hold so personally dear, such as our individuality. If we commit, that will surely be the end of us as unique individuals. Most of us had similar fears when we entered our coupleships.

So, to counter those fears, we may well have "mouthed" the words of commitment but deep down given ourselves escape plans. "If things get too bad, I can always leave (have an affair, get a divorce, kill myself [or my partner], go insane, go back to Mom and Dad, and so forth)." But a commitment is not a contract that comes with an escape clause. It is a pledge, based on our own honor as a human being, to live up to our words. There is no negotiating with commitment. There is no "have your lawyer and my lawyer work out the details."

Commitment is one of the finest gifts human beings can give. Commitment comes after much consideration and goes to the heart of being fully human—*no matter what,* we are in this process together. With commitment the most amazing thing can happen: intimacy! With intimacy, we are more fully able to explore who we ourselves can be. Though it may seem strange, this fact remains; with commitment comes freedom—the freedom to fully be ourselves.

Our commitment today

Today we will review our commitment. Is it steady? Do we trust the Higher Power of our coupleship as well as the RCA program of recovery to work for us?

My commitment today

Today I will let go of my fear of commitment. I will "act as if" my commitment is safe in the hands of my Higher Power without any thoughts of leaving.

39. Conflict as a Road to Health

Life with our partners brings to the surface those facets of ourselves that need emotional healing. When we come together, we each bring with us belief systems formed in our families of origin. The belief systems we bring to the coupleship may never be entirely compatible with those of our partner because our individual wounds are different.

Some members of the helping professions think that we actually attract people who will clash with our belief systems that need to be altered. This view sees relationship conflict as a path to becoming a better human being. What is certain is that experiencing conflict in our coupleships is inevitable. We can look at conflict with our partner as a negative thing or we can see it as an opportunity to change ourselves—and the coupleship—for the better.

Discovering why we are feeling angry or upset with our partners often leads us to places in our past where we have unresolved issues. In our Tenth Step, we can keep our side of the coupleship clean by taking responsibility for our personal upsets. To keep our coupleship in balance, we can resolve these issues in our individual recovery program or with a therapist or spiritual advisor. By learning to work through these conflicts with our partner in a mature way, using the tools of RCA such as a Fair Fighting Contract, we begin healing old personal wounds as well as our coupleship.

Our commitment today

Today we will review our Fair Fighting Contract (or Conflict Resolution Contract). Are we honoring our agreements? What help do we need from our support systems to turn conflict into a positive solution?

My commitment today

Today I will look at my part in handling conflict. If I am avoiding or denying, I will ask for courage. If I am reacting in anger and striking out, I will work on this with my individual support system.

40. Valuing Our Differences

Some people choose partners not because they are so much alike, but often because of something that they admire in the other, or that is complementary. Nevertheless, as life goes on we may find ourselves at odds with our partner, sometimes for the same qualities we first found so attractive! Perhaps we like to plan for the future, but our partner wants to live each moment to its fullest. As months or even years pass, we find ourselves saying, "If only you could be more like me."

Contrary to popular belief, there are *no* perfectly matched couples. Many of us participate in RCA because we realize that we have our own family-of-origin issues that may get in the way of a successful coupleship. Some of us entered our coupleships with the illusion that our coupleship and our partner would be a certain way. The more we try to encourage our partner to change, the more our communication will tend to break down. We become frustrated, lonely, angry, and resentful.

Our commitment today

Today we will practice valuing differences within our coupleship, knowing that these differences make us stronger as a team.

My commitment today

Today I will first work on acceptance of myself and then expand this acceptance to include my partner. I will embrace the unique qualities that my partner possesses. I will look to see one way my differences complement my partner, and one way my partner's differences complement me.

41. Anger and Resentment

Most of us were filled with anger and resentment. Each day brought incidents that ignited our anger and continued as resentments. No incident was too trivial to stir up these seething emotions, driving out respect for our partner. We thought the resultant emotional wasteland was our partner's fault. But our problem was *spiritual bankruptcy*. Rather than taking responsibility for our own problems, we would transfer (project) our uncomfortable emotions onto our partners by finding fault. We were then relieved of the responsibility of changing ourselves.

Early in recovery, we began to learn to be responsible for our own feelings. Other people weren't responsible for our feelings. It was just that *we* had allowed others to control our emotions. We realized it was almost as much an error to *take* offense as to *give* offense. But by *taking responsibility* for our own emotions, we took back control of our own happiness.

Now that we are beginning to maintain a spiritual relationship with our Higher Power, we are beginning to be happy. If our partner seems to be annoying, the solution is less with our partner than in regaining a personal relationship with our Higher Power. We change our relationship with our partner by changing ourselves rather than our partner. Then we can love our partner again. Without projecting our own insecurities onto our partner, the person we admired and loved in the beginning is back again. This is the miracle!

Our commitment today

Today we will affirm as a couple that our happiness as individuals and as a couple flows from our relationship with a power greater than ourselves.

My commitment today

Today I will look to my Higher Power for my happiness, in order to free myself to be a friend and companion to my partner.

42. Letting Go of Despair

Twelve-Step recovery bolsters our ability to let go of despair. Learning to turn over our hopelessness to our Higher Power, even when there seems no end to our pain, is a blessing we receive each time we are willing to remember The Promises of RCA.

We hear that we come into relationships for a reason—to learn lessons about life and ourselves. We try to be mindful of these lessons, and purposefully to offer gratitude for the presence of our partner in our life. Each day we can look at the events in our life to see how they have served their purpose: to help teach us the lessons we need to learn on our spiritual journey.

Our commitment today

Today when we begin to feel overwhelmed, we will work the RCA program. Instead of sliding into despair, we will trust our Higher Power.

My commitment today

Today I will strive to accept the things I do not understand by remembering that things happen that I cannot control.

43. Disappointment

Before we came into recovery, most of us couldn't trust anyone—much less our partner. Where once we had seen perfection, our partner had become someone who was not reliable—someone who lied, concealed, misled, and behaved in ways we could not trust. Where had that person gone who was accepting, full of love, and nurturing, making us feel good by just being there?

Early recovery was a shock. We learned there were *no* "perfect" partners. The process of being "in love" had blinded us to our partner's faults. What we experienced were other human beings seen through our distorted perceptions as perfect.

Our conceptions of trust were from our early childhoods when parents were experienced as trustworthy people, able to make us feel good whatever was going on. We tried to put our partners on that same pedestal. Finally, we learned we needed a *spiritual* connection, there whenever we needed it. No human could do that.

How much easier it is to get along with our partners now. We no longer need to put our partners on pedestals (or make them scapegoats). We are attempting to have relationships with human beings—not people who constantly let us down in our attempts to make them our Higher Power. We can develop equal relationships. We can trust our partners as humans who love us.

Our commitment today

Today we will look at our coupleship disappointments. Have idealism and unrealistic expectations set us up for a fall? We will select an affirmation that is realistic for us.

My commitment today

Today I will treat my partner as my equal, a worthy human being like me—with many fine traits and room to grow.

44. Coupleship

When we first began attending RCA meetings we didn't really distinguish between using the words "relationship" or "coupleship" to describe what we were together. However, with time in RCA we came to appreciate that RCA sees a significant difference in the two terms.

A "relationship" can be, and frequently is, a "one-sided" attachment. I can have a *relationship* with a person, a pet, a possession, or even a job. However, in RCA, a "coupleship" is a much more dynamic relationship. It is a relationship characterized by mutual reciprocity. When two people freely "choose" to be in partnership not only for their own benefit, but to benefit their partner, they have entered into a *coupleship*. They develop mutual goals and share a vision.

Whenever two people commit to form a coupleship it initiates a couple *dynamic* that is independent of the two individuals. This can become greater than simply the sum of what they each bring to the relationship. This *coupleship* develops a life of its own, and being dynamic, it will change in ways that are sometimes predictable and sometimes unpredictable. The "Promises" tell us some of the more predictable changes many of us will experience by following the RCA program. When a couple commits to working the Steps together, they set their coupleship along a spiritual path.

Our commitment today

Today we will work together to transform our relationship into a *coupleship,* a partnership with shared goals and vision. We will share our excitement for both the predictable and unpredictable changes that lie ahead.

My commitment today

Today I will set aside my expectations of what my relationship with my partner should look like. I will be open to the evolving process as we work the Steps of RCA together and our coupleship develops along a more spiritual path.

45. Fun

Before recovery, "fun" was euphoria induced by alcohol, drugs, or sex, usually with the mistaken perception we had control over ourselves, our partner, or others. Everyday life was dull and boring, but "fun" made it livable. Even as the pain increased, we could not see that we were isolated from ourselves, our partner, and our Higher Power.

Then the consequences of our behaviors made it clear that something was *terribly wrong*! We *had* to change our lives. We began to change ourselves through individual recovery programs and our coupleship through the RCA program. Early recovery was difficult, and generally lacked anything like fun, but we were able to find some peace and serenity with ourselves and as couples in the fellowship of recovering people. As we worked the Steps, we began to experience a sense of belonging we had never felt before.

However, many of us were still biased toward work. We still had to learn how to play and have fun together. With practice and time, laughter, spontaneity, and happiness have begun to enter our lives. This is a part of our RCA balance. We have come to prefer our real happiness now to what we had before.

Our commitment today

Today as a couple we will explore the times we have had fun together. We will make time for these activities in our lives.

My commitment today

Today I will appreciate spontaneity and playful attitudes in my partner and myself. I give myself permission to enjoy life.

46. Letting Go of Control

Before we found recovery, we tried to control events and people around us as best we could. We would be OK if only things went our way—the right way. We had to control the future so we could be OK when we got there. How much needless expenditure of time and effort went into trying to control! Back then, the most effective way of dealing with any subject was worrying about it.

Recovery, particularly Step Three, introduced an idea that seemed impossible. The secret to being OK was not in controlling what was going to happen, but in taking care of ourselves so we could be OK *regardless* of what would happen! What a radical idea that was!

In practice, we have found that keeping from being too hungry, angry, lonely, or tired (HALT) keeps us out of a lot of misery. Regular attendance at our RCA meeting is a big help. Having a sponsor couple and sponsoring other couples helps us to keep our focus. Reading RCA literature keeps us in contact with proven guidelines. Service work gets us out of ourselves. If we are doing all these things, we will likely find we are OK as the future rolls around.

Our commitment today

Today we can take an inventory of the things we *can* change: taking care of ourselves personally and as a couple. We can affirm that as we do these things today, we can trust God to take care of the future.

My commitment today

Today I will dare to trust a Higher Power to care for me—and my partner—in the future. I will keep my attention on practicing the program principles, knowing that they will keep me in balance.

47. Money

Many people misquote the old saying "Love of money is the root of all evil" as "*Money* is the root of all evil." As the actual saying posits, it is the importance that we attach to money that causes problems. Money itself can be used to harm or to benefit.

Issues surrounding money are one of the top three (along with sex and power) that vex coupleships. Working the Twelve Steps of RCA can help us understand that we are worthy of having our basic financial needs met and help us develop better attitudes regarding scarcity and plenty. As we release our emotional attachment to money, fear of economic insecurity begins to leave us.

In practice, it is less important how we decide to handle the coupleship's money than that we do decide and have a well thought-out plan. Some couples have joint accounts for paying bills as well as separate personal accounts. Others keep their money together and pay everything out of one account. Some couples have two accounts and each pays predetermined bills. The important thing is that whatever the arrangement, both individuals see themselves as members of a partnership and confront the issue of how money will be handled in the coupleship.

Many of us do not have the knowledge or the tools to be money experts. It is not uncommon for couples to seek outside help when money problems surface. Developing a personal and couple support system is also valuable. Praying together for knowledge of our Higher Power's will for us is a helpful way to begin any coupleship meeting in which money will be discussed.

Our commitment today

Today we will discuss our financial hopes and fears, and invite our Higher Power into our financial life.

My commitment today

Today I will examine my part in creating a safe, sound, and sane relationship with money.

48. Service is Therapy

My partner and I find that doing service is therapeutic to our coupleship. Sowing the seeds of recovery and doing service benefits us. If nothing else, it lets us see ourselves as part of the solution instead of part of the problem. Whether it is sponsorship, service on the RCA Board, taking a service position in our own meeting, telling others about RCA, or leaving literature at a Twelve-Step club, we benefit personally.

This is our fellowship! It is up to us to make RCA grow. Giving the gift of recovery is an integral part of the Twelve Steps. We ask ourselves, "Can we add another dollar to the basket? Can we talk to the new couple who came in or give them a call to ask why they haven't been to a meeting in a few weeks? Can we help our meeting find childcare or go to a meeting we've never been to before? Can we help a Board Committee with a project? Can we set up guidelines that are helpful to our meeting such as no cross-talk, shaming, or blaming? Can we sponsor another couple or lead a meeting or plan a non-meeting social event or a half-day RCA get-together? Can we organize a workshop? Can we plan a fellowship activity that members can invite their friends to?"

As a result of the spiritual awakening these Steps have provided, we try to carry this message to other couples and practice these principles in all aspects of our lives. And when we do this, the benefits will amaze us; the Promises we repeat at each meeting will come true in our lives if we work for them.

Our commitment today

Today we can look at one way we can be of service, and commit to it.

My commitment today

Today I will take the initiative. I will call a Meeting of Two, or make an outreach call, or take a service commitment.

49. The Courage to Be Vulnerable

Many of us have a dog that is so comfortable and trusting that it sleeps flat on its back in the middle of the floor with its legs all askew and doesn't even open an eye when we step over it. Now that's vulnerability! The dog trusts that—no matter what—we will not harm it. This kind of safety is what we strive for in coupleship. We want relationships in which we trust that our partner will never purposely harm us. The RCA Steps provide us a spiritual awakening for our coupleship. That is why we work the Twelve Steps together. Most of us have been hurt enough. Now we want something more nurturing—something safe.

Working the Twelve Steps allows us to practice being honest, open, and vulnerable with our partner. We are able to communicate our true feelings and express our deepest thoughts, and we discover that our partners don't judge us or leave us for being who we are. After we have completed the Steps, we continue to practice vulnerability by working the Tenth Step on a daily basis. We also pray and meditate together, which is a very intimate thing to do and enhances our vulnerability.

Some of us meet every day in our "Meeting of Two" to talk about how we've been feeling that day. Others have regular meetings. Many couples continue to meet with their sponsor couple. Many hold family meetings with their children and become role models for honesty, intimacy, and vulnerability. We are hopeful that the next generation will not be quite so fearful as many of us have been. They will receive a new legacy and grow up speaking and hearing the language of the heart.

Our commitment today

Today we will commit to using an RCA tool that helps us to be vulnerable.

My commitment today

Today I will inventory my ability to be vulnerable. I will commit to using an RCA tool that helps me to be vulnerable.

50. Taming the "Critical Parent"

"That's not the way to do that!" Do we say these or similar words to our partners? Do we tell our partners they don't do things "right" and then try to tell them the "right" way? Is our way almost always the "right" way? And is their way almost always the "wrong" way?

If we constantly judge our partners by what we want them to do without understanding that as adults, they are perfectly capable of making decisions, then we are acting as *critical parents*. When parents constantly judge a child as inadequate or incapable, the child usually grows up with little self-esteem. As adults, particularly with critical partners, it takes a lot of emotional energy to overcome all of the negative input. Of course, everyone makes mistakes from time to time, but these are opportunities for learning. As partners, we need to let the people we love be adults by treating them as adults—not as children we need to parent. Pointing our fingers and playing the "You're not good enough" game will not change our partners for the better. It just drives a wedge between us and destroys any opportunity for intimacy.

Healthy adults allow each other to be themselves, and to learn their own lessons. How do people know if they act like critical parents? Well, just for one twenty-four-hour period, we could try to not say one critical thing to our partners. If we find ourselves stopping in mid-sentence or mid-thought, then we may be acting as critical parents. Awareness is the first step in turning this destructive behavior around.

Our commitment today

Today we will treat our partners with kindness, caring, and loving communication.

My commitment today

Today I will monitor my thoughts for criticism, note where I am judging my partner or myself, and reflect on how to be more accepting.

51. Balance and Stability: The Three-Legged Stool of RCA Recovery

The three legs of our Recovery Stool (each person's individual recovery as well as the coupleship's recovery) are interdependent. Our personal recovery programs support us individually, which in turn supports our work on coupleship healing. Without personal, individual healing, it is difficult to fully participate in healing our coupleships. Coupleship healing not only supports couple intimacy, it also assists in our individual recoveries. Without some coupleship healing, our individual healing becomes more difficult, lacking a supportive environment. And without treating our coupleship as a distinct entity needing healing, it is difficult to heal either the coupleship or ourselves. Each leg is important to the whole—all interwoven, all interdependent. Without any one of these three legs, our lives tend to lose balance. We need all three legs for stability.

Our commitment today

Today we will discuss how our individual recoveries are helping to keep our coupleship alive and well.

My commitment today

Today I find ways to maintain my individual well-being—physically, emotionally, and spiritually—so I can be a healthy partner in my coupleship.

52. Couples on a Spiritual Path

A wise man once said, "People on a spiritual path have a spiritual practice, and they practice their practice, and they are faithful to their practice, and their practice is faithful to them."

As couples in RCA, we have begun a path of spiritual practice together. We have made a commitment to place the good of our coupleship above ourselves as individuals. In practice, our spiritual paths include such things as attending RCA meetings together, sharing at our local fellowships, working the Steps, and meeting with our sponsors. These practices open us up to healing. They help us share ourselves with our partner more intimately and honestly than we ever have before.

So as a couple, we do our best to be *faithful* to our new spiritual practices together. We see how these practices have helped other couples, and that gives us new hope that we can be healed too, if we are committed to these spiritual practices. We try to maintain open minds, trusting in the process of the RCA program and its fellowship. Our faithfulness is demonstrated by our *consistent practice.*

Today most of us are not the same as when we walked into our first RCA meeting. It doesn't usually happen overnight; in fact for some of us, it happens fairly slowly. A spiritual path is not a straight line. There are many peaks and valleys along the path. We can easily see that our valleys of today are much higher than our previous peaks. It is our commitment to these practices that has carried us out of some very desperate valleys.

Such is the way of spiritual paths. Looking over our shoulders it is clear that the changes in each of us, and in our coupleship dynamics, have been achieved as a natural result of our Twelve-Step practices. As a result of being faithful to our coupleship's spiritual practices, our practices have been faithful to us, and the rewards are "beyond our wildest dreams."

Our commitment today

Today we will be grateful for the Promises of RCA that we have received. We will not forget the paths we have walked together from despair into hopefulness. We will renew our commitment to our spiritual practices by sharing with other members of the fellowship how it works for us.

My commitment today

Today I will do my part to ensure that I do not allow myself to rest on my laurels. I will remain steadfast to working the program and living my spiritual practice. I will do the footwork, trusting the process even if I see no immediate results.

Chapter VII

Keynote Addresses

These three keynote addresses span the development of RCA from the first RCA Convention in 1991 to the 2009 RCA Convention. Pat Carnes's Founder's Address delineates the beginning aspirations of RCA. The 2002 Hawaii Convention keynote address tells the story of how RCA was started in Sweden. The 2009 Fort Lauderdale Convention address describes how one couple that had been in RCA from the beginning experienced those years in RCA and what it meant to their coupleship.

Founder's Address to the First RCA Convention held August 7–9, 1991 in Minneapolis, Minnesota

Pat C.

I can recount in my life that there were times when I got involved in things, and I really didn't know where they were going to end up. I feel that this is true about this moment. I would like to start with my history and what I think the significance is for me personally. It starts with a story with which I think many of you will identify, because the common denominator of co-dependency and addiction is abandonment and feeling the isolation and loneliness on which addictive and co-dependent obsession thrive.

I have been thinking a lot about my life as a kid. I grew up on a farm. My nearest friend was about a half mile away. In addition to the compulsive working, my Dad's drinking, and all the other things going on in our house, I was left alone a lot. My Dad was a professional animal trainer, and we had animals. I found that my friends and the beings in my life that I looked to for comfort were the surrounding animals. Throughout much of my life, one of the things I have searched for has been community. I have gravitated toward things and those organizations that could provide me with a sense of community.

I remember that as a graduate student I was so frightened of being with people. I wondered if I would be accepted. The grad students had coffee breaks in the morning, and I would anguish about attending because my hand would shake when I would hold that cup of coffee. Of course, the more I would try to control it, the more my hand would shake.

I would always be embarrassed that I might spill the coffee. That little terror I had experienced in much of my life and I wanted to feel accepted in the community. This was in the early '70s. I did not know about Adult Children of Alcoholics, and I did not know about many of the things that now we take for granted. At that time professionally, one of the things I was attracted to was the notion of family therapy. We did know that people progressed more with family and marital counseling approaches than by doing things individually. In fact, there was already research in the early '70s about the fact that it was unethical to try to treat people individually for problems that were of a family and marital nature. Often people got worse with individual treatment. So, the ethical thing was to use family and marriage approaches; but I looked around me, and there were not many people doing that kind of counseling.

In 1976 I was asked to start a treatment center. When the hospital asked me how that treatment should be configured, I said that it should be family-centered; in other words, we should have whole families come in. At that time, that was pretty unusual thinking. We started a ten-week program where whole families would come in. The kids would be there, starting at about age six. We started out with chemically addicted families, and eventually we extended treatment to sexually addicted and incest families and used the same formula. These people who came for treatment with their spouses and children had individual and peer group meetings in the afternoon and family group in the evening. Afterwards at about 9:30 or 10:00 p.m., five or six of these families would head down to the pie shop and buy themselves a couple of pies and go over to someone's house and do group all over again until about 2:00 a.m. Then they would go to work the next day, and they would come into the treatment program at three o'clock in the afternoon saying, "Boy, treatment wears you out!"

The problem they were having was that they just didn't go to bed! It took me a while to figure out what was going on. Then I realized that they were just so hungry to be a part of a group. They had wanted to be part of a group, an extended family, where they were with older people and younger people who were bonded as families. They felt that this was the way it was supposed to be, and somehow they had missed this in life. The reason they didn't want to go home was because it felt so good to be together. Never before had they belonged to a group of people like this. As I watched those families, one of the things that impressed me was that there was a sense of community. Many of those people are still close and connected with one another to this day.

As I reflect on this, I think that we live in a culture that is almost antithetical to community. When we note the history of how people lived together in earlier times, it was a community of people who raised a community of children. This is the first time in history that we have asked just two people to raise children. If you were in a community of people raising a community of children and you saw a child doing something wrong, then you felt partially responsible to stop that kid, to set some limits, or do something appropriate. Now, when we see someone else's kid doing something wrong or hazardous, we say, "Someone should do something about that." We don't feel like we have a right to intervene, because we don't have the connection to do that. The point is that in earlier times, there was a sense of connectedness.

Now, that is not to say that in earlier times there was an ideal family life. Until the last century, there were large parts of this world in which the father of the family had the right to terminate a child's life. We have made extraordinary progress in terms of our ability to visualize how childhood can be very different. The point I am making is that there was a sense of community, and while we have made progress in some ways, we have really stepped backwards in other ways. The people we really feel sorry for in this day and time are single parents who are raising kids by themselves. The reality is that there may be some couples sitting here that are sweating it out alone raising kids where there are just two parents involved. Indeed, the aunts and uncles, the other people and all the varied parts of the community that were usually involved in a child's life are missing today. We could spend a whole evening just pointing to the ways that we seem to be dismantled and disconnected from one another.

The next important event in my life was my exposure to a base community. The Catholic Church in Central America started base communities because of the shortage of priests. In base communities, family units would commit to one another liturgically, emotionally, and in social action. Six or seven families would become very involved in each other's lives as a community. There was a time in the late 70s—and at that time I was married—when we got involved in a base community. There were six other families in our base community.

In some ways these were the three best years of my life. For three years, we did things together. There was this incredible feeling that you had other adults to talk to, people who witnessed your life. I could get involved with their kids, and they could get involved with my kids. It took the pressure off being a parent in some ways. It took the pressure off being a partner in some ways. In other words, there could be women and men friends in that group, and we could have that intimacy.

That experience had a very profound impact on me, because I knew I wanted that in my life. In some ways, this was part of the genesis of thinking about the "We Came To Believe" program. I know, conceptually, that when people struggle with relationships, in fact, relationships have a life of their own. A relationship is more than the individuals who make it up.

One of the things that we used to do at that first treatment center I mentioned earlier was an exercise conducted which we would do about every ten weeks. One of the assignments was given to people as they came in the door. We would have the children there; we would have the adults there, both single folks and partnered folks. We would ask the kids to pick out new brothers and sisters. Then they would have to pick out new parents. And then as a new family, they would have to go out and spend the evening together and do something none of them had ever done before.

Now, it had a little risk to it! You could have a woman in the group who hadn't talked to another man in seventeen years, and suddenly she's got another woman's husband, for example. What you did, you see, is to change the rules on them.

Initially when those families would first come into treatment, referral sources would say: "These are all the things that are wrong with the family: They don't know how to send 'I' messages; they don't know how to listen; they don't know how to differentiate; they don't know how to problem-solve; they don't know how to resolve conflict; they don't know how to deal with anger; they don't know how to set boundaries—the list is endless. They don't know how to have fun; they don't know how to do things."

But the amazing thing is that when you put them with other people's kids and other people's partners, they knew how to be respectful and how to observe boundaries. They knew how to send "I" messages and listen and have fun. They could be themselves and enjoy one another! And they had a great time.

And they'd come back at the end of the evening and always, inevitably, somebody would get reflective and say, "Why is it that I can be this way with the people I don't live with? And then, with people whom I care about the most, I can't be that way?"

See, it isn't that they didn't know how to do those things. What they were experiencing was clearly their illness. In other words, the pathology in their relationship had a life of its own. I know this is one of the things that happens to all of us, because we have the inheritance that we bring with us from our families of origin. We also have whatever we have created between us. Those systems are very strong.

What really has happened is that we have seen an extraordinary amount of progress in what we can do individually with people. But we have not taken our knowledge and instituted it in a way that a couple could take those Twelve Steps. If you were a family therapist who was starting from scratch and trying to figure out an ideal way for a couple to deal with those central dilemmas which every couple faces, you could not devise a better system than the Twelve Steps. But no one ever, ever, developed that system for couples to do.

So, the other part of our work that was important to me was the "Don't Call It Love" survey, which involved a thousand people, some of whom are here tonight. We interviewed them as couples and as individuals. When we really started looking at the data, one of the things that became very clear was that the people who made it the furthest, who were doing the best, who were feeling great about themselves and feeling the most whole, were those people who had support for their coupleship!

In other words, there are lots of people who had support individually, but they didn't have support for their relationship. Let's use Mark's example from his talks about couples' fighting: "I get my army and my supporters in my group, and you get your army and your supporters in your group." Couples didn't have the witnessing of supporters who had the whole picture, and couples did not get support from people with the complete perspective. As we observed this, it partially prompted us to start the "We Came To Believe" weekends.

Now, it seems to me that there is basically only one problem that couples have, and I would like to talk a little about it. The ideas may sound very simplistic, but actually this is the truth: The basic thing that all couples have to deal with is how to be separate and individual and how to be paired at the same time, and how to do those two things simultaneously.

I would like to stop for a moment and just reflect a little bit about what the dilemma means for us as recovering people. Let's talk about: What does that mean in terms of our own individual pieces? In terms of the pieces we bring that are ours? The part about being separate and the part about being ourselves? I think that there are lots of resources available to us. And also, what is the inner life of ourselves that we need to listen to? I believe that spirituality is truly being able to look around in your life and notice the metaphors. To be able to seek—out of those metaphors, those analogies, those things where we are constantly listening to what's going on—and to say, "How is that like my life? What is the message in that for me?" Because the messages are all around us if we listen to them.

I had a dream earlier this year, which I think illustrated that for me. Some of you know this part of my story. One of the struggles in my life is that my father is an alcoholic who was sober for thirty-five years and started drinking about four years ago. And about eighteen months ago, it really plunged me into a whole new round of therapy. And here I am. I'm forty-six years old. I've been in this field; I've been in recovery for fourteen years; I've got to waste my time going to therapy; and there I was. It's been a very powerful year for me in terms of some of the things I did not know that I now have learned. It's like there are big pieces of a puzzle that have just come to me.

The dream that I had was very helpful to me because the dream was about two hawks. There was a snowstorm. As the hawks were flying by me, I could see that the male hawk had been injured somehow. He was flying and he was keeping up. There was a female hawk and a male hawk and the male hawk was keeping up, but I could see that it was a struggle. So I grabbed them out of the air, both of them. I expected that the injured hawk was going to struggle and try to get away. I was surprised because the hawk knew that I was trying to help and heal him. As I pulled him close to me, he nestled next to me and was loving me in response. I was moved by that. As I was walking back to the house, I stumbled, and I dropped the hawk. And I thought, "That blew it, because for sure he'll fly away." But he waited for me, and I picked him up. He nestled against me again, and I brought him inside. The tip of his wing had been broken, and the children and I set his wing.

As I told that story to my therapist, we both ended up crying. In many ways the dream was a metaphor about how therapy has been for me, in that I've worked very hard at it. I felt the good will of my child—that there was a part of me that was willing to be healed and to stay there while the adult part of me took care of me. It was a very powerful thing for me to listen for, because I think that is the suffering that all of us deal with in our individual recoveries. It is the gift you bring to your partner. And it is that willingness and the suffering, I think, which are some of the gifts of recovery.

You know, I've been really struck by commercials that sort of make fun of Twelve-Step meetings, where people get up and say I'm a such-and-such-aholic and what have you. In some ways, at first, I kind of cringe when I hear it, because for me, they are mocking something sacred. Yet, on the other hand, there is also the fact that the recovery movement is impacting this culture, and others are having to deal with it. And while it is appearing in commercials, something has made a difference.

The other thing that I think we bring to a coupleship as part of our individual recoveries is that we learned how to "de-people" the room. Whenever you come to a relationship, you bring all of those interactions that you had with others in your formative years. The critical issue is to become clear about "what is about your family of origin" as opposed to "what is about yourselves."

I know that, for me, that dream has involved some really intense struggles in this past year. One of the gifts in my life is a man named Louie Anderson. You may have read some of Louie's stuff. One of the things in his book is videotaping his family. I thought, "What a great idea." So I found my videotape camera, and I told my folks that I wanted them to have a talk about their childhoods and their growing up and their marriage. It was a very powerful experience for me.

I'm the second child in my family. I have an older sister who was born dead. It was in 1941, on All Saints' Day that she was born dead. My uncle was a physician, and his partner delivered the baby. My uncle swooped in and grabbed the baby. My mother never saw. As she told the story, in those days there were no grief groups. There wasn't anybody to talk to; there was no debriefing for her. And she was in the Red Cross and as you remember, December 7th wasn't far behind. So when she got out of the hospital, she immediately was immersed in all the activities of the Red Cross, in the early days of World War II. The fact was that the first time she ever talked about it since 1941 was on that 1980s tape. I was real struck by it, because for myself, I was aware of her tremendous sadness.

And then, I realized that played a part in my own addiction, my own recovery. One of the things I've had to learn is about my interaction patterns. How, in my life, I have sought out very sad women. I learned how my life might have been very different. Picture with me now: I was the second kid. My father was away at war. My mother lost her first child, so when I came, I became a special child for her; one that took up a lot of her energy and her focus and her sadness. The result for me was that it set up a series of dynamics of which I didn't really have a clear picture. What I learned is that I had carried these dynamics into my marriages.

I think that part of your activities as members of RCA—and that one of the things which you bring with you from your individual recovery to your relationship—is that you have to take care of your individual business. We all have stories about the families we come from, and the ways that we impose those things, or find matches in our relationships.

The second task you have to deal with is bonding. How do you connect and make commitments to people? I myself am now having to deal with the issues of dating, which is interesting in my family. For openers, just explaining to people what I do is interesting. In my dating, there are complications when I have felt it important to talk about my recovery as a sex addict. There is never a really graceful way.

I remember one occasion and a woman who was a very dear friend. We started dating, and the level of connection was such that I thought it important for her to start knowing a little bit about me. So I said: "You know, it would be really important to me that you read this book, *Out Of The Shadows*." So she read the book. And when she finished the book, I said: "I have some things to tell you," and I did tell her. It was about a month later that I'd read a great novel called *The Wolf's Hour,* which is a novel about werewolves. I said, "You know, you really ought to read this book." She gave the book back to me and she said it was a good book. I don't know where this came from in me, but there is this impish side of me, and I said, "There's one other thing I need to tell you about me!" . . . and for just a moment, I could see it had crossed her mind. One of the things I got out of that relationship is that I think that she is one of the people with whom I learned what it's like to be me in a relationship.

I feel presumptuous in front of you folks. I mean, we joke about my being the honorary single member of RCA; but you guys are the people who have labored the good fight and are here now. You are doing it. So it is sort of presumptuous of me talking about having relationships. But the part that I've learned out of my dating experience (which has got to be the same as yours) is that the criterion for success of the relationship is when I can be with you and feel most myself. The degree that those pieces aren't there is the degree of my discomfort.

One of the things that I have seen RCA couples do, and which I think is an astounding and wonderful gift, is couples exchange pictures of each other as children. So you always have in front of you a sense of the vulnerability of your partner, and that there is this child within you to whom you also need to attend. I think that part of bonding (like my hawk dream) is that we can attend to each other's vulnerability and build our trust that adults can in fact be trustworthy.

I believe also that the toughest part for those of us who come out of shame-based systems, is that righteousness can be in our way and lead us down a path in which we can be very blind. I am sure that there are such times in your families; this has happened to everybody in here, I know. There has been a time when you are absolutely certain something was such, and you swore it was, and everybody in the family said, "No, you don't know what this is like." And you said, "Absolutely not," and you knew it. Only later it became clear with incontrovertible evidence that you were wrong. I hate that thought. And I learned one of the things that can be most deadly for me is righteousness, especially if that righteousness is connected with my anger.

Not long ago, I was really upset and angry and in a very righteous place. I stomped into my bedroom, and I flipped on the TV. There were the Ninja Turtles, the Teenage Mutant Ninja Turtles! For those of you who don't know the story, there is a character in that show called Splinter, who is kind of an overgrown rat and who is also like a Zen monk. He says these very wise things. He is the one who has raised these four Mutant Ninja Turtles and taught them their martial arts and given them their wisdom. Splinter's words came right out of the TV and said (he was talking to Raphael), "You know, Raphael, your anger will destroy you." I backed up and I sat down, and I listened to Splinter's two-minute dialogue with Raphael about how his anger was going to eat him from within and destroy him. It was the best thing I've heard in a long time.

The point is: all of us need to be aware, because of the nature of how shame works, that one of the greatest impediments to bonding is the fact of our righteousness and our anger. This is not about holding onto our truths and standing for our boundaries and all those things, but I'm talking about that blaming dynamic, that feeling where my happiness is somehow impaired because the other person isn't doing something right. My experience both in watching people recover and in my whole life and as a family and marital therapist is this: people think, "I need that approval." And after you have seen that one hundredth couple in therapy, it just seems incongruent. We do our own happiness make!

So the value, I think, of what you guys are doing is that you are really creating a revolution in the Twelve-Step communities! The Twelve Steps are a very disciplined way to live your life as a couple. We are in a stage in our history where we are going through a traumatic revolution. We are seeing it in terms of watching the democracies across the world. None of us two years ago (1989) could have forecast what is happening in terms of democracy. What we don't realize is that there are other kinds of revolutions that are happening. It was at the same time that the Magna Carta was written in 1215 that across Europe whole movements around courtship were also happening. And the notion, which was new in Western Civilization and new on the planet, was that you got to choose your partner. Joseph Campbell talks about that as being one of the most extraordinary revolutions in mankind's history. And, in fact, just to give you perspective on this, last fall an article came out about studies of couples in China. China is an incredibly interesting place for family study. Couples who had their marriages arranged, which is how it has been for lots of people on the planet, were compared with couples who chose their partners. The couples who chose their partners were dramatically happier, especially the women, than the people who had their marriages and partnerships arranged. Now, the important thing about that, you see, is: I believe that a relationship is a continuum of choice. Every day it brings a choice. And it is in the wrinkling of that choice, you see, that a lot of people get stuck. This is because the relationship becomes sort of a given. "This is what I have got to do," as opposed to recognizing that "this is my choice."

Every relationship has its suffering. I like Scott Peck's phrase; he says, "Every relationship is an ordeal. The question is how to make it the best ordeal you can find." The reality is that this is a tough challenge. What you are about and the significance in all this is that the recovery movement has really started a new culture and whole new ways of being. People have popularized principles that have been learned in therapy.

People are interacting on different levels now than they were twenty years ago. I listen to my children. The thought that I could have had the psychological awareness at sixteen that they do, drives me nuts! My sixteen-year-old daughter looked at me and said, "You know, your parenting has become counterproductive." She says, "Your consequence is going to make me more defiant, and I am going to act out more, and it's going to be your fault."

This is the same child with whom I failed to connect during a trip I had taken. When I travel, I usually connect with my kids daily, and for three or four days I had not connected. It had been a particularly hectic trip and for a number of reasons we had not hooked up. When I came back, she looked at me and said: "Dad, when you live between two houses, you don't have a geographical place which is your center. So, people are my center. When I don't hear from you, I lose my center." All you can say to a kid who says something like that is, "I can't wait to see your children!"

The recovery work we are doing is bringing these notions of different ways of relating. The fact is that we in recovery are twenty million strong in this country. You can't have 10 percent of this population doing what we do, and not have the ripple effect on the rest of the population. We will never raise children the same again, because of what Twelve-Step communities are doing.

And as you know, people criticize. We have our critics, usually academics, and forgive me, but sometimes they also come out of their own pathology. In their criticisms, one of the things they really have to deal with is the fact that people are doing Twelve-Step programs because it is renewal to them and because it makes a difference and because their lives are better. And so, what's happening is that the recovery movement is becoming popularized.

I look at John Bradshaw, for example, who wrote the book *Homecoming*. People in New York are still trying to figure out what happened, because that book sold 610,000 copies in three months. No nonfiction book in the history of this planet has ever done that! Novels, perhaps, but no nonfiction book has ever done that. Which says there is a need there.

People in the academic community and the critical community can't figure out what this means. The fact is when we start dealing with those vulnerable, inner-child feelings within ourselves, transformations occur. It's the recovery movement that's helping us get better. It is the recovery movement that says, "You know, I've produced a lot of suffering." The healing starts! We are becoming more responsible for our own healing. No longer are there going to be just physicians telling us what to do. In fact, one of the things that's happening is that the biggest watchers of continuing medical education are—guess what? It's not physicians. On Sunday mornings, there are programs designed to teach doctors about what this illness is. There are only about 63,000 physicians who watch those programs. Six million other people watch them! Six million people and they have a common characteristic. They have a chronic disease of some kind, of which one of the leading ones is alcoholism.

What you have is more and more people taking responsibility for their healing. So physicians are having to deal with the fact that some of their patients know more about their illness than they do. And God knows in sex addiction, that is the truth. Many times addicts and co-dependents have had to teach their therapists about themselves and their illnesses. We are making a difference and that suffering can be a badge of courage.

I also believe that it is the Twelve-Step communities which are bringing spirituality back to this country and that people are living in the spirit. And I believe that there's a rift between those forces that have destroyed it and how the Twelve-Step communities have grown. I do believe that there is stuff that is emanating. What this is about, and what I'm now saying is that you as a recovering couple sort of have that extra added quality, and that you are adding another message. Historically, a characteristic, and (now I'm going back to AA) one of the things that people coming out of shame-based, co-dependent, addictive families have ended up doing is viewing things in very black and white ways. They become rigid about it. So they take recovery and make it rigid. In other words they "sacredize" the Twelve Steps, and make it so they can never change anything. And, you see, the Twelve Steps need to change. If you went to a meeting for everything for which you qualified, you would not have a life left! RCA is the one group that you can come to with whatever things you've got! And during the meeting, it's OK. This is the one place you can do that.

The second thing is that you are putting a value on coupleship after a time when we have been extraordinarily mindful about the individual, the new generation, and the culture of narcissism. You are coming to a time where you are giving the message about the value of bonding, and that it is a good thing to be in a bonded relationship.

I have some hopes for you. This is the second time that I have been present when a fellowship got started in my lifetime. I remember the early days of SAA. I remember how frightened we were, and how we had this men's spirituality group. We didn't want the church to know quite what it was that we were doing. Out of the first ten members of SAA, nine of them were therapists, and God knows we didn't want our clients to know! So we started another group that was the Wednesday night group. However, what happened was that in the first two or three years we grew very slowly because of fear. We always had this logic that we have to figure out what we are doing before we tell anybody else, which I think was perfectionism on our part. I think what we needed to do was let many people in the door, and let them start talking from where the problems were. I believe that this Board has done that in the spirit of inviting you in, and investing you with the responsibility to help articulate what needs to happen now. One of the things I hope that you are willing to do, because you truly are different from the other fellowships, is perhaps to write a group conscience of what's said. All of us are new in this program. My plea to you is that you be open to doing that.

The second thing is to recognize that we are as imperfect as we are. This organization will have its imperfections, just like in our relationships we have imperfections. We need to be tolerant and to allow things to unfold. You know, sometimes things take an incredible amount of time.

I had an experience earlier this year that was very moving for me. I had been involved with a woman twenty years ago, and I lived with her for about a year. It was a very devastating experience for me. Some of you have heard my monologue on the "Velcro woman." Basically, that was this relationship. She clearly was also a sex addict.

One of the things that happened for me was that I got a phone call from her this past year, and she asked me out to lunch. Her story was that she is now recovering, and her therapist had assigned her the task of going out and getting a Twelve-Step workbook. She couldn't find the one that she had been assigned, but she ran across *A Gentle Path.*[1] For her, it was two days of a great deal of pain. And she said, "You were even thinking about those things back then, and I was in such a funk that I had no idea what you were trying to say, and I'm sorry." She spent the rest of that lunch making amends for all the things that happened. And, I found myself saying that this is what making amends is. It allowed me then to make amends for all the hurts that I caused. I found my inner self just making a gigantic shift with that healing. And what I realized was that it took twenty years for that to happen! Twenty years!

When we think of the program, we think that it should happen in one year or it should happen in two years and what-have-you. For some of these things to come together, there is God's timing. I find myself very impatient and wanting all these things to happen at once. I believe that the timing for this particular

1 Patrick Carnes, *A Gentle Path Through the Twelve Steps,* Compcare Publishers, Minneapolis, MN, 1989.

experience in my life was absolutely perfect. It gave me some things that were very, very helpful, and the timing was perfect. From the perspective of this organization, you need not look at the timeline as one year or two years, but you need to think of decades of time.

I truly hope that what happens this weekend is that RCA becomes a non-Minneapolis- based organization. These people here have labored very hard. It is a lot of work. I don't know how you guys are going to work things out, but my hope is that the representation on the Board will fully reflect a nationwide perspective. You may still have a Minneapolis post office box and central office and keep all the mechanics of that here. The point is that the Board, however, needs to reflect a national perspective. So, if you are sitting there, and you are saying that it sounds like something you could do, but you live in Fresno or wherever, remember the RCA Board needs to have you folks as part of it.

My other hope for you is that you do not hide your recovery. I have traveled around this country, and there are a lot of you who are not here tonight. I have met RCA groups all over, and I know there are places where I have met people and those people are not here. My hope is that you continue your outreach, that those folks will get an opportunity to come, and we really do let the world know what RCA is all about.

I hope you have a good time. I know a lot of you, and so I trust that this weekend will be a lot of fun for you.

I hope this group makes some effort to reach out to minorities and oppressed people. I was recently talking with an RCA couple in North Carolina who have an amazing story. One of their recovery issues (and this man is a sex addict) is that his son announced to him that he was gay, and that he had a lover and that he wanted his parents to accept him. The mother was moved by the integrity of the son saying that this was the truth and that he wanted his lover to be accepted by his parents. She welcomed this young man. This was not true of the father. He was troubled. It was his RCA community that told him to "lighten up." Today he cherishes this young man, and it was one of the real milestones in their RCA recovery. I was moved by the lesbian couple seated at the back. My invitation is that we not blind ourselves again to the needs of oppressed and misunderstood individuals.

It may seem like a simple thing to put one of these conferences together, to agonize over trying to maintain your recovery, but also going to meetings and Board meetings to get things done. It is a lot of work, you guys. These are true troopers up here in this front row. I want to take a moment and recognize their contribution. I watched you. I know what you did. You deserve the credit. You've done well.

It has been a pattern in my life to start things that I guess I needed myself. And here I am once again. I have a final wish for myself. You see, I know what you guys have got, and I know what the potential is for you, and my wish is that someday I'll be able to join you.

Thanks.

Keynote Address Given at the 2002 RCA Convention in Honolulu, Hawaii

Annliz and Per

Annliz

I am recovering with Per. I came to my own program, Al-Anon, when Per got sober. It was a tremendous relief hearing others in the same situation; I believed I was alone. Listening to others was very useful. I do not come from an alcoholic family, but there are other things that I now am seeing as I am working the program.

I met Per for the first time 1975; he was a patient in the hospital I was working in. It was not love at first sight. It took two years, I think. So one day after he had been calling me several times I went to visit him. I was thinking, a cup of coffee, that's all. I am still here.

After some years I had been thinking that this couldn't be right. He drinks too much. It was no fun to meet friends, to go to a party, go out for dinner, meet our families, etc. Then my work started to get him sober. It was hard work, as some of you know. We went to different doctors and treatment homes, Per following me to all these places, but he was too busy, he had to work, etc. So I gave up my friends, I never went out to do things for myself. I took care of Per so he could go on drinking. I had to have the control.

But one day—it was when we had a vacation week—Per was drinking every day. He began to cry. He asked me if I could help him to be sober. I said, "I can't." I was not crying, yelling—I only said, "I can't, you have to do this alone, I am so tired of this." I did one thing, I called the treatment home for him; I called Monday and a week after, he was there. And since then he has been sober and that was twelve years ago.

So, when we had been in our own programs for some years, we discovered that something was missing in our lives. For example, we did not do anything together, just the daily duties. We had no communication, a bad sex life, and non-intimacy. We just talked about paying the bills and things like that. So one day, a member in my Al-Anon group asked if Per and I were interested in starting a group for couples. I went home to ask Per and he said, "So what, we have nothing to lose." So we started an RCA group; we were four couples. Giant step. None of us knew how to share in this kind of meeting. What could you say, what could you not say, and so on. In the beginning we had no place to meet, so we borrowed Per's brother's office. We were three couples for a long time (one year). We wanted to feel safety before we took in newcomers, so we could take care of them.

There are two couples left since the start five years ago. We have seven groups in Sweden with meetings every week. One group is resting because they have no place to meet. When a new group is started we go to them, helping them with the first meeting. For us, Per and I, if we had not found RCA, we would not be together today. RCA is very important for us. We don't have the world's best communication, but it is much better than it was before RCA. We are doing things together today, seeing other couples, going out for dinner together, and sometimes we even have fun. Just to work the Steps together gives us a better relationship. If we are having a hard time, it feels much better after a meeting.

Since we started RCA five years ago, we have been having a convention every year, the last weekend in March. This year it was the first weekend in April and we were twenty couples.

The problem in Sweden, as everywhere else, is to get people to do service. We have translated the Steps, Traditions, Reflections, and all that we need for the meeting. But it takes time.

Per and I are the Service Office in Sweden. We try to give the other groups information and they can contact us if they have something they are wondering about. They can also buy medallions and books from us. I think I will stop here and thank you all for being here and giving us the possibility to be here. Thank you.

Per

I am recovering with Annliz. I am really happy to be here at this RCA convention in Honolulu. This is our fourth convention in the United States and it is very exciting to meet RCA friends. If someone had told me twelve years ago that I would be talking at an RCA convention in Hawaii, I would have told that person he was crazy, for twelve years ago I was an active alcoholic. I was so sick that even the alcohol did not help anymore. I began drinking early; I was twelve years old the first time I got drunk. I began drinking more and more. The alcohol was soon the most important thing in my life. I met with my first alcoholism doctor when I was fifteen years old, and after that I met with a lot of therapists and psychologists and others working with addicts. The alcohol came first, not girls, friends, and family.

The consequences of my drinking got worse and worse. I went on drinking for twenty-five years. I was thirty-seven when I got in touch with AA. After November 1990, I have not needed drinking. I go to two AA meetings a week. It was a big relief and release not to drink. Annliz, my parents, brothers and sister, friends, and workmates took a sigh of relief! It has been a lot of AA meetings and service in AA; most of it has been good.

But the years went on and the relation to Annliz was calm but emotionally really cold. Something was missing. Annliz had her own Twelve-Step program and I had mine, but we didn't get any closer. We had nothing in common. We lived under the same roof but it was not good. I loved Annliz but I could not accept that I was powerless in our relationship. So we had nothing to lose when we got the possibility to start RCA in Sweden.

Keynote Address Given at the 2009 RCA Convention in Fort Lauderdale, Florida

Karl and Pat

Karl

Here we are. Your keynote speakers for the 2009 RCA Convention. I'm Karl and I'm in recovery with Pat.

Pat

Hello, I'm Pat in recovery with Karl.

Karl

As you can see we're nothing special, just an ordinary RCA couple. Well, Pat is special in so many ways, but taken as a couple, we're nothing special. Yet as Pat was saying the other morning when we were chatting with another of the RCA old-timers: "We're so lucky! We have had the opportunity to have a rich, full life."

And we owe so much of that to RCA! If we hadn't come into RCA when we did, with the extraordinary people we did, I don't know where we would be today. Certainly not together, loving and joyous and free! As John Prine says of a less than stellar couple in one of his songs: We're the big door prize! Because in spite of all our faults, we love one another, we've made over thirty years together, and we're going to be a couple until the Lord separates us! We don't have to be anything special. We can be screwed up as hell. But if we love and respect each other for who we are—not for who the other might think we ought to be—if we stick it out, in the tough times as well as the good, then we're the big winners!

And Lord knows, no one would have guessed that we would be winners seeing us coming into what became RCA. We were a mess! I was a nasty and demoralized drunk. I won't take Pat's inventory, but I suspect she would admit to qualifying for this program in spades! We were blaming, shaming, bullying, and just plain bad! Bad for each other, and bad for anyone unfortunate enough to try to help us. But many people in this program stuck with us! And here it is a mere twenty-one years later, and look at us—old, broke down, and loving each other every minute we have left!

I'm sure that one reason we were selected to give the keynote address tonight was based more on our *longevity* in the program than our great work in couple recovery. Along with two other couples (who wish to remain anonymous), Pat and I have been in RCA since before it was RCA—and believe me, we have *needed* every minute of it! We began our journey in Oakland, California in the Kaiser ADAP in February, 1988. (For the uninitiated, ADAP stands for Alcohol and Drug Addiction Program.)

I assume that another reason we were asked to talk was that we came from a somewhat different stream from that of the 1988 retreat in Golden Valley, Minnesota where Pat Carnes introduced a Twelve-Step approach to couples ripped apart by sexual addiction. As I understand it, the retreat was so revolutionary in the lives of the participants that they wanted it to keep going. They began to meet regularly calling themselves Recovering Couples Anonymous. The dates were approximately the same, but as of yet neither group had heard of the other.

Since we have no particular expertise—just longevity in the program, I propose that we keep this simple. Pat and I will talk about what brought us into recovery and how that led to the founding of a couples' group which met in a Berkeley, California child care center called The Snuggery. Initially part of Al-Anon, this embryonic group finally merged with the fledgling RCA to produce the organization we all know and love today. Finally, we'll talk about Pat's and my history in RCA and what we have learned—what it has meant to us.

Back at Kaiser ADAP, I was grudgingly being introduced to recovery from alcoholism (and as I was later to learn, a whole host of other addictions including drugs, sex, food, tobacco, gambling, co-dependency, and most forms of relationship addiction—plus I am sure, many others less clearly defined). In my experience, addiction is the gift that keeps on giving. As soon as I think that I'm recovering from one addiction, I realize that I need to confront two new ones.

My worst addiction—bar none—was to tobacco. I thought I would never be able to quit smoking. I had lost track of how many times I had attempted to quit before I finally succeeded. If I remember correctly, it was in 1986, and I was taking my coffee break to buy a tube of TOPOL, a smoker's toothpaste. I don't suppose I'll ever know why I was able to actually quit that time, when I had failed so miserably so many previous times, but there was something inherently ridiculous about buying toothpaste specifically to remove the stains left by smoking. I twitched for almost two years, but since that morning, I've never smoked another cigarette.

But a surprising thing happened; as I was quitting smoking cigarettes, my marijuana and alcohol consumption skyrocketed. And my problems with Pat got even worse. *(If you quit cigarettes cold turkey, stay juiced and stoned most of that time; you'll have relationship problems, too!)*

Pat and I had always had violent arguments. About six months into our relationship we went to see a relationship counselor. There was a lot of love and passion, but it was marred by arguments and an inability even to confront, much less resolve, any of the relationship issues: You know them: *money, sex, and power.* We spent about forty-five minutes of our fifty-minute hour explaining why, although we loved one another, we just couldn't seem to get along. The counselor patiently listened to both of us, then sighed and told us it was unfortunate, but some couples just had more tolerance for bickering than others. She thought we would likely stay together, but likely also keep bickering!

On a chilly January night, 1988, I met Pat coming home from work on the front steps to our home in Berkeley. I was drunk (on Tequila; we had just returned from Mexico). She was tired and stressed. A fight erupted immediately—the sort of screaming, violent horror that induces the neighbors to call the cops "before he kills her!" It didn't help that I was waving a steak knife (I had been using it in the kitchen) to emphasize my more *subtle* points. One of my brothers (who had been staying with us) tried to intervene. Most of that evening is blissfully blacked out of my memory, but I do remember making a crack about his wife wearing his balls for earrings just before the lights went out! Sometime later I vaguely remember the police arriving, and my drunkenly demanding that the officers remove both my brothers from the house as unwelcome guests. I don't remember much else.

Pat

Unfortunately, I remember this day quite vividly. Our backgrounds were completely different. I had no clue about addictions; drinking to me was occasional, and for fun. My family had a lot of problems, but they weren't drinkers. My father would have a beer occasionally on a hot day, and I remember my parents having a shot of whiskey after my father came home from work. It wasn't forbidden—just no big deal.

I couldn't understand what was going on I guess . . . and I didn't know where to go. Karl had literally swept me off my feet when I met him with ideas of traveling, music, and seeing things I hadn't dreamed of. I dumped a long-term relationship for him.

On this night, with his brothers there, we all just split. Interesting that his brothers seemed to have had no concern at all for where I went . . . but I took the dog and we searched for a motel that would take us both. I called a brother of mine who lived in the area (last resort for me) who told me to stay with them . . . I did for awhile. But, then things changed. Karl quit drinking . . . he has an aunt who was (and is) in AA. She helped more than I could ever imagine. I stayed with my brother and sister-in-law for a while, but then came back home. I believed Karl when he said he wouldn't drink again. I never knew him to lie about anything.

Karl

The next morning I awoke on the floor with the worst hangover I could ever remember, the cat licking my face, and a horrible suspicion that I had done something really shitty—the details of which were teasingly out of reach in my booze-soaked brain. What was clear was that both my brothers and my wife had moved out, taking even my dog with them. I was utterly alone (except for the cat) and wretchedly miserable. I just knew that my life was over! It was a belief I was to retain for quite some time. At that time I was in such a state that if I hadn't been *incapable of doing anything positive,* I would have done away with myself.

I don't remember anything in detail of the next several days. Somehow, I came to realize that Pat was gone for good—if I didn't do something about my drinking. I didn't know what to do, so I called my HMO (Kaiser Permanente) and inquired if they had any program for drunks. They assured me they did, but it would be several days before they could schedule an intake session—meanwhile I was encouraged to go to Alcoholics Anonymous.

For me, at that time, Alcoholics Anonymous was a mixed blessing at best. I was ashamed to go to meetings, but AA meetings were the only relief I had from the terrible depression that was consuming me. I was this totally miserable, hunched-over figure in the back of the meeting room who never said a word if I could help it. I suppose I hoped I would get the program by osmosis.

I hated to self-identify as an "alcoholic." To me, at that time, my problem was that I was in love with a woman I couldn't live with, and I couldn't live without. You would drink a bit too much too if you were entangled in a no-win relationship like that! Sometimes things just got out of hand without my realizing it until too late. I never intended to make loud, threatening, drunken scenes. In fact, I never really intended to get drunk. It was just that that first drink felt so good, it had to be followed with another. I had a drinking problem on account of my relationship problems—but I wasn't really an alcoholic!

Then there was all that "God talk" in AA meetings. You have to understand, I'm a "preacher's kid." If you grow up in a household where religion is the family business, you either go into the same business, or you get as far away from it as possible! There is no middle ground! And besides, alcoholism (or whatever was my problem) had nothing to do with my religion or lack of it. It was a medical or psychological or social problem—but certainly not a religious problem! If I had to become a psalm-singing, Bible-thumping evangelical down on my knees praying that God would save me, then I'd rather remain a drunk!

The Kaiser ADAP Program incorporated the usual Twelve-Step approach, but there was a twist. From the Kaiser perspective, it was almost useless to treat the alcoholic *in isolation*. The alcoholic came from a family matrix and would return to it. In that alcoholic family matrix a dance had developed, and everyone had his or her assigned steps. If a drunk sobered up, that threw a monkey wrench into the whole family dance, and no matter how they might protest that they really wanted him sober, in various subtle ways, he would be pressured to resume his usual role in the family dance.

Ideally, one would treat the whole family so that they were all recovering from their addictions, co-addictions, codependences, and other dysfunctions all at the same time. Since this was usually impractical, Kaiser insisted that at least one's significant other be in their program with the drunk. One woman, I recall, came with her teenaged son—all that was left of her family.

Thus the Kaiser ADAP program was filled with couples—learning that they *both* needed to recover—not simply the "designated addict." Recovery was not something that the drunk was to do alone and come home "cured." But just as we had danced the dance of addiction together, we needed to dance the dance of recovery together. It was a profound insight into the nature of family systems and addiction and remains the cornerstone of "couple recovery" and RCA to this day!

Pat

When Karl asked me to come to this meeting, I had never heard the word "co-dependent." I thought it was a good thing . . . why not? It meant that I was "helping." Boy, was I wrong! I went to the Kaiser meetings, and also went to Al-Anon meetings religiously. I had moved into a new world, and realized quickly that I was leaving my other life behind. My family certainly didn't understand, but there were people we met in these meetings that did. It was a relief for me to actually be able to talk openly about things. The one thing that occurred to me while going to the Kaiser meetings was that I expected everything to be simply wrapped up in a few months and we could go on with our lives, but without drinking, and presumably getting along better because of it. If someone had told me that we would still be working on our relationship twenty years later, going to meetings and being part of groups in "recovery," I would have told them they were crazy.

Karl

The Kaiser phase lasted about six months. Then we were told to go and continue practicing our couple recovery outside the confines of Kaiser ADAP. The problem was that although there was AA and Al-Anon, there was nothing that replicated the support and recovery we had come to believe was essential. Nothing supported us as a couple.

And nothing excited us as the Kaiser ADAP approach had. I don't know quite how to explain this, but when we entered recovery for our various addictions and co-addictions, we were thoroughly demoralized. It seemed that our lives were over. We might go on living, but it would be a hard, outcast life with seemingly no hope of redemption.

By the end of the Kaiser phase we were perky and upbeat. We all knew that our addictions and our relationship issues were interrelated, but we had had no idea how to address them. AA and Al-Anon were good at focusing on our individual recovery, but in the Kaiser program we had worked together with our significant other to confront our addiction and our relationship problems together as multi-facets of the same edifice. It felt good to work together! We were beginning to talk the same language, and were beginning to work with other couples towards common goals. We were seeing that our issues were reflected in the issues of other couples who were working the same program. We were getting along, sometimes for the first time in years! We had been at the door labeled: "Abandon hope all who enter here" and we were coming out with more hope than we had had for years! Then Kaiser told us to go out in the world alone!

In addition to the classes and meetings we had had as part of Kaiser ADAP, several couples had gotten in the habit of going out together afterwards for pizza and coffee, where we discussed what we were learning while socializing as couples. I suppose this "meeting after the meeting" was the germ of what became the West Coast's couple recovery. Several couples from Kaiser (two to three of them still in RCA to this day) decided that if there were no meetings to support our couple recovery, well, hell's bells, we could just make our own support and recovery. We just needed a place to meet.

We didn't have the image of the three-legged stool in those days, but we understood that we needed a combination of personal, individual recovery and couple recovery to be truly on the road to recovery. We also had heard horror stories about how few couples were still together five years after one or the other got into recovery alone. If we didn't recover together as couples, finding support for our coupleships, we were likely to lose our mates—and what was worse, we were convinced we would have to confront the same dysfunctional issues if we attempted a new coupleship later on. RCA posits that if we don't resolve our coupleship issues with our current mate, we will just have to face them if we try with another mate. I think those fears were justified.

We also believed that couple recovery was the toughest, but the most important recovery we would encounter. It was where we got into recovery's deepest issues, confronted our deepest fears, and we did all this unable to hide from our most intimate critic. Coming from a family approach to addiction, we knew that our addictions and intimate problems were interrelated. But, if we could work through these issues together, we might become truly free. It was one thing to learn how to live life without drugs or alcohol—but to learn how to live life joyously as an intimate mate, parent, and friend—that would be something! To begin, we just needed the courage to start doing something really scary and a place to meet.

One couple, who were friends with some others in our little group and who were concerned about couple issues, got permission from her boss for us to meet in the evenings at her child care center, The Snuggery.

Pat

I was at an Al-Anon meeting in Oakland one night when at the end of the meeting, a guy stood up and said that he and his wife wanted to get together with other couples in recovery. He gave the address of the place and the time and date for the meeting, and encouraged people to come try it out. I went home, talked to Karl, and he was all for it. When we went to The Snuggery one Friday night, it was the beginning of RCA for us. We are still in contact with several couples from that small group many years ago. At least three couples from that initial group are still among our best friends. They have seen us go through more severe ups and downs than we ever imagined possible. But they were always supportive and not at all judgmental, unlike some family and friends who really didn't understand and couldn't figure out why we didn't just bag it.

Karl

We've talked a bit about "service" at this Convention. I have heard more than one couple explain that there were no couples' groups available in their home area, and their relationships were virtually at an end, so they started their own groups. Now that is "service" with a capital "S." That's what the group in Golden Valley did after their retreat. That's what a couple right here in Florida did, and the flourishing RCA movement in Florida would likely not exist if they had not taken their fears, their shame, and their pain, and bundled it as energy to be in service to others, thus healing themselves.

This is precisely what some couples did in the San Francisco Bay Area in September 1988. We didn't do it. We were friends of the couples that did, and we tagged along on their energy, guts, and faith. And we are extremely thankful we did.

In the early days, we didn't really know what sort of group we were. Since most of us were drunks or related to drunks, we toyed with the idea of affiliating ourselves with Alcoholics Anonymous. However, since most of the literature we used came from Al-Anon, and we were focused on couple recovery, we initially decided to affiliate with Al-Anon. Al-Anon seemed quite happy to have us. For a time it seemed we might be the new cutting edge of how Al-Anon might be developing. It was all very exciting!

Then when our fledgling group decided that we would like to participate in regional and national affairs, we discovered there was a rule against any addict holding office in Al-Anon! Half our membership was disenfranchised! But more importantly, our group was focused on the equality of all participants in the coupleship. We were all engaged in a coupleship—dysfunctional to be sure—but it was a coupleship dance we danced together! The coupleship couldn't recover if one partner in the coupleship were demonized and disenfranchised.

I'm sure Al-Anon has good and sufficient reasons for the adoption and maintenance of that rule. But what it said to us was that Al-Anon had a fundamentally different perspective from our group. Al-Anon was focused on the *individual* recovery of persons affected by addiction. We were focused on the recovery *of the coupleship, and all individuals within it.*

As a group, then and now, we salute the great work Al-Anon was, and is, doing. Pat will tell you what a great help Al-Anon was to her. But their focus is on the *individual* impacted by addiction, *with or without* the survival and recovery of the coupleship. It was clear that our group could no longer fit in that rubric. We began shopping for another Twelve-Step group with whom we could affiliate.

For a while we considered affiliating with CODA, but not all of us would self-identify as co-dependents *(though looking back I think a lot of that might have been denial).* However, the compelling factor was, again, their focus on the individual. *(In the meetings I attended, most of the participants were not even in a relationship!)* We, of course, were focused on individuals' recovery from co-dependency not in isolation, but in partnership with their mates.

Pat

No matter where we looked, Twelve-Step programs were all focused on *individual* recovery. Family or couple recovery, where it existed at all, was an add-on, not the core focus. Then one of our members ran across an article in *Recovery* magazine about a virtually unknown Twelve-Step program dedicated to healing families threatened by sexual addiction, which had recently started in Golden Valley, Minnesota. The more he read, the more he thought we just might have a fit. Although premised on very different sorts of addiction, their approach to the impact of addiction on the family and the need for the family to heal together seemed implicit. After he explained what he had discovered, the meeting voted to explore affiliation with Recovering Couples Anonymous.

The rest, as they say, is history. The two streams merged and became the program we still call Recovering Couples Anonymous. It is no longer simply the recovery program of sexually addicted families, or of chemically addicted families, but of any families impacted by most any dysfunction—which, of course, is virtually all of us.

Karl

Pat and I have gone through many transformations since we entered this program. I think my wife would agree that had we not entered the Kaiser ADAP program over twenty-one years ago and continued on through the various stages of the growth of RCA, we would not be together today, and we would not enjoy the happiness we do today. It has been a godsend to us, individually and as a couple. You are seeing a miracle right here in front of you!

Pat

I totally agree with everything Karl has said about our process (and this is actually pretty rare in our everyday lives). I'm not usually a group sort of person. I don't mind doing things on my own, and usually when I'm in a group, I stay in the background. We never discussed feelings in my family . . . we just dealt with what came our way and didn't complain about it. Karl's family talks (all the time). I remember the first time I met them, I don't think I said a thing, and I don't think anyone noticed.

Karl

I have recently been privileged to work on the editing of the latest edition to the *Blue Book*. Those of us on the literature committee have been forced to think long and hard about the deeper meaning of all aspects of our program. It has given me a renewed appreciation for the gifts this program has given me and us.

I would like to share a few of them with you. These are only a few of the gifts we have received. If we were to describe all of the gifts we have received, we'd be here all night. I'm sure no one would appreciate that. Please remember too, I am speaking only of myself—or at most, my coupleship. As they say in the car ads: "Your mileage may vary!"

First, I would like to say that even very "small" gains in mutual understanding can be huge in the long run. One of the benefits of participation together in the Kaiser ADAP program, and later through all the years in RCA, was that Pat and I developed a mutually acceptable and understandable language.

Pat

You have no idea what that meant to us! I am Northern, urban, Catholic, and the youngest child of seven. Karl is Southern, Protestant, rural, and the eldest of five. All our bred-to-the bone cues were off. We thought we understood what we were communicating to one another, but our body language and our interpretations of what the other meant were all off. Simple misunderstandings could leave us spiraling through weeks of mutually insane infighting. We had zero trust, because we thought the other person was always lying to us. It was just that we didn't understand each other's cues.

The Kaiser ADAP and RCA gave us a common perspective on addiction and a common language to express it. We learned to use "I" statements instead of "You" statements. We learned to ask our partner to "mirror" what he had just heard instead of assuming we had been perfectly clear. And over the years, in meetings and discussions with friends in program, we developed a mutually understood vocabulary. We could sometimes hear what the other meant to convey. This new vocabulary still is not perfect, but it has meant a world of difference to our coupleship, and our trust in each other.

Karl

Lesson number 2: You don't have to do the program well to reap dividends. You just need to keep coming back. Pat and I have been "in program" for twenty-one-plus years. We were never what you might call "good program people." We were reluctant to accept, much less put into practice, the precepts of either our sponsors or the program itself. Whether it was the "God" talk or the insistence that I focus on me, and not the foibles of my partner, I was reluctant to accept program suggestions for my life—much less put them into enthusiastic practice!

No doubt had Pat and I been more amenable to following the program's "suggestions" from the beginning, we would have reaped greater dividends earlier. But if I had been the sort of person to accept external direction for my life, I wouldn't have been in program in the first place! You get what you can get when you can get it. When the student is ready, a teacher will emerge.

Pat

What worked in our case was that we kept coming back. Through all those pointlessly hurtful stupid fights, we knew we got at least some relief if we went to a meeting or worked a Step with our sponsors. A little bit of sanity would enter our lives. Somewhere along the way, we came to understand that what worked with others might help us, too. Maybe we just got worn down fighting so much, and finally gave up our emotional attachment to personal pride—a need to always be "right" if it killed us! The miracle came late to us because we were arrogant and stubborn, but it wouldn't have come at all if we hadn't been willing to just keep coming back!

Karl

Lesson #3: It ain't Pat's fault! Yes, my life would have been easier if Pat had been different in ways more to my liking. No doubt her life would have been easier had I been more to her liking. I wasn't. She wasn't. And no matter how much or how hard we tried, we couldn't make the other conform to our idealized image of the perfect mate. And God knows we tried long and hard to do just that!

In the RCA *Blue Book* it says that we each must take 100 percent responsibility for the health or dysfunction of our coupleships. That just sounded wrong to me. How could we each have 100 percent responsibility for our coupleship? Well, it might not make strictly logical sense, but it does make perfectly good "psycho-logical" sense. It is like one of those Zen *koans* which present you with an insoluble problem as a way of stimulating you to see reality through new eyes.

My problem wasn't whether I was right or Pat was right. It was *how could we be happy and joyous together*, and that couldn't be brought about by critiquing her faults, no matter how right I might have been in the critique. That was no way to build trust and a sense of common destiny—which is what I really wanted.

Since I couldn't change Pat's essence—at the most, I might get her to conform outwardly in some minor ways—I had to consider whether she was "in essence" the woman I had fallen in love with, and if so, how I could reconnect with that woman. In other words, if I were unwilling to immediately run like hell for the nearest marital exit, it was up to me to figure out a way to restore mutual faith and trust. And to trust that if I did my damnedest to do that, Pat would respond in kind. It has been hard, but I have tried—and so has Pat. She is still the person I fell in love with many years ago—and so much more!

Pat

Another gift of RCA is the remarkable people we have come to know and love in this program. People who, despite crushing burdens of addiction and intimate dysfunctions, somehow managed to transform their personal problems into a source of strength for themselves and others. We still rely on the close support we have received from people we met in Kaiser ADAP twenty-one years ago. They have seen us at our absolute worst and been a non-judgmental support for us during all those years of agonizing growth, and they are still vitally important to us today. There are no deeper friendships than the friendships formed with people who have stood shoulder to shoulder with you through really bad times. Ask any combat veteran about the buddies he served under fire with! Well, these friendships have been much longer and much more intimate! Without those friendships, Karl and I wouldn't have made it here.

Karl

On a similar note, I think that when the recovery community can forge bonds with one another outside the meetings, they and the meetings flourish. If those in a recovery meeting don't form these community bonds—don't develop relationships outside the meeting, half of the expected recovery does not take place, and their recovery will be stunted, and the meeting will likely fail. *The meetings that play together recover together.*

And lastly: It might seem like the end of the world at first, but in reality it is an adventure! I started to say that Pat and I got into this for all the wrong reasons, but on second thought, they were just short-sighted reasons. I started this not believing much of anything and figuring that whatever had been the good part of my life was over. I figured I was a ne'er-do-well, and my entry into an addiction program was proof of that. My major hope was that if I conformed to the program for a while, she might not leave me, and maybe I would learn to control my drinking and drugging.

I remember a woman walking down a hallway in early recovery whining to her husband, "If I can't drink wine, how will we go out to dinner? Does that mean that we can't go to anywhere nice? Do we have to eat at McDonald's for the rest of our lives?"

At that time I felt just as vacuously defeated about my life, and my chances of ever finding happiness. I had no idea that I was entering the greatest adventure of my life, and that I would come to experience love and understanding beyond my wildest dreams!

Pat

For me, there is no doubt that without RCA, my life would have been completely different. I learned to listen to people talk without interrupting. I learned to say "I feel" rather than "You should." It hasn't been perfect . . . but I wonder if there is anything that is really perfect. We have been to many conventions over the years, and spent a few years serving on the Board, and we have come away from each and every RCA experience learning something about ourselves. I just retired from a job that I spent over thirty years at. People from work asked what I'd do, wouldn't I miss it? I always said no. I really believe that a big part of that feeling is that Karl and I at least understand each other and know that our lives have been extremely rich. I feel lucky more than anything else. Thank you all for being here.

Appendix

The Language of RCA

Words and special phrases you'll hear at meetings

Twelve-Step Program Terms

Newcomers to RCA and Twelve-Step fellowships can be baffled by terms that old-timers may assume everyone knows. So just to be sure that you are "in the know," we've listed some of our special language here:

The Serenity Prayer

"God, grant me the serenity to accept the things I cannot change, courage to change the things I can, and wisdom to know the difference."

Although not original to Twelve-Step programs, this prayer is frequently used in the Fellowship to connect or re-connect to our spiritual source. In RCA, we substitute the words "we" and "us" for "I" and "me."

The Slogans

Easy Does It

This slogan brings us back into balance and out of the stress zone of taking on too much too fast.

HALT

Don't get too **H**ungry, **A**ngry, **L**onely, or **T**ired; these are basic principles of self-care.

Keep It Simple

Remember to avoid making things harder than necessary.

One Day at a Time; Just for Today; 24 Hours at a Time

These are keys to focusing on the "now."

RCA Program Terms

Affirmations

Positive statements we make to become open to the possibility of change.

Acknowledgement

Stating our awareness of a situation.

Blaming

Avoiding responsibility by putting the blame on another. Blaming often makes matters worse, as it leads to defensiveness and rebuttal.

Baiting or Button-pushing

Saying or doing something to re-open an old injury, thus triggering a negative reactive response in our partner.

Book-ending

The practice of calling or meeting with a sponsor couple before and after making a difficult decision or taking a difficult action.

Checking in

Briefly sharing our feeling about ourselves, our life, and our coupleship, usually at a meeting, but also with sponsors or at a Meeting of Two.

Contract (see also Written Agreement)

A written agreement with our partner to define acceptable behavior in specific circumstances, for example, a "fair fighting" contract that defines acceptable behavior during an argument. Contracts are arrived at through negotiation, agreed to by both partners, signed, and often witnessed by sponsors.

Cross-talk

Any interaction or interruption that distracts attention from the sharing. This includes vocalizations such as gasps, "ohs," dramatic facial expressions and body language, as well as verbally responding to the content. All sharing should be directed to the entire group and never to any specific individual, particularly a partner.

Fair Fighting Contract

A written agreement defining acceptable behavior when fighting or in conflict. (See sample contracts in following section.)

"I" Statements

Learning to keep the focus *off* our partners and *on* ourselves. Instead of "You were so rude to keep me waiting for an hour," a partner might say, "I felt hurt when you were late and didn't call." "I" statements deal with our own emotions and physical sensations.

Meeting of Two

A meeting between partners in the format of an RCA meeting; for instance, beginning and ending with a prayer, and invoking the Safety Guidelines to assure respectful communication.

Moratorium

Calling a halt to a discussion that feels frustrating or upsetting for a specific time period, giving each partner time to cool off.

Old Behavior

Reverting back to pre-recovering behavior. Responding in non-productive or hurtful ways as a result of unconscious or reactive patterns.

Respectful Communication

Listening respectfully to another to understand what is being communicated. Thinking before speaking, and speaking with respect.

Safety Guidelines

Guidelines for communication in RCA meetings, and in Meetings of Two (p. 55).

Shaming

Attempting to induce a feeling of pain in one's partner by blaming him or her (for the dysfunction of the relationship) as a means of control.

Sponsors

A couple you choose to be your mentors in working the RCA program.

Taking Another Person's Inventory

Putting the focus on what another is doing wrong instead of keeping the focus on one's own program of recovery.

Written Agreement (see also Contract)

Agreement or contract with our partner to define acceptable behavior in specific circumstances, for example, a "fair fighting" contract defines acceptable behavior during an argument. Written agreements are arrived at through negotiation, agreed to by both partners, signed, and often witnessed by sponsors.

Contracts and Written Agreements

When we came to RCA, we wondered how our trust in a Higher Power could help us remove our shortcomings. Where could we get help to know how to communicate, fight fairly, have a healthy sex life, etc.? Many of us have found contracts or written agreements to be important resources. No matter how new you are to RCA, we urge you to adopt the RCA Safety Guidelines (see p. 55) as one of your agreements in your first contract. This can be very helpful when you are discussing anything "touchy" or intimate.

We suggest exploring the following topics as you create your contracts:

Sexuality

These are typical questions we have found helpful in addressing our sexuality: Have we considered seeing a therapist for insight and direction regarding specific attitudes and behaviors? Have we discussed making celibacy an agreement in our contract to take sexual pressure off our relationship? Do we need agreements regarding our sexual boundaries? If we tend to avoid sex, can we include agreements about giving and receiving pleasure? We may need contracts about how often, who initiates, etc.

> *"I agree that I will playfully and joyfully initiate sex, spontaneously, but not less often than once a week, so that Jimmy knows that I care about him and am not just going along with it because he wants it."*

Selected excerpts from Sexuality Contracts

The purpose of this agreement is to identify and plan actions and activities we can take with—or for—each other that nurture our feelings of love for one another. We agree to have a "day date" or a "night date" at least once a month.

Some examples of what a Day Date or Night Date might look like:

- A walk somewhere in nature
- Romantic foreplay and sex
- A meal at a new restaurant
- A movie or video together

We also agree to set aside time twice a month or more to talk about our feelings, our sex life, and ways to enhance our intimacy.

Finance

These questions illustrate why many couples found a contract useful to clarify their roles and boundaries in these situations. What have been our patterns when one partner is financially dependent on the other? When both partners are producing income and sharing? What behaviors have been instances of unhealthy dependency, enmeshment, and power struggles? What have been our spending patterns? What have been our saving patterns? Do we have a budget? Have we considered seeing a financial counselor?

Sample Financial Agreement

The purpose of our Financial Agreement is to create a safe and loving environment in which we can have healthy discussions regarding our finances.

We agree to routinely pray together at night, expressing our gratitude for the abundance that is ours to share. We turn over our financial concerns to our Higher Power, and ask our Higher Power to remove all our blocks to a sense of financial security.

We agree to balance our checkbook within seven days of the statement's arrival.

We agree we will not charge without our mutual agreement to do so.

We agree to review this Financial Agreement together each Monday evening.

Neither partner will spend more than $200 without discussing the expenditure with the other partner.

Division of Labor

Here are some questions we have considered when devising a division of labor contract. What has been the impact on the division of labor in the household when both partners work outside the home? When only one works outside the home? When neither partner is working? Do we feel that the division of labor is fair?

Contracts are especially helpful in defining division of labor responsibilities. A list or schedule of tasks for each family member to complete can be helpful. This way, no one partner assumes the whole burden of household responsibilities.

Communication

How do we talk to each other? Are we respectful, sarcastic, or rude? Do we call each other names, throw things, yell, or bring up issues from six months ago? We encourage you to look at the Safety Guidelines for guidance in how to structure a contract about communicating. The use of "I" statements can help partners communicate their feelings in a healthy, non-blaming manner (e.g., "I feel angry when you . . . " "I feel sad," "I am depressed," or "I am lonely," rather than saying "You did . . . " "You said . . . " "You always . . . " or "You made me . . . "). This helps each of us take responsibility for our behavior, and avoid blaming others.

Recreation

How have we played together? Do we value taking time to relax and play? We may have lost our playfulness as a couple. Do we feel guilty when we use time playfully? Why is having fun such hard work sometimes? A recreation contract encourages couples to take time out to have fun together. Some couples schedule a "date night" or time as a family to enjoy each other's company. Some families have game nights. This can be a good way to get away from the TV, the computer, household chores, kids' sporting events, and other tasks.

Parenting

Who is responsible for the children and when? Do we agree on discipline and on the values we wish to pass on to our children? Do we discuss consequences of actions ahead of time and then follow through? How have we been confused about our parenting roles? Have we allowed our children to "divide and conquer?" Or have we maintained unity in parenting? A contract can be helpful in delineating how we address our parenting roles. It may also be useful to include the children in the contract so they understand the rules and how they participate. Family meetings are very helpful; we can use them to discuss family rules, as well as the consequences for breaking them.

Fighting

How do we fight? Are we respectful or must we win at any cost? Conflict is healthy, and an essential part of intimacy. But if we fight *unfairly* we run the risk of losing intimacy, causing resentments, and losing our relationship.

Fighting contracts vary from couple to couple and are based on our own experiences as a couple. For example, if one of the patterns we have identified is, "We always quarrel unfairly after 11:00 PM; we're just too tired to fight fairly," a fair fighting agreement might be, "We won't start an argument after 11:00 PM" We might agree not to argue in the car or in front of the kids, etc. Some general rules that many couples have used are:

- In order for a constructive argument to take place, both partners must agree that there is indeed an issue in conflict, and agree on an appropriate time and place to discuss this conflict. When agreement of a time and place is reached, all other "fair fighting" rules take effect.
- We will not name-call, shame, cause damage, use offensive language, or blame our partners.
- We will use "I" statements to express our needs, feelings, and boundaries.
- We will have a time limit. When the time is up we agree to reschedule a time to continue the dispute. We can call a "time-out" or take breaks.
- We agree to avoid dramatic exits and to refrain from physical abuse.
- We agree not to threaten divorce or permanent separation.
- If one of us needs an individual time-out to get in touch with feelings, to think about things, or to feel safe, we can say, "This is not about my leaving the coupleship or avoiding the conflict issue, but I am taking a break and will be back. Do you agree to meet in one hour (or tomorrow morning, etc.)?"

For those of us who don't know how to fight or don't like to engage in any kind of conflict at all, we will agree to be honest about our feelings (including anger), even if this is only for fifteen minutes. If we can't fight fairly by ourselves, or if we fear confrontation, we will discuss our disagreements only in the presence of our RCA sponsor or our couple's therapist.

Rules vary according to the history of each relationship. The rules may seem oppressive or cumbersome at first. Still, we have found that while we needed to be very intentional about them in the first months, the rules eventually became more automatic as they replaced our old behaviors and became routine. The goal is to be able to express and hear anger in a healthy way. We have experienced the ability to resolve conflict and fight fairly as a great gift of intimacy. We write out our fighting contracts, with each agreement stated clearly, and ask our RCA sponsors to witness them.

Creating a Fair Fighting Contract

Before we can create a Fair Fighting Contract, we need to look at the ways that we may not have communicated fully in a respectful and healthy manner. We suggest that each person compile a list of unhealthy, disrespectful behaviors they may have exhibited in the past such as: being self-righteous, belittling, name calling, yelling, hitting, threatening to end the relationship, or saying hurtful remarks to our partner. These are a few examples of unhealthy behaviors that you may choose to write on the list. It is suggested that each individual make a list.

As we each create this list it is helpful to pay attention to the feelings that may come up. Do we feel fear, anxiety, or shame as we recount the behaviors? If we have negative feelings that should indicate to us that we violate our own internal moral codes when we practice these behaviors, and they certainly do not help our relationship, these feelings may help us realize our need to make changes. Have we modeled behaviors that we would want our children to follow?

After each of the individual lists have been completed; we suggest that you look at both lists and think about what respectful behaviors would be more helpful to your coupleship and family.

Next, after examining the combined list, try to create a list of healthy, respectful behaviors. Part of creating a Fair Fighting Contract is for each individual to feel safe during conflict. If both agree to the respectful behaviors on the list, they will each be able to focus on what is being said during the discussion. We urge couples to do this exercise with their sponsor couples or counselors. If we feel safe we may be more willing to talk to our partner about our feelings or requests. Some couples may choose not to voice their anger, frustrations, or other feelings for fear of a heated argument ensuing. If we choose not to talk to our partners about our feelings we may end up distancing ourselves from our partners and sacrificing intimacy.

When the contract is completed, the couple needs to agree to the contract in order for it to work. If both partners are not committed to following the agreement, the behaviors will not change, making the contract worthless. Old behaviors are very difficult to change. The important thing is willingness to try. Awareness of our behavior is a start, and then if we fall back into old behavior, we can say we are sorry, take a deep breath, and try again to behave in a healthy manner. Eventually it gets easier when the new behaviors become more of a normal way of behaving. Using "I" statements as in the Safety Guidelines, may seem strange at first, but eventually it becomes a normal way of expressing our feelings. Over time the new behaviors come to replace the old unhealthy ones.

The contract can be modified or changed over time as children grow up, health issues occur, and the couple's recovery gives them more insight and personal growth. Some couples have more then one behavior contract. They have one for conflict, one for intimacy, and a family contract that includes their children with the parenting or family contract. The contract is a reminder and a symbol of the couple's vow to make healthier choices to improve their coupleship.

Sample Fair Fighting Contract

A Fair Fighting Contract might look something like this:

The purpose of this agreement is to create a safe and intimate environment for times when we are in conflict. These "Fair Fighting" guidelines and boundaries allow us to express our feelings in a healthy way and ensure that each partner is heard.

1. We agree that we are allies and on the same team.
2. We agree to review this agreement frequently.
3. We each agree to uphold this agreement.
4. We will start by reading the RCA Safety Guidelines.
5. If either of us needs a "time-out" to cool off, we agree *in advance* that the first time-out will be for a limited time (for example: 15–30 minutes). The person requesting the time-out agrees to state something like, "I need a time-out for 15 minutes. I am not leaving the relationship. I just need time to calm down." More time can be requested as needed.
6. We agree to limit discussions of highly emotional topics to 20 minutes. When the time is up we will reschedule a time to complete the conversation. We agree not to attempt to discuss highly emotional topics before 9:00 AM or after 9:00 PM.
7. We agree we will not name-call, shame, use offensive language, or blame each other.

8. We agree we will not be physically or emotionally abusive, which includes, but is not limited to, shoving, hitting, door-slamming, or throwing objects. We also agree not to engage in threatening behavior that we know our partner fears, such as threatening abandonment or exile. If either one of us is in fear of the other due to the conflict, we agree to state these feelings honestly. We will then continue the discussion only when both partners feel safe—for example, when we meet with our sponsors.
9. We agree to identify the issue that needs discussion and to keep the conversation focused on this issue.
10. We agree not to attempt to resolve a conflict or engage in "fighting" behavior at the following times: while driving; while in bed; during the workday or at a place of employment; when hostile behavior may escalate; and/or when either partner is feeling low, vulnerable, tired, hungry, or "not up to the task."
11. We also agree not to attempt to resolve conflict while in public or around family members.
12. We agree to reach out to our sponsor couple, or another couple, if either of us feels unable to remain respectful in our attempt to resolve the conflict.

We enter into this agreement willingly and lovingly:

Partner ____

Partner ____

Date ____

Sponsor ____

Sponsor ____

Date ____